Morality Politics in American Cities

STUDIES IN GOVERNMENT
AND PUBLIC POLICY

Morality Politics in American Cities

Elaine B. Sharp

with the research assistance of:
Yvette Alex-Assensoh
Susan Clarke
Richard DeLeon
Janet Flammang
Michael Rich
Marjorie Sarbaugh-Thompson

 University Press of Kansas

Published by the University Press of Kansas (Lawrence, Kansas 66049), which was organized by the Kansas Board of Regents and is operated and funded by Emporia State University, Fort Hays State University, Kansas State University, Pittsburg State University, the University of Kansas, and Wichita State University

Library of Congress Cataloging-in-Publication Data

Sharp, Elaine B.
   Morality politics in American cities / Elaine B. Sharp ; with the research assistance of Yvette Alex-Assensoh . . . [et al.].
     p. cm. — (Studies in government and public policy)
   Includes bibliographical references and index.
   ISBN 0-7006-1373-0 (cloth : alk. paper) — ISBN 0-7006-1374-9 (pbk. : alk. paper)
   1. Municipal government—Moral and ethical aspects—United States. 2. City and town life—United States. 3. Social problems—United States. 4. Church and social problems—United States. 5. Christianity and politics—United States. 6. United States—Politics and government—2001—Moral and ethical aspects. I. Alex-Assensoh, Yevette M. II. Title. III. Series.
   JS331.S46 2005
   320.6′0973—dc22   2004025499

Printed in the United States of America

10 9 8 7 6 5 4 3 2 1

British Library Cataloguing-in-Publication Data is available.

The paper used in this publication meets the minimum requirements of the American National Standard for Permanence of Paper for Printed Library Materials Z39.48-1984.

Contents

Figures and Tables

Preface

In his 2003 book *Hellfire Nation: The Politics of Sin in American History,* James Morone argues that morality conflicts are essential to the unfolding American experience. From its Puritan foundations through its Victorian battles over temperance and women's proper place in society to the moral crusades of Christian conservatives in the last two decades of the twentieth century, there has been a "moral urge at the heart of American politics and society" (4). Contemporary battles over gay marriage and the pledge of allegiance are only the latest fronts in the long-running battle that inevitably faces a nation built on moral fervor.

Journalistic coverage of these battles at the national level has been common since the 1980s. But a number of years ago, I noticed a curious thing. While much was being written by both journalists and scholars about abortion politics, gay rights issues, drug policy and politics, and other divisive social issues, the literature about these "culture war" conflicts was focused at the national level. Despite the fact that communities and their governing officials also grapple mightily with issues rooted in religion or morality that evoke strong sentiments among the general public, relatively little was being written about that struggle. This led me to edit a collection of case studies titled *Culture Wars and Local Politics* (Sharp 1999). That volume provided the opportunity to develop some hypotheses to account for the startling differences in city governments' handling of these issues — hypotheses that could be pilot-tested with the case studies contributed to that volume. That pilot testing suggested that differences in cities' governing institutions, social subcultures, and even economic circumstances were part of the answer, as were cities' intergovernmental relationships.

But I was still bothered by the puzzle of how to get beyond ad hoc case study selection to a larger number of systematically chosen cases that would allow full-blown testing of those hypotheses. This motivated the development of a project that examined a set of morality issue decisions in ten study cities. By taking a systematic sample of study cities and examining all decisions (or, as we called them, incidents) involving a defined set of morality issues in those communities, my research collaborators and I were able to uncover a large number of cases for analysis. The results of the quantitative analysis generated by that project appeared in articles in *Political Research Quarterly* and *Social Science Quarterly* (Sharp 2002, 2003).

But there was still a problem. In order to pursue quantitative analysis, individual cases of decision making about morality issues had been largely torn out of historical context and sequence. As important as the quantitative analysis was, it was also important to understand the cities' responses to these morality issues by examining the historical context of each community's experience with the particular issue. And we had the means to do so, at least within the limits of recent history, because the initial raw material generated by the fieldwork for the project consisted of a series of historical narratives of each study city's recent experience with each issue chosen for study—narratives developed from a combination of newspaper archives and personal interviews with local officials and activists.

What is more, we were sitting on a gold mine of interesting stories about how real people grappled with real issues. Some of these stories are more elaborate and interesting than others, depending on the extent of each city's involvement with each issue, but as a whole, they include material that is sometimes startling and dramatic. Sharing these stories would put people back into the picture and make for more interesting comparisons of communities' experiences with some highly volatile issues.

But there was another problem. In order to encourage those we interviewed to be as open and frank as possible, we promised them anonymity. And since those interviewed occupy one-of-a-kind positions in their communities (e.g., mayor, public health director, leader of a high-profile abortion protest group, director of an embattled abortion clinic, leader of a needle-exchange activist organization), the only way to ensure their anonymity was to make the cities themselves anonymous, using pseudonyms rather than real city names. This follows a long-established tradition in the social sciences, best known in the Lynds' 1956 study of Middletown and evident in recent scholarship as well. This tradition has recently come under attack, however, such as Alan Wolfe's (2003) diatribe in the *Chronicle of Higher Education,* which claims, among other things, that "nearly everyone" he interviewed for his projects agreed to have their real names appear in the books. Nevertheless, Wolfe's publishers, on the advice of their legal departments, chose *not* to use real names, on the grounds that individuals who gave permission might later change their minds.

Indeed, although high-level officials may be accustomed to being "on the record," we should appreciate the possibility that other local officials and citizen-activists could get into considerable trouble for sharing their insights with us. It is precisely for this reason that my colleague Steven Maynard-Moody and his coauthor Michael Musheno (2003) masked the identity of the communities whose police, teachers, and vocational rehabilitation workers provided personal narratives of their handling of difficult cases. Similarly, when I recall the high-level public health official who told me of his agency's under-the-table support for an officially illegal needle-exchange program, I am reminded of the utility of pseudonyms to mask identities. In short, there is still good reason for the Middletown approach in social science.

Throughout the book, I tried to provide contextual information about the communities, as well as details about events surrounding the issues under study, without actually giving away the identities of the cities. Undoubtedly, some readers will believe that they know one or more of the communities. But as long as the cities are not officially revealed, those who were promised anonymity cannot be conclusively identified.

I would like to acknowledge the National Science Foundation, which provided support for this project through grant 9904482. I would like to acknowledge the invaluable contributions of the colleagues who served as faculty associates on this project: Yvette Alex-Assensoh, Susan Clarke, Richard DeLeon, Janet Flammang, Michael Rich, and Marjorie Sarbaugh-Thompson. In addition to their crucial fieldwork in six of the ten study cities on which this book is based, these individuals functioned as colleagues in the best sense — providing intellectual support and personal enthusiasm for the project while entrusting me with the products of their fieldwork. Finally, on behalf of my colleagues, I would like to thank all those public officials and private citizens who agreed to be interviewed and, in some cases, took considerable time to brief us about the unfolding of morality issues in their communities. These individuals were invariably generous and gracious in sharing their stories, including their very personal and sometimes even painful involvement in the events. Without their contributions, this book would not be possible.

1

Local Governance and Morality Policy: Emergence of a Neglected Issue Area

A PROTOTYPICAL ISSUE

In September 1999, controversy erupted in New York City over an exhibit that was about to open at the Brooklyn Museum of Art. The exhibit, which was reported to feature sculptures of sexually mutilated people, a painting of the Virgin Mary daubed with elephant dung, and real animals that had been mutilated, evoked the outrage of several groups. The president of the Catholic League for Religious and Civil Rights stated that the exhibit "has gone beyond the vulgar, the blasphemous and the scatological" and asked for a boycott of the museum. The president of People for the Ethical Treatment of Animals said that it was "cheap, low and ghoulish to use, dominate and dissect animals," as had been done in some of the artwork (Feiden 1999).

Wasting no time, Mayor Rudolph Giuliani immediately condemned the exhibit in a press statement that took the policy position that no taxpayer dollars should be devoted to the exhibit (Feiden 1999). One week later, the mayor announced that city funding for the Brooklyn Museum of Art would be halted until the museum canceled the show. The mayor's action constituted a serious threat to the museum. Its budget included $7 million a year in city funding for operations, plus additional amounts for capital improvements, such as a planned $20 million expansion project—negotiations for which were halted by the mayor's office (Willen 1999). The mayor also threatened to replace the museum's board of directors and to evict the museum from its facilities (Polner 1999).

The museum's director, Arnold Lehman, stood by the ideals of artistic freedom of expression and indicated that he would resist the mayor's efforts to determine the content of the exhibit. One of the mayor's political competitors, Democratic City Council Speaker Peter Vallone, criticized Giuliani's actions as a "legally dubious attempt at government censorship" (Polner 1999). Early on, there were some reports that the mayor's office and the museum were negotiating, and city officials claimed that an agreement was pending—one that would have the museum completely remove the painting of the Virgin Mary from the show and move several other controversial pieces of art to a separate room. Word of this dismayed Norman Siegel of the American Civil Liberties Union, who argued that if the agreement were true, it amounted to censorship and showed that the "mayor has bullied the museum into submission" (Polner 1999).

But instead of an agreement, the controversy led to litigation. When museum directors refused to accede to the mayor's demands, the Giuliani administration began withholding monthly payments and sued to evict the museum on the grounds that because the art was unfit for children, the museum had broken the provisions of its lease calling for it to educate schoolchildren and the public. Museum officials in turn filed a First Amendment lawsuit against the city (Hays 1999).

In November 1999, U.S. District Court Judge Nina Gershon ruled that the mayor's actions constituted a First Amendment violation and issued a temporary injunction ordering that the city restore funding and cease its efforts to evict the museum. In her ruling, the judge stated: "There is no federal constitutional issue more grave than the effort by government officials to censor works of expression and to threaten the vitality of a major cultural institution as punishment for failing to abide by governmental demands for orthodoxy" (Barstow 1999). Unrepentant, Mayor Giuliani called the judge's decision "the usual knee-jerk reaction of some judges" and vowed that there would be an appeal, especially in light of evidence that museum officials had "raised money for the exhibition by soliciting hundreds of thousands of dollars from companies and individuals with a commercial interest in the display" (Barstow 1999). Meanwhile, museum officials moved ahead with legal preparations to make the injunction permanent.

In March 2000, with the exhibit already concluded and the date for the mayor's deposition in the museum's lawsuit nearing, the city and the museum reached a settlement under which Mayor Giuliani would restore the museum's funding and cease his efforts to evict the museum. In addition, the city agreed to pay the nearly $6 million for renovations that had been held up by the dispute and assented to a provision that banned the mayor from targeting the museum for funding reductions in the future. The museum thus came away with what appeared to be a total victory, although spokespersons for the city strove to save face by pointing out that the city had not been asked to pay the museum's nearly $1 million in legal fees and that the $6 million for renovations was less than the museum had wanted (Feuer 2000).

A NEGLECTED SUBJECT

This high-profile case of municipal controversy over an issue of morality is presumably widely known and remembered, despite Mayor Giuliani's retooled image in the wake of the September 11, 2001, attack on the World Trade Center. But what lessons can be drawn from it? How should it be interpreted, and how might it fit into broader understandings of politics and governance in American cities? Most attentive citizens both in New York and elsewhere might conclude that this episode simply reflects the mayor's combativeness and sense of moral superiority, the political power of the Catholic Church, and the inevitable controversy generated by the artistic community's avant-garde sensibilities. And until recently, urban scholars would not have attempted to fit this case into mainstream theories of urban politics and governance.

Indeed, decision making on morality issues—issues in which the primary stakes involve religious convictions or similar fundamental principles (Mooney 2001, 4)—has traditionally been outside the purview of urban politics and governance. Despite the many critiques it has weathered on other grounds, Paul Peterson's (1981) classic categorization of city politics into developmental, allocational, and redistributive spheres of activity is still largely intact, encompassing virtually all the subject matter covered by contemporary scholarship on urban politics. And none of those spheres of activity is explicitly defined to include morality issues. In contrast with the emphasis on noneconomic stakes inherent in the conceptualization of morality issues, each of Peterson's spheres is defined on the basis of its "impact on the economic vitality of the community" (Peterson 1981, 41).

Although it emerged as an alternative to Peterson's framework, regime theory (Stone 1989) has also taken the field in a direction that emphasizes economic development and overlooks morality issues at the local level. The building of governing coalitions is the central focus of regime theory, and those coalitions are conceptualized as being rooted in material stakes and divisible benefits. But morality issues such as the Brooklyn Museum of Art controversy are distinctive because they are rooted in deep-seated religious beliefs or moral values.

This is not to say that economic stakes are not involved at all. The Brooklyn Museum of Art case shows that, along with moral indignation, there can be large financial stakes in such controversies. Indeed, conflicts over many morality issues can have material consequences. Owners of nude dancing establishments or other sexually explicit businesses certainly have a financial stake when indignant citizens press for regulations to close such establishments. And although opponents of gambling casinos include religio-moralistic forces, gambling proponents certainly include investors with financial stakes. However, the conceptualization of morality policy hinges on the fact that at least one party to the conflict is mobilized largely because proposals or existing practices are viewed as an affront to religious belief or a violation of a fundamental moral code (Mooney 2001).

In short, the Brooklyn Museum of Art controversy exemplifies what Kenneth Meier (1994) calls "the politics of sin"—a phenomenon that has been neglected by urban scholars. In fact, the history of urban scholarship suggests that, until recently, this case would have been treated as an idiosyncratic episode, largely irrelevant to urban politics and governance. Just as many Americans might roll their eyes and mutter, "Only in New York," so might many urban scholars assume that such controversies are extraordinarily rare, confined to special cases or unique situations far removed from the meat and potatoes of "regular" city politics and therefore altogether inappropriate raw material for developing or applying theories of politics at the local level.

But ongoing developments put a different light on the matter. The stream of local controversies over morality issues has continued to flow long after federal legislation and court cases have quieted protest activity outside abortion clinics; it has continued in a post–September 11 era, when one might have expected other issues to supplant morality issues. Instead, the sheer volume of cases in which local officials grapple with morality issues suggests that this is a neglected area of urban politics and governance rather than a sprinkling of idiosyncratic episodes that have no relevance to our efforts to find meaningful patterns in urban politics and governance. Consider, for example, the following "postcards from the edge" of urban politics.

In September 2002, Portland, Maine, was about to be sued by Catholic Charities Maine over the city's insistence that all agencies receiving grant funding from the city provide domestic partner benefits for their employees—that is, the same health insurance benefits for unmarried, same-sex partners that spouses enjoy. The Salvation Army had already refused to do so because of its religious position against unmarried couples living together and had lost a $60,000 grant for a senior center and meals-on-wheels program as a result. At stake for Catholic Charities was an $85,000 grant to support a variety of counseling and child-care programs (Bouchard 2002a). Ultimately, the controversy was resolved when Catholic Charities came up with a method of skirting Catholic doctrine against premarital sex and homosexuality and providing the domestic partner benefits. Specifically, employees of Catholic Charities could specify one other adult who lived with them to be eligible for health insurance benefits, without having to designate that person as a "domestic partner" (Bouchard 2002b).

In January 2003, the city of Woonsocket, Rhode Island, was embroiled in a controversy over a needle-exchange program designed to provide clean needles to intravenous drug addicts to prevent the spread of HIV and other diseases through the sharing of "dirty" needles. The needle exchange, staffed by employees of the state's health department, had been operating for only a couple of months out of a van that appeared for two hours each week at a location next to a city park. Woonsocket Mayor Susan Menard vociferously opposed the program, stating, "I don't want them in Woonsocket, and I will do whatever's necessary to get them out." The mayor had allies in the legislature, including a Woonsocket police detective and a Woonsocket firefighter who were also state representatives. The two representatives, who were "philosophically opposed to giving needles and other paraphernalia to intravenous drug users," introduced a bill to ban needle distribution within 300 yards of parks, schools, and churches (McFadden 2003).

Nude dancing was the subject in Portland, Oregon, in November 2002. In a case involving a small community in eastern Oregon, the state's appeals court had recently ruled that nude dancing is not a form of expression protected under the state constitution's freedom of speech provisions. The city council in Portland, which had "long expressed frustration at its inability to check the proliferation of nude dancing establishments," seized on the ruling as an opportunity to introduce new zoning regulations that would restrict nude dancing. One city council member was proposing a 1,000-foot exclusion zone to separate sexually oriented businesses from schools and homes, as well as an ordinance to prevent a concentration of such businesses in particular neighborhoods. That member had asked the city attorneys to be ready with ordinance language as soon as the appeals court's ruling was upheld by the state supreme court (Stern 2002).

In February 2003, a federal district judge ruled that the case filed by the city of York, Pennsylvania, against the Reverend Jim Grove could proceed to trial (Associated Press 2003). Grove had been charged with disorderly conduct, harassment, and marching without a parade permit in November 2002 when he led a band of antiabortion protesters carrying large posters of dismembered fetuses in the city's Halloween parade. A number of citizens along the parade route claimed that the protesters had screamed and pushed the posters at them when they had tried to shield their children from the sight (Associated Press 2002). If convicted on the disorderly conduct charge, Grove could receive a one-year prison sentence and a $2,500 fine.

The issue was gambling in the summer of 2002 in Des Plaines, Illinois, a suburb of Chicago. Eight years before, a referendum on casino gambling had registered majority opposition in the community. But in August 2002, the city council nevertheless voted seven to one to develop casino gambling in the city. This meant that the city would have to put in a bid with the Illinois Gaming Board to get a gaming license that had become available when another community's casino development effort failed (McLaughlin 2002a). The city council's vote in favor of a casino occurred despite opposition from a local group—

Citizens of Des Plaines against Gambling Expansion—that had formed with the help of the Reverend Tom Grey, a nationally prominent antigambling activist (McLaughlin 2002b), as well as Bishop C. Joseph Sprague from the Northern Illinois Annual Conference of the United Methodist Church (Higgins 2002). Whereas city officials were enticed by the $25 million in revenue the casino was expected to generate each year, opponents pursued a passionate campaign based on allegations that a casino would bring gambling addiction and crime to the community (McLaughlin 2002c).

These examples, drawn from an array of ordinary cities of various sizes, suggest that morality issues of one kind or another are a staple of local politics and an important part of urban governance. They also exemplify the range of local morality issues considered in this volume—gay rights, abortion protest, legalized gambling, needle exchange (and related drug-control programs), and a host of controversial issues involving the sex industry (e.g., pornography, prostitution, sexually explicit businesses). Although this set is not necessarily exhaustive, it includes a wide array of morality issues and, arguably, most of the morality issues that are distinctively relevant to local government.

MORALITY POLITICS AND CULTURE WARS: THE EMERGENCE OF ANALYTICAL FRAMEWORKS

In addition to the existence of actual controversies in U.S. cities and counties over issues involving morality-driven stakeholders, two important lines of scholarly discourse have provided grounds for moving this topic onto the mainstream agenda of urban scholarship. They have identified morality-based conflict as a key phenomenon in contemporary politics in the United States and provided preliminary frameworks for understanding the character of this important phenomenon. The two lines of scholarly discourse of relevance here are (1) the ever-growing body of empirical research focusing on morality politics, primarily at the national and state levels, and (2) the largely theoretical or interpretive writing concerning "culture wars" in the U.S. context.

With respect to the latter, a series of writers have pointed to the emergence of a new cultural divide in American politics, eclipsing the more familiar social class division that was once the focus of analysis. Although earlier writers such as Daniel Bell (1976) were on the trail of a very similar argument, James Davison Hunter (1991) is perhaps the most notable contemporary proponent of the culture wars thesis. He suggests that "there has been a fundamental realignment within American public culture (and beyond) that cuts across traditional religious divisions" (Hunter 1996, 244). On one side of this cultural divide are orthodox forces based on a "culturally conservative impulse rooted in a transcendent metaphysic that is more or less universally binding"; on the other side are those who espouse "a culturally progressive impulse that grounds moral authority in human experience" (Hunter 1996, 245). According to Hunter, this division between the orthodox view, with its emphasis on unchanging standards of truth and goodness, and the progressive view, with its rejection of universals and emphasis on contingent standards, drives a broad array of conflicts over public policy, religion, the family, the arts, and the basic meaning of American society.

Hunter's work has sparked considerable criticism and debate. But it has also offered an organizing framework for scholars interested in the politics of highly contentious issues, such as abortion, that do not fit well within the usual interpretations of American politics. Coming hard on the heels of American experience with the political mobilization of the Christian right and its continuing involvement in issues such as abortion, pornography, and gambling, the argument was both timely and compelling. Rather than treating periods of conflict over highly volatile issues as bizarre episodes that are the exception to the rule, the culture wars thesis suggests that contentiousness, high levels of polarization based on a clash of fundamental views, and possibly even overt violence are hallmarks of the new way in which politics is organized in American society.

Meanwhile, a distinct but closely related line of scholarship on "morality policy" was sparked by the publication of Kenneth Meier's *The Politics of Sin,* a multimethod analysis of public policy on drugs and alcohol. He treats these two issue areas as examples of morality policy, which is defined as a special form of redistributive policy in which "one segment of society attempts by governmental fiat to impose their values on the rest of society"; hence, values are being redistributed rather than income (Meier 1994, 4). Consistent with the work of culture war analysts, Meier's theoretical framework suggests that morality policy is distinct from other issue areas because citizens' deeply held values are being threatened, leading to a passionate, highly salient style of politics in which both sides engage in simplified and value-based discourse (Meier 1994, 7–8). However, Meier emphasizes that, like other issue areas, morality policy is shaped by industry forces (e.g., producers of alcoholic beverages), political institutions, and bureaucratic processes as well.

It is sometimes claimed that morality policy is defined by the extent to which at least one party in a conflict defines the issue in terms of sin and morality; thus, morality policy does not necessarily include any objectively predefined set of issues (Mooney 2001, 3–4). Nevertheless, the morality policy studies that have emerged tend to focus on topics that might just as easily have been defined a priori as morality issues. These include examinations of national and state-level politics and policy making with respect to abortion (Meier and McFarlane 1993; Norrander and Wilcox 2001), the death penalty (Mooney and Lee 2000), gambling (Pierce and Miller 2001), gay rights (Haider-Markel 1999), pornography (Smith 2001), and statutory rape (Cocca 2002).

Given the occurrence of ongoing local controversies over many of these same issues and the availability of both the culture war and morality politics frameworks for interpreting them, it is not surprising that scholarship on the local government manifestations has finally begun to emerge. Growth in the volume of research focusing on city and county governments' adoption of gay rights policies has been especially notable (Bailey 1999; DeLeon 1999; Chong and Marshall 1999; Rosenthal 1999; Button, Rienzo, and Wald 1997; Klawitter and Hammer 1999; Dorris 1999), but there has also been research on local governments' handling of abortion protest (Woliver 1999; Clarke 1999), gambling (Deitrick, Beauregard, and Kerchis 1999; Goodman 1995), and prostitution (Weitzer 2000; Miller, Romenesko, and Wondolkowski 1993).

This spate of research has generated a number of important insights that contribute to the explanatory framework outlined in the next chapter. However, the existing body of work has several important limitations. Some of it is based on single-city case studies. Although this approach has the advantage of offering richly detailed, contextualized information that allows a deep understanding of policy developments in a particular city, single-city case studies do not allow the generalization of results across cities; nor are they structured to help explain differences in morality policy among cities. Other research on local morality policy involves quantitative analysis of a particular morality issue in a relatively large number of cities. Such an approach has the important advantage of providing a generalizable explanation of differences in morality policy across cities; however, it has three important disadvantages. First, the detailed, contextual information available in a case study approach—particularly the historical perspective—is sacrificed in favor of using statistical inference to draw conclusions. Second, studies in this genre tend to focus on only a single morality issue at a time, leaving the matter of cross-issue generalization underdeveloped. In addition, efforts to compare results across issues are hampered by researchers' use of different sets of theoretical frameworks and different independent variables in their analyses. Finally, in part because of the imperatives of measuring the dependent variable in a standard fashion across cities, and in part because of the vagaries of data availability, quantitative studies of morality policy tend to be narrowly focused on the adoption of a particular policy (such as a gay rights ordinance). A more complete understanding of a city's stance on any given morality issue involves much more than this, including information on whether relevant policies were adopted readily or reluctantly, whether there are large differences between the policy as adopted and the policy as implemented or enforced, and whether officials engage in actions and rhetoric that amount to the making of symbolic policy above and beyond officially legislated policy.

This book takes the middle ground in the methodological divide between "large N" quantitative studies and single-city case studies. It is based on ten study cities, strategically chosen to allow for systematic comparisons and contrasts among them (see chapter 2). The patterns generated by these comparisons and contrasts can yield evidence about the importance of various explanations for different local governmental stances on a given morality issue. At the same time, the manageable number of study cities allows for a detailed examination of each one's recent handling of the five morality issues explored in this book: abortion, gambling, the sex industry, gay rights, and drug-control programs. These historical narratives provide detailed evidence to support the classifications used to compare and contrast the cities' experience with each of the morality issues; they can also corroborate the inferences drawn from those comparisons by offering direct evidence of the considerations in play as local officials grappled with these issues.

Apart from their evidentiary importance, though, the historical narratives presented in this book are interesting in themselves.[1] Readers with a particular interest in casino gambling or gay rights or any of the other issues covered in this volume will, of course, be especially curious about the developments in those topics. But the experiences of these ten cities with these five morality issues are inherently engrossing because of the pure drama that enlivens many of the histories. In the pages that follow, you will meet local officials in a confrontation with the Vatican over funding for abortion services; officials in another city engaged in a multiyear legal battle with a major research university over its refusal to provide health benefits to gay and lesbian partners of faculty members; officials in another community mounting a massive legal attack on topless clubs, using a special prosecutor paid with hundreds of thousands of dollars amassed by a citizens group opposed to the clubs; local officials risking possible legal action for supporting a program to provide clean needles to drug addicts; and much more.

Despite their occasionally dramatic character, however, these episodes of local controversy and decision making about morality issues can be explained. That is, they exhibit patterns of variation across cities that reflect what we would expect on the basis of key theoretical frameworks. For citizens and local officials caught up in a controversy, the particulars of the unfolding issue may seem unique. But objective comparisons with other cities can generate important insights about which theoretical frameworks have the "reach" to account for what happens in this realm of local politics.

2
Studying Morality Politics

Local officials grapple with a number of important morality issues, but if they all ultimately adopted the same policy stance and took the same implementation actions, local morality politics and policy making would not be particularly interesting. But as the case histories in this book show, there are enormous differences in how these issues are handled in different cities. Officials in some cities eagerly legislate the agenda of gay rights activists, while officials in other places are hostile to similar proposals. Officials in some cities adopt needle-exchange programs, while officials elsewhere stoutly refuse to even consider them or to tolerate programs that have begun operating informally. In some cities, official crackdowns on pornography or other sexually explicit material are at least as vociferous as Mayor Giuliani's in the example featured in chapter 1; other officials adopt a much more permissive attitude toward the operation of the sex industry in their communities. There are equally striking differences in the handling of abortion protest and in local governments' stance on casino gambling.

How can we account for these differences? That is the focal question of this book and the primary reason for presenting the histories of the handling of particular morality issues in the various cities. But exploration of these comparative case histories should not be undertaken without some conceptual road map to point out possible explanations and thereby define the relevant evidence to consider in the case histories.

The literature on morality policy and culture wars offers a plethora of suggestions for that road map. The character of abortion policy at the state level, for example, has been found to be a function of the direction of public opinion in the state, the overall position of state policy on a liberal–conservative spectrum, party control of the legislature, the magnitude of the Catholic population, and the extent to which women are serving in the state legislature (Norrander and Wilcox 2001). The most extensive multicity study to date of the adoption of gay antidiscrimination ordinances found that whether a city adopts such an ordinance is a function (sometimes negative, sometimes positive) of city size, the extent of nonfamily households, the number of openly gay public officials or candidates, the availability of service establishments for gays, the extent of church affiliation within the city's population, the prevalence of conservative Protestant adherents, and the existence of a state gay rights law (Wald, Button, and Rienzo 1996). With respect to sexually explicit materials, Smith (2001) found that the aggressiveness of state enforcement of obscenity laws depends on the prevalence of fundamentalist religious adherents in the population, the extent to which the public has permissive attitudes toward pornography, the degree of female political empowerment in the state, the extent of political party competition, and state per capita income level.

Even these three examples show that different researchers tackling different morality issues include somewhat different variables in their analyses. It might seem, then, that there is no common explanatory framework that can be used to guide our inquiry. However, a broad-based synthesis of existing research on morality politics and culture wars, coupled with basic theoretical perspectives from studies of urban politics and policy, suggests the importance of four key explanations for the character of official action on morality issues at the local level: a cultural (or, more accurately, subcultural) explanation, an institutional explanation, an economic explanation, and an intergovernmental explanation. These four explanatory approaches provide the framework for the analysis in each chapter, and they were the basis for the selection of the case study cities, which are introduced later in this chapter.

SUBCULTURAL EXPLANATION

Morality issues involve core beliefs and frequently feature the activity of social movements and identity groups; they are also directly implicated in the "culture wars" (Hunter 1991, 1996) that provide an important new dividing line in American politics. Not surprisingly, then, a crucial theoretical framework for understanding city governments' handling of morality issues is cultural analysis. Although there are frequently complaints about the lack of an agreed-on definition of *culture* (Eckstein 1988), social scientists have long used the term *culture* to refer to "beliefs, values, and affective commitments" that groups of individuals hold in common; these beliefs, values, and affective commitments are expected to provide the basis for individuals to interpret reality and perhaps even to define their own identities (Crothers and Lockhart 2000, 1). In the late 1980s, writers such as Ronald Inglehart (1988, 1203) noted that the "incompleteness of models that ignore cultural factors is becoming increasingly evident." In the years since, there has indeed been a renaissance of interest in using culture to explain political developments.

But political science's interest in how cultural differences might drive political and economic outcomes (Jackman and Miller 1996) is burdened by a variety of problems. In his cataloging of these, Ross (2000, 56–57) notes that there is a unit-of-analysis problem, because "culture is not a unit of social or political organization with readily identifiable boundaries." And even if there is agreement on the group or spatial unit that is alleged to have a particular culture, there is substantial variation among individuals within any culture, leaving some critics to wonder just what it is that members of a culture share. In addition to these problems, culture is supposed to be stable and enduring. Hence, there are problems in using cultural differences to explain relatively rapidly developing changes in politics or policy. Finally, critics have raised questions about the mechanisms by which culture leads to the effects attributed to it (Ross 2000, 58–59). In addition to these problems, there are unresolved differences over the meaning of *culture,* the cluster of variables that is most important for inclusion in cultural analysis, and the resulting categorization of cultures. As a result of all these problems, Ross argues that "culture is not a concept with which most political scientists are comfortable" (2000, 40).

Much of the earliest work using cultural analyses of political phenomena treated the nation-state as the appropriate unit of analysis, thereby ignoring the first problem in favor of an assumption that a nation-state is equivalent to a society with a single culture. Such an approach exacerbates the second problem, for clearly there is substantial variation in values, lifestyles, beliefs, and practices among individuals, communities, and even regions of the United States. Those interested in cultural analysis at the community level have taken a different approach. Though acknowledging that there may be enough shared identity and shared meaning to think of the United States as having a culture, they recognize that the substantial differences in values, lifestyles, beliefs, and practices across communities indicate the presence of *subcultures* in the United States.

Daniel Elazar (1970, 1984) was one of the first to develop a specific formulation of the content and character of these subcultures. Drawing on historical migration patterns of various nationality and religious groups, combined with interviews, personal observations, and analyses of published works on those groups, Elazar developed a typology of three distinct subcultures— individualistic, moralistic, and traditionalistic—and mapped states and substate regions into one of the three types or one of six hybrid types based on the initial three.

Although Elazar's formulation was used in numerous research applications, it exhibits several of the problems outlined earlier. The unit-of-analysis problem is manifested in his use of entire states or large substate regions without any strong basis for viewing these geopolitical units as a society with a shared culture; in addition, the size of these units is such that the variation within them is substantial. Even more important is the failure of Elazar's formulation to deal with the issue of cultural change. Over time, there has been substantial change in the ethnic and religious composition of many communities. Yet Elazar's typology does not take into account the layering of these demographic changes onto historical patterns of migration (Lieske 1993, 889).

These weaknesses inspired Joel Lieske (1993) to develop a new mapping of subcultures in the United States. This one uses cluster analysis of forty-five county-level demographic characteristics intended to measure, with 1980 data, urbanization, agrarianism, population mobility, social status, income inequality, family structure, age distribution, distribution of religious affiliations, and racial composition. Although this generates an updated typology that is grounded in a rigorous empirical analysis, the typology is unsatisfying. It includes an unwieldy set of ten subcultural categories that, despite the number of characteristics used in the analysis, amount to no more than descriptions of the dominant nationality groups (Germanic, Nordic, Anglo-French), religion (Mormon), race (Black Belt), or region (Heartland, Border).

Departing from the approach developed by Elazar and Lieske, the cultural analysis in this book draws on the work of a host of writers who have pointed to important trends in the postindustrial era, including changes in women's social roles; the increasing prevalence of postsecondary education; the rising number of nontraditional households, such as unrelated individuals living together and female-headed families; and the growing importance of human services employment (Rosdil 1991, 81). Donald Rosdil argues that in cities where these trends have developed the furthest, "large, robust countercultures which challenge traditional societal values" have emerged, and these have created a social culture in the city that is unconventional or post-traditional. Cities having such unconventional cultures are depicted as being dominated by a set of political values that include radicalization (in the sense of antisystem beliefs and values), a propensity to support new social movements, and a left-liberal predisposition (Rosdil 1998). By contrast, in cities that have experienced little in the way of postindustrial change, the overall social culture can be characterized as conventional or traditional.

In a related vein, Ronald Inglehart (1977) points to trends such as increasing levels of education, geographic mobility, and technological and economic changes that are gradually, through the socialization of those coming of age after World War II, transforming the political culture of advanced, postindustrial societies. Inglehart posits that these trends have led to a value shift, placing more emphasis on the satisfaction of higher-order needs, such as the need to belong and for esteem and self-realization, and less on lower-order needs, such as satisfaction of material needs and security. This change in values is a manifestation of cultural change, and it has political culture implications as well. Although there will be pockets of traditionalism, vanguard cities in advanced postindustrial nation-states will increasingly be characterized by a style of politics that involves the salience of lifestyle issues, the decline of class-based conflict relative to conflict based on other social cleavages, the declining legitimacy of traditional institutions, and the rise of identity politics.

In a similar fashion, Terry Clark and colleagues have argued that, although it is more dominant in some locations than in others, a "new political culture" began to emerge in many advanced, postindustrial countries by the 1970s. According to Clark (1998, 3), this new political culture is more likely to emerge in places "with more highly educated citizens, higher incomes, and high-tech service occupations." With Inglehart, Clark argues that the new political culture is manifested in the decline of class-based conflict and traditionally defined left-right issues; the decline of party identification in the mass public; the "heightened, sometimes heated, importance of ethnic, linguistic, and regional cleavages"; the emergence of politically mobilized religious fundamentalism; and the rise of new social movements (Clark and Inglehart 1998, 9–10).

These various analyses provide theoretical support for an approach to political culture that distinguishes cities with unconventional cultures from those with conventional or traditional cultures, and they provide hints about how this cultural difference can be expected to influence the way officials deal with morality issues. In particular, we can assume for the moment that local public officials reflect their subcultural milieu, either because, as products of that subculture, they share its values and preferences or because reelection (or reappointment) imperatives force them to be sensitive to those values and preferences. Although this assumption will shortly be made conditional on the institutional arrangements within which public officials function, it is a reasonable beginning—one that is consistent with both national- and state-level research showing that elected officials are particularly likely to be responsive to public opinion on highly salient, value-based issues (Page and Shapiro 1983; Burstein 1999), and one that is consistent with Clark and Inglehart's (1998, 10) notion that public officials are the critical actors or Weberian "carriers" of cultural change.

At the most basic level, then, we might expect the character and trajectory of official action in unconventional communities to be more consistent with the agenda or values of the progressive left (e.g., favorable to gay rights, supportive of needle-exchange and other innovative programs involving drugs), whereas officials in conventional cities would have the opposite policy stance. Conversely, in conventional cities, we would expect official action to be con-

sistent with traditional values and supportive of the conservative, "family values" agenda promoted by conventional, conservative forces (e.g., more permissive toward antiabortion protesters, more hostile toward gambling, more
restrictive of pornography and sexually explicit businesses).

INSTITUTIONAL EXPLANATION

There are strong grounds for theorizing that the expectations and pressures
stemming from the local political culture (including the identity movements
and interest groups that reflect that culture) are not equally important in shaping governmental responses in all cities. Rather, a long line of scholarship in
political science suggests that the influence of these cultural expectations and
interest-group pressures is mediated by local political institutions—local governing structures or authoritative decision-making arrangements (Lineberry
and Fowler 1967; Morgan and Hirlinger 1991; Clingermayer and Feiock 2001).
But what political institutions should be of particular interest? And what does
theory have to say about how they mediate between cultural or group inputs
and governmental outputs?

Given the types of issues involved in morality policy making, a host of political institutions are arguably relevant in some way. For example, because public health departments are often instrumental in decision making about needle-
exchange programs, institutional differences (e.g., level of professionalism,
degree of autonomy from overarching officials such as mayors) might be expected to make a difference in how cultural and group inputs factor into decision-
making outcomes. Likewise, county-level institutions—most notably the district attorney's office and county courts—are relevant to many morality issues.
For example, district attorneys are key figures in deciding whether to prosecute purveyors of pornography on obscenity charges, and county-level judges
have been singled out as key actors in the development of courts that take an
alternative, treatment-focused approach to minor drug offenders. Presumably,
then, institutional differences with respect to district attorneys and judges (e.g.,
whether they are elected or appointed) could be expected to have a bearing on
the extent to which community pressure influences decision making. And although this book examines cities, other officials in the counties in which those
cities are situated are sometimes integral parts of the story. Hence, institutional
differences in the structure of the county executive or the county legislature
may also be relevant.

In short, decision making on morality issues involves a complex mosaic
of institutional arrangements, even though some are relevant in only a few

cases or for only a certain type of issue. Although the role of each of these arrangements is considered here, the institutions that distinguish reformed from nonreformed general-purpose city government are the primary focus of this book's approach to the institutionalist explanation, in part because that set of institutional arrangements is relevant for all types of morality issues, in part because the primary focus is on city government, and in part because such a long line of research in urban politics focuses on those institutions and provides richly developed theoretical perspectives for understanding how they might shape policy outcomes.

Three kinds of institutions are key to the distinction between reformed and nonreformed city governments. First, with respect to the chief executive, reformed cities have city managers rather than mayors; they are appointed by the city legislature on the basis of professional management credentials. Although city managers serve at the pleasure of the legislature, they have full executive powers, including the hiring and firing of cabinet heads and budget formulation. This arrangement attempts to separate the more political, policy-making powers of the legislature from administrative functions; thus, it relies on nonelected professionals whose neutral competence insulates those functions from partisan politics. Although city managers may be actively involved in policy formulation through the provision of information and recommendations to the legislature, they are not expected to play a leadership role in policy making, nor, as unelected officials, can they play a strong leadership role in the sense of speaking for the community. By contrast, nonreformed cities lodge executive powers in the hands of directly elected mayors. Because of the reelection imperatives facing mayors, administration in nonreformed cities can be more politicized. By the same token, because nonreformed cities have an elected official as the chief executive, there is greater potential for strong, unitary city leadership.

The second institutional arrangement of relevance to the reformed-nonreformed distinction involves city legislatures, which go by various names (commission, board of supervisors, city council). Because it is the most common reference, the term *city council* is used here. Reformism with respect to the city council means that members are elected at large rather than from the single-member districts (i.e., wards) characteristic of elections in nonreformed cities. At-large elections are "reformed" institutions in the sense that they substitute council members with a citywide constituency (and presumably citywide concerns) for more parochial, district-elected council members (with neighborhood-level interests or, even worse, ward-based machine politics, with its emphasis on votes in exchange for favors). By the same token, at-large elections in principle diminish responsiveness to neighborhood-based needs and make it more difficult for some groups, most notably racial minorities, to elect representatives.

The third institutional arrangement signifying reformed government is the use of nonpartisan ballots — again, to break the back of party-based political machines. However, the use of nonpartisan ballots is not really reliable for distinguishing reformed from nonreformed cities, for a variety of reasons. In many cities that are officially nonpartisan and ostensibly use nonpartisan ballots, there are nevertheless a variety of slating organizations that develop candidates, provide financial support for them, and in other ways function much like a conventional political party. Furthermore, in many large cities in the United States, one party is so dominant that the movement to nonpartisan elections would be relatively meaningless.

Reform-style institutions such as at-large elections and the council-manager form of government are structural arrangements that theoretically insulate governance from community demands and activist pressures, substituting professional and technical considerations for political imperatives in decision making. By contrast, nonreformed institutions, such as district elections and mayoral control of administration, offer, in theory, a more politicized system that is more vulnerable to demands. Thus, the institutionalist explanation involves a more complex version of the subcultural explanation acknowledged earlier. To the extent that subculture involves a mélange of community expectations, pressures, or demands for particular courses of action, those demands can be expected to operate with greater force in nonreformed cities because of the enhanced accessibility and political motivations of their officials. Subcultural differences can be expected to make less of a difference in city officials' stances on morality issues in places with reformed governing institutions, which tend to buffer local officials from community demands.

This is the essence of the institutionalist explanation, and there is considerable empirical support for it, at least as applied to nonmorality issues (Feiock and Cable 1992; Clingermayer and Feiock 2001). And there is every reason to expect that differences in formal governance structures would in similar fashion influence communities' handling of culture war issues.

ECONOMIC EXPLANATION

Initially, it might appear that the status of the city's economy and the sphere of developmental activity designed to affect the local economy are completely separate from and irrelevant to the city's handling of morality issues. As argued in chapter 1, morality issues are a distinctive sphere of activity, in part because they involve the mobilization of stakeholders whose motivation is moral or religious values rather than money, jobs, or other material benefits. For this reason, some analysts of morality issues largely eschew economic explanations, or they include economic variables in their analysis but indicate that they are not expected to contribute to the explanation (Wald, Button, and Rienzo 1996, 1158). However, there are theoretical grounds for expecting there to be a connection between the politics of morality issues and the politics of economic development.

Although the investment necessary for economic development is in the hands of private-sector actors, local public officials are held accountable for encouraging that investment. They are actively engaged in efforts to do so, including the issuance of tax abatements and other financial inducements, programmatic efforts to develop the necessary infrastructure, and informational campaigns designed to tout the city's advantages as a place to do business. Pagano and Bowman (1997) show that, in the competition for economic development, city "image" is a crucial matter. City image is a "collective vision of what the city could, or should, become" (48)—an image developed by city leaders in conjunction with their perception of who their competitor cities are. City image in this sense is a "guide for purposive action" (50), suggesting which projects, plans, and policies should receive public-sector backing. But city image is also a symbolic representation, a message to potential investors. And "a positive and attractive image is one of the tools a city can use to lure investors" (51). By the same token, a negative, unattractive image is damaging to a city's efforts to lure investors. Although physical structures are often the most obvious examples of a positive image (e.g., a new convention center) or a negative image (e.g., decaying buildings in an old warehouse area), social features can also either damage or enhance a city's image. For example, in cities that are convulsed with social conflict over abortion clinic protest, officials' responses to the conflict will be shaped in part by concerns about how that conflict damages the city's image as a good place to do business. Similarly, where activists are pushing for needle-exchange programs on public health grounds, city officials may be concerned that such programs would amount to publicly airing the city's "dirty laundry" (i.e., its drug problem). In short, the politics of morality issues intersects with the politics of economic development to the extent that any morality issue heightens the city's profile in a way that may be viewed as undesirable.

Concerns about city image may be particularly important when the city's collective vision of its economic future includes an attempt to market itself for convention and tourism business. A large number of cities are in this category, in part because the central city has lost its key role in manufacturing and cannot successfully compete with the suburbs for wholesaling and retailing investment (Judd 1999, 35). Analysts note that city governments' efforts to compete for convention and tourism business involve investment in a standard set of physical developments: atrium hotel, festival mall, convention center, domed stadium, aquarium, office towers, and waterfront redevelopment (Frieden and Sagalyn 1990, as cited in Judd 1999, 39). More important, these facilities are located in what Judd (1999, 36) calls a "tourist bubble"—that is, a separate section that is insulated from the rest of the city, so that everyday problems such as crime and poverty are not visible to tourists. Although it may be possible to shield tourists and convention-goers from such problems by constructing facilities that are physically distant from the ordinary city, it may be more difficult to keep them from contact with morality issue controversies. Whether the city's image is one of provincialism or cosmopolitanism, social conflict or tolerance of diversity, depends on the reputation the city develops when morality issues become controversial and visible.

It is a truism that city leaders are intolerant of anything that might be construed as frightening to tourists. At the simplest level, one might expect that officials in all communities would be hostile to activism on any morality issue, on the grounds that the attendant controversy would be bad for business. But that hypothesis is too simplistic. The precise way in which morality issues factor into the politics of economic development depends on the specific morality issue in question and on the particulars of the city's development plans. For example, local officials might be especially responsive to decency activists when adult entertainment establishments stand in the way of redevelopment projects designed to transform an erstwhile red-light district into an upscale shopping area; however, local officials might be nonresponsive to decency activists protesting over "offensive" art displayed by a major art institution that is a keystone in the city's efforts to market itself for cultural tourism. Similarly, those opposed to gambling on moral grounds may find that public officials are either receptive or hostile to their antigambling cause, depending on whether casino development fits into city leaders' collective vision of how the city can successfully market itself or whether casinos are viewed as "unlikely to anchor an economically integrated and diversified local tourist sector" (Deitrick, Beauregard, and Kerchis 1999, 233).

In short, the ways in which morality issues intersect with economic development considerations can be highly variable. The key to the economic development explanation is that intersection of the two issues is more likely to occur in cities that are desperate for economic investment. That is, although all cities confront pressures for economic development and have corresponding concerns about city image, these pressures and concerns are much more

substantial in declining, economically distressed cities than in cities with secure economies. Hence, when there is a conflict between morality forces and
economic development considerations—for example, when antiabortion
protest creates a conflictual environment that could be threatening to tourism,
or a needle-exchange program raises concerns about the city's image as a center for drug problems—economic development considerations are highly likely
to trump morality considerations in economically distressed cities but are less
likely to do so in prosperous communities.

INTERGOVERNMENTAL EXPLANATION

City officials do not make decisions on morality issues in isolation. As noted
in the section on the institutional explanation, they often must act in conjunction with county officials. But apart from these local interrelations, city officials' actions on morality issues will be strongly influenced by both the federal
government and the state government. At the most general level, the federal
and state governments function to shape local action in many spheres through
the resources they provide in the form of information and grants-in-aid. Hence,
we should not be surprised to find federal and state efforts to use funding and
information as incentives to push local officials in particular directions on
morality issues as well. For example, the federal government impaneled a national commission to study the impacts of gambling, which recommended a
moratorium on new gambling despite its admitted economic benefits; similarly,
Congress has refused to sanction the use of federal monies for needle-exchange
programs.

More important, both the states and the federal government have engaged
in policy making on many of the morality issues considered in this book, generating laws and judicial rulings that constitute explicit mandates on local
government that can either empower or constrain local officials. With respect
to constraints, what local government can do is often limited by federal or state
action, especially in states where there is little in the way of a home-rule tradition. For example, if state law does not allow gambling, city and county officials cannot pursue casino development. Or if state law bans the distribution
of syringes to drug addicts, even for public health purposes, local officials are
constrained from institutionalizing needle-exchange programs. Conversely,
state governments, and sometimes the federal government, can expand the
range of choices that local officials are empowered to make. Again drawing on
the gambling example, if a state government adopts a highly permissive gambling statute, local officials have the option of using it to aggressively pursue

casino development. Or if a state's high court upholds a local ordinance restricting nude dancing, local governments throughout the state have a new tool to use in regulating sexually explicit businesses.

Virtually the entire body of scholarship on intergovernmental relations in the United States is guided by the theme of conflict versus cooperation or collaboration (Agranoff 2001). The character of intergovernmental relations with respect to morality policy should also be considered along this dimension. In addition to the contrast between empowering and constraining, the policy-making action of states and the federal government may be either consistent with local policy makers' predilections or at cross-purposes with them. That is, they may either support or conflict with the actions that local officials are predisposed to take on the basis of pressures stemming from the prevailing local subculture. The mobilization of culturally conservative forces in conventional communities, for example, can generally be expected to push local decision makers to aggressively repress the growth of sexually explicit businesses. However, the effects of that mobilization may be apparent only if the community is located in a state where state law and judicial rulings allow aggressive local responses; in similar cities located in states that do not allow aggressive local responses, local officials may be limited to symbolic gestures, such as rhetoric signaling their opposition to sleazy businesses. In other words, the intergovernmental explanation, like the institutional explanation, specifies a mediating role for intergovernmental arrangements. Hence, the impact of local subculture on city officials would be most apparent where state law is consistent with the values of the local subculture and least apparent where state law conflicts with local values.

However, such a straightforward approach treats local governments as passive targets of state and federal action or inaction, ignoring the possibility that local officials might take action to compensate for or counteract the policies of higher-level governments. In principle, such compensatory action can operate in two directions. Local governments might engage in action to overcome obstacles or constraints created by the state or federal government. For example, in states that do not authorize needle exchange, local officials in communities with strong pressures for such programs might find legal subterfuges that allow them to institute needle-exchange programs in defiance of state law. Alternatively, local governments might try to avoid taking an action that federal or state policy empowers them to take. For example, if a state allows needle-exchange programs but the local context makes such programs controversial, local officials might simply avoid addressing the issue, perhaps even permitting the police to continue to arrest activists engaged in private needle-exchange operations.

Table 2.1 Typology of Local Action vis-à-vis State Government:
Needle Exchange

	For Cities Predisposed to:	
Status of State Policy	Adopt Needle Exchange	Avoid Needle Exchange
Constrains needle exchange	Compensatory action	Legitimated inaction
Empowers needle exchange	Legitimated action	Underutilization

The various possibilities outlined so far are summarized in the typology in table 2.1, using needle exchange as the example. As the table suggests, the relationship that local governments have with their respective state governments (or with the federal government) on these morality issues is theorized to depend on the consistency between state policy and local policy preferences (i.e., only where there is inconsistency would we expect to find either compensatory action or underutilization of powers provided by the state). The task in the chapters that follow is to determine whether there is evidence for the sort of action theoretically specified in table 2.1.

THE STUDY CITIES

As noted in chapter 1, much of the research on morality politics at the local level has been driven by case studies focusing on only a single city (or perhaps a pair of cities). Although much has been learned in this fashion, such case studies have obvious limitations related to the generalizability of the findings. The explanatory frameworks outlined earlier invite us to use an investigatory approach that allows for systematic assessment based on comparisons across cities. However, to fully and accurately depict what happened in a particular community on even one morality issue (let alone a variety of them) requires the sort of richly detailed information and evidence that must be gleaned from fieldwork using newspaper archives, analysis of other documentary sources, and interviews with relevant government officials and issue activists. This time-consuming and expensive data collection approach inhibits the inclusion of a large number of cities.

However, it is possible to gain a great deal of explanatory power from a relatively small number of study cities if those cities allow for systematic comparisons and contrasts (King, Keohane, and Verba 1994). In particular, the chosen study cities must have maximal variation on key explanatory variables and minimal correlation between explanatory variables. Setting aside the intergovernmental explanation, which plays only a secondary role in this inquiry, there are three key explanations for variation in city governments' handling of morality issues, focusing on (1) the sociocultural character of the community, (2) the institutional arrangements of local governance, and (3) the economic status of the community. From the fifty-two cities in the United States with a 1980 population of at least 300,000, ten cities were chosen that exhibit the greatest amount of variation on a variable chosen to represent each of the three explanations and allow for comparisons of cities that differ with respect to one variable while being similar with respect to the other two.[1]

Although study cities were initially selected on the basis of a single variable representing each of the three core explanations, the work in this volume relies on a more refined and updated classification of the cities into the analytical categories of the core explanations, based on a multivariable assessment of each city's sociocultural type and economic development status. Economic development status for each city is the average of standardized scores on three indicators: population change 1990–1998, household median income in 1989, and unemployment rate in 1997. Community subculture for each city is the average of six indicators of unconventional culture, all for 1990: same-sex-partner households per 100,000 households; percentage of individuals not living in households with married parents and children under age nineteen; percentage of women in the labor force; percentage of the workforce in professional, scientific, technical, or educational categories; percentage of the population aged twenty-five and older with a bachelor's degree or higher; and percentage of the county population not adhering to a church. The resulting study cities are presented in figure 2.1, which shows each city's sociocultural and economic categorization, along with one of the relevant institutional features—type of chief executive. In addition, it may be useful to know that the study cities exhibit fairly good regional representation, with four cities from the West or Southwest, two cities from the Midwest, one city from the Northeast, two cities from the Southeast, and one from the mid-South.

Because the six-item index of unconventional (versus conventional) culture is both innovative and crucial for much of the analysis that follows, it may be useful to establish some evidence of its reliability and validity. Fortunately, a unique opportunity to do so was made possible by the Social Capital Benchmark Survey (SCBS) that Robert Putnam and colleagues conducted in more than thirty communities in 2000–2001 and by the efforts of Richard DeLeon and Katherine Naff (2003), who used the SCBS data to develop and test the new political culture index, which is intended to measure the same phenomenon of unconventional culture that is of interest here. Their seven-item index includes measures that closely parallel those used in the index of unconventional culture (e.g., whether an individual is a church adherent and the percentage of

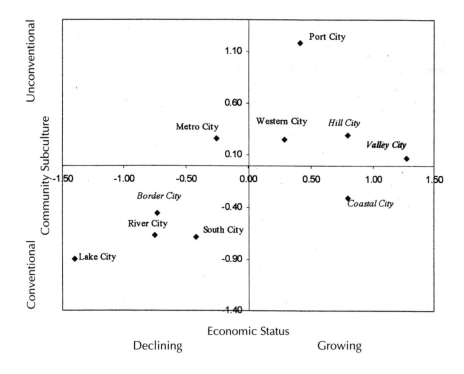

Figure 2.1 Study Cities, by Economic Status, Community Subculture Type, and Chief Executive Type

Roman type indicates cities with mayors only; italic indicates cities with city managers; bold italic indicates cities with city managers and directly elected mayors. Economic development status for each city is the average of standardized scores on three indicators: population change 1990–1998, household median income in 1989, and unemployment rate in 1997. Community subculture for each city is the average of six indicators of degree of unconventional culture, all for 1990: same-sex-partner households per 100,000 households; percentage of individuals not living in households with married parents and children under age 19; percentage of women in the labor force; percentage of the workforce in professional, scientific, technical, or educational categories; percentage of the over-age-25 population with a bachelor's degree or higher; and percentage of the county population not adhering to a church.

respondents who are single, working women), as well as some additional items (e.g., the percentage of respondents who have a gay or lesbian friend and a composite indicator of the racial diversity of respondents' friendships) that go beyond what is possible with Census Bureau and other aggregate data. By comparing the index of unconventional culture (updated with 2000 data and applied to the thirty-odd SCBS communities on which DeLeon and Naff based their analysis) to the new political culture index, we can examine the believability of the measurement scheme that undergirds much of the analysis in this book.

The new political culture index yields substantially better results with respect to reliability than does the index of unconventional culture; the average inter-item correlation is 0.64 for the former, compared with 0.29 for the latter. The problematic elements of the index of unconventional culture involve the Census Bureau's measure of individuals employed in the scientific, technical, and educational sector and the Glenmary Institute's county-level measure of church adherence. With these two items removed, the simpler four-item index of unconventional culture has a much more respectable average inter-item correlation of 0.43. Reassuringly, however, if unconventional culture in the study cities was measured with the four-item index, the cities would still be ordered and categorized in the same way.

Even when the six-item index of unconventional culture is used, it is clearly measuring much the same thing as the new political culture index; the correlation between the two is 0.84. And in terms of validity, the index of unconventional culture performs well. In addition to its high correlation with the DeLeon and Naff index, the index of unconventional culture shows strong construct validation, in that it is strongly related to concepts for which it would be expected to serve as a predictor, based on theoretical grounds. For example, the correlation between the index of unconventional culture and the percentage of SCBS respondents who describe themselves as politically liberal is 0.834 (the corresponding correlation with the new political culture index as the predictor is 0.945). Further information on the index's measurement validity and reliability is presented in Sharp (2004).

Thus, classification of the study cities with respect to unconventional versus conventional subculture and the other key explanatory dimensions was based primarily on statistical information. However, our fieldwork generated supplementary evidence in the form of newspaper articles and comments from those we interviewed that corroborates their categorization. That material is the basis for the capsule descriptions that follow, which also give the reader a more qualitative "feel" for the cities than figure 2.1 can provide.

But first, a side note: In this book, pseudonyms are used for the study cities themselves and for individuals, organizations, and specific places within each city. To some readers, this practice may be aggravating, subverting the desire to factor in personal knowledge they might have about the study cities. However, the use of pseudonyms is necessary because the individuals interviewed for the study were promised anonymity. Oddly enough, the pseudo–city names remind us that the intent is to move away from the mind-set that treats a particular city's experiences as being unique to that city. Each study city occupies an important place in an explanatory framework, and the emphasis here is on the theoretically relevant context that each city provides rather than the uniqueness of each city.

Unconventional Cities

Valley City. Valley City, one of the four unconventional, growing cities in this study, is headquarters to a large number of leading high-tech companies and is a major export city. In the early 1990s, Valley City was hit hard by a recession and a $15 million to $20 million budget shortfall, but by the mid-1990s, economic prosperity had returned and there was talk of high-tech employment making Valley City a land of opportunity, where one could make one's fortune with skill and luck. Valley City's population grew faster than all but one of the other study cities. Its 1990 median household income of over $36,000 was the highest among the study cities. The economic boom of the late 1990s also drove up property and housing values to among the highest in the nation.

The city is frequently described as a liberal, progressive place. Its ethos is that of a live-and-let-live, risk-taking, can-do, Sun Belt city. However, there is also a small-town feel of trust, consensus, and friendliness among both citizens and politicians. Voter turnout is high, but there is a low level of political activism in the form of demonstrations or civil disobedience, and there is minimal conflict among social groups. In fact, a reporter who visited the local human relations commission was told that "this place is seething with rest," a relative calm that local officials attribute to the area's affluence and political culture. The pioneer spirit that led to wave after wave of settlers in the area is another reason for the peace. People came ready to try something new, to experience different places and people. Likewise, a former mayor emphasizes Valley City's lack of factionalism; its lack of entrenched, powerful interests; its large number of newcomers; and its wealthy and well-educated citizens.

Valley City is a hybrid reformed city. That is, it has a council-manager form of government, with an appointed, professional city manager. However, it has an eleven-member city council elected by districts and a mayor who is directly elected at large. The mayor is a member of the council and has powers that make the office somewhat more than the figurehead position it is in most cities with city managers. In particular, the council traditionally follows the lead of the mayor with respect to which issues are on the agenda.

Western City. Western City is a growing city, with a 1990 population 5.4 percent larger than its 1980 population and a nearly 7 percent increase from 1990 to 1998. Historically, Western City and its home state suffered the vagaries of boom-and-bust cycles characteristic of economies dominated by energy-sector activities. The state and city entered a prolonged recession in the early 1980s, and because of a lack of diversification, both Western City and the state responded sluggishly to national economic recovery in the 1980s. From 1988 through 1991 especially, the state was undergoing an economic transformation dogged by industrial consolidations, slow job growth, and declining real estate values. Economic turnaround began in the early 1990s, and by the end of the decade, the state had the third most diversified economy in the United States. The business climate was earning straight A ratings for performance on employment, earnings and job quality, structural diversity, entrepreneurial energy, infrastructure resources, amenity resources and natural capital, and innovation assets. In contrast to the energy resource–dominated economy of the 1980s, major economic sectors now include agribusiness, engineering, tourism, biotechnology, telecommunications, computer software, and storage technology.

In the latter 1990s, the city's mayor called on the city's urban renewal authority to push forward on downtown revitalization and to accelerate development in an area slated for entertainment and tourism development. In 1999, *Fortune* magazine's ranking of the best American cities for business put Western City high on the list, citing the high proportion of people with college degrees, the high degree of economic diversity in the city, rising rates of personal income relative to housing costs, low taxes, and a magnificent public park system.

To many local leaders, the economic future involves international trade and tourism. Western City's airport is one of the busiest in the country, though it ranks lower in terms of international passengers and lags even further on cargo operations. Enhancing the airport's international traffic is an important priority for city officials, and in 1997, Western City created an international trade office. These global aspirations make city officials especially sensitive to the city's image as a diverse and cosmopolitan community.

However, the business community is relatively disengaged from public policy issues other than economic development. On many policy issues, the business community is concerned but confesses that it is not well orchestrated and lacks the "generals" to provide leadership. This is believed to stem from the fact that Western City is a regional rather than a corporate headquarters city. Hence, the business community and its leadership are more transient; people pass through on their way up or down the corporate ladder. Furthermore, there may be fewer large businesses in the Western City economy than in the past. This means less coherent corporate leadership, more diffuse leadership that varies by issue, and more ad hoc, issue-based mechanisms for coordination than in the past.

Western City's placement among the unconventional cities stems in part from its particularly high scores on two elements of the index of unconventionalism: Western City is one of three study cities where nearly two-thirds of women are in the workforce, and with 54 percent of the population not adhering to any church, it is the third highest of the study cities in terms of lack of formal religiosity. It is actually below average on the number of same-sex-partner households identified by the Census Bureau, but gays have a substantial presence in the city. In particular, they have played a significant role in recent mayors' electoral coalitions and can therefore count on city officials to support their concerns.

Like Valley City, Western City's unconventional political culture is also shaped by its period of accelerated growth, which brought newcomers to the city. As one local activist sees it, morality issues are important controversies in the city because of the economic base, the influx of newcomers, the changing demographics of the city, and the empowerment of previously "quiet communities." Western City is distinctive because of its size—it is "not large enough to have a legacy of dealing with such conflicts," but it is "not so small that there is a family/small-town sense of dealing with people on a day-to-day basis."

The governmental structure of Western City is largely nonreformed, with a strong mayor-council system. The city council consists of thirteen members, eleven of whom are elected from districts. The mayor's office has very strong formal powers. Despite its formally nonpartisan elections, Western City has had a majority of Democrats on its city council since at least 1963. Although Western City has become an increasingly "minority" city, its politics is not dominated by ethnic and racial cleavages. Black representation on the city council has actually been above parity, and the city has elected minority mayors several times.

Hill City. Hill City has a reputation as a center of high-tech industry—most notably computer-related activity. The city has also experienced substantial growth in the health care sector, including medical products industries. Finally, tourism and hospitality are important components of its substantial service sector. The city has grown rapidly in recent years. Partly for that reason, environmental and land development issues are clearly dominant in the political life of the community, overshadowing virtually all other matters in terms of both citizen activism and government agendas.

The city's growth is also linked to its politics, in a variety of ways. Hill City is a predominantly white (62 percent) city with a substantial Hispanic population (23 percent) and a smaller black population (12 percent). It is frequently described as having an activist, liberal-oriented local politics, and the local newspaper touted it as being "the most socially tolerant in [state name], a live-and-let-live oasis." Several local leaders, including the city manager, also emphasized that the city has a liberal, progressive, tolerant political culture. That political culture has perhaps been reinforced by the growth in major technology-related companies that began in the late 1980s. As the city manager explains, "You've got these companies that bring in people from all over the country, and perhaps from all over the world." He believes that this helps account for the community's general tolerance. However, several community leaders volunteered concerns that the city's recent growth might lead to the loss of its traditional tolerance and progressivism, especially if the newcomers bring a more business-oriented, conservative element to the community.

Hill City scores particularly high on two indicators of unconventional culture. Nearly two-thirds of women are in the workforce, and more than one-third of the population over age twenty-five has at least a bachelor's degree. One city council member links the city's highly educated population to its "enormously participatory" but "bifurcated" character. That is, there is not a lot of voter participation. "If we can get 15 to 20 percent of the voters to vote in a council election, we're lucky. . . . But that top 15 percent is a bunch of rabble-rouser activists. . . . I mean they are fantastic. They're all Ph.D.s and masters' in this and masters' in that . . . [a] highly educated community." He went on to describe city council meetings where some 700 people had signed up to speak, even though there was only one item on the agenda. Another informant, a district attorney, notes, "Neighborhoods are very important to Hill City. . . . Hill City has a tradition of being activist and everybody has their say. . . . This is why city council meetings go to three o'clock in the morning."

The city council is known for liberal stands and policies, such as a recent social equity initiative that would provide $4 million for child care, job training, neighborhood service delivery, and affordable housing. In the spring of 1995, an organization was formed to try to elect conservative members to the city council, which had come to be dominated by a coalition of liberal, environmentally oriented members. But in the 1996 election, only one of the three conservative candidates even qualified for the runoff election, and he did not win. The city's reputation for electing liberal, environmentally oriented candidates was further solidified in the 1997 election.

Hill City has a council-manager form of government. Its seven-member city council is elected at large, with a variant. The ballot designates seven council spots, and each candidate must indicate which council position he or she is running for. One of the numbered spots has come to be accepted as a de facto seat for a Latino representative.

Port City. Port City has a growing population and a booming economy. Its predominantly service economy and its especially large government sector reflect its role as a major regional headquarters for state and federal offices. Job growth has been driven by the booming high-tech industry, including jobs in computer software development, biotechnology, and microelectronics, as well as by technology-intensive occupations in existing manufacturing, retail, and service industries. In the late 1990s, the growth of Port City's high-tech sector, fueled by massive investments of venture capital, accelerated to the point that it was having major negative impacts on housing costs, traffic, and parking in some of the city's most diverse and vibrant neighborhoods. Residential and commercial vacancy rates were only 1 to 2 percent, and in some neighborhoods, that figure was zero. Thousands of new dot-com businesses and young high-tech professionals crowded into the city with a gold-rush mentality, hoping to make their fortunes. The resulting gentrification-induced displacement of working-class and low-income families put land use and development policy, as well as the demand for growth controls, high on the city's political agenda.

Port City has an extremely diverse multiracial and multiethnic population, with large numbers of Asians and Latinos and a smaller number of African Americans. In the 1990 census, whites were a bare majority, but they are now only a plurality (with the Asian population continuing to grow rapidly) in what is now a majority-minority city.

The sociocultural context of Port City is distinguished by the presence of a sizable unconventional subculture predisposed to challenge traditional social values and to support progressive positions on a range of morality issues. Port City has a high percentage of nonfamily households, a high percentage of college-educated residents aged twenty-five or older, and a high percentage of females in the civilian labor force relative to national norms. Port City also has a large gay and lesbian community.

In terms of religion, only about 44 percent of Port City's residents are Judeo-Christian adherents. Perhaps more important, only about 6 percent are adherents of fundamentalist and evangelical Protestant churches, identified by Button and colleagues (1997, 177–79) as among the most active opponents of gay rights and other socially liberal causes.

The institutional governance of Port City is predominantly nonreformed— most notably, it has a strong mayoral form of government—though some elements of the reform package are present. For example, the city has formally nonpartisan elections; however, elections here are highly politicized and strongly contested, with the active involvement of many groups. Although the city had at-large council elections during the 1990s, in 1996, voters endorsed a return to district elections for the council starting in November 2000.

Metro City. In sharp contrast with the other unconventional cities, Metro City is declining in terms of jobs and population. It is the core city of a large metropolitan area that has experienced significant growth in the last two decades. But in contrast with its fast-growing suburban counterparts, Metro City's population has been steadily declining since 1970; it lost nearly 15 percent of its population in the 1970s and another 7 percent in the 1980s. Metro City is a majority-minority city, with roughly two-thirds of its population black and emergent growth in the Asian and Hispanic populations.

The metropolitan area has an excellent transportation infrastructure, manifested in its interstate highway system (three major interstate highways intersect near downtown) and its world-class airport. This, along with relatively low land costs, a limited union presence, and pro-business state and local governments, has contributed to much of the regional growth that occurred over the past two decades. The metropolitan area's convention and tourism industry has remained strong due to a number of first-class trade facilities and the city's exposure through major sporting events. However, during the past two decades, there has been a dramatic decentralization of employment in the metropolitan area, with economic growth in the suburban areas coming at the expense of Metro City itself.

Although it is categorized as a declining city economically, Metro City has an unconventional subculture. On some of the dimensions used to assess subculture type, Metro City might appear to fit awkwardly in that category. For one thing, churches are important, and church adherence levels are relatively high here, reflecting the importance of the black church in this predominantly black city. However, the city ranks fourth among the ten study cities on educational attainment, with more than one-quarter of its population having at least a bachelor's degree, and it is second highest in share of the workforce in quintessentially postindustrial occupational categories. But Metro City's unconventional culture is perhaps most markedly on display with respect to household arrangements. It has the fewest number of households composed of married parents with children, and it ranks second in its rate of same-sex-partner households. In June 1999, one local newspaper noted that gays "support their own shops, bars, and restaurants, visit gay doctors and auto mechanics, exercise at gay gyms, worship openly in churches and temples, read their own newspaper, and enjoy the neighborhoods they helped revitalize—most notably Crafton—as close to a 'gay community' as can be found anywhere in America." Another story from July 2000 proclaimed that Metro City "has emerged as a Mecca for gay men and women, with people coming from throughout the region to enjoy one of the country's most thriving and open gay communities."

Metro City has had a strong mayor-council form of government since 1973, when a revised charter gave the mayor appointment and reorganization powers that had previously belonged to the city council. The city council, which was reduced in 1995 from eighteen to sixteen members, is predominantly a nonreformed arrangement of district elections for twelve members; the other four members, including the council president, are elected at large. African Americans are incorporated into the highest levels of Metro City's government. The city has had an African American mayor continuously since 1973, and a majority of the city council (nine of sixteen, including the council president) was African American in the late 1990s.

Conventional Cities

River City. River City is an old industrial city that has, over a number of years, engaged in a transformation to a postindustrial economy. While retaining some vestiges of its industrial past, the River City metropolitan area has emerged as a leader in the growth of environmental, biomedical, and advanced manufacturing establishments. It is a corporate headquarters city, ranking among the top ten U.S. cities for Fortune 500 companies, including two banking corporations, a food industry giant, a natural gas company, and three major corporations engaged in the production of construction materials. By the same token, since 1996, more than thirty new biomedical technology ventures have formed in greater River City.

Despite these positive developments for the metro area as a whole, River City is a declining central city. This is most evident in its ongoing loss of population. From 1990 to 1998, River City's population decline of nearly 8 percent placed it last among the ten study cities on that dimension. River City's declining economy is also evident in the relatively low incomes of city residents. River City's average household income in 1989 was second lowest among the ten study cities.

River City is an odd amalgam of cultures, with some elements of a newer, more cosmopolitan structure beginning to be overlaid on an older one that is traditional and parochial. The newer, more cosmopolitan side of the city's sociopolitical culture is linked to the emergence of white-collar professionals in the medical, research, and high-tech sectors. This cosmopolitan part of the community is geographically concentrated, based in two specific neighborhoods with a large university population and where the health care industry has brought in a lot of professionals and "progressive folks," according to the local director of the American Civil Liberties Union (ACLU).

The older, traditional culture represents the city's social and economic past, when working-class white ethnics from southern and eastern Europe worked in manufacturing jobs in the city. One legacy of the city's traditional culture is the importance of churches, most notably the Catholic Church. Another legacy is the seemingly confusing combination of sociopolitical ideologies. Some informants are likely to describe the community as "a very small town in some ways" and "rather conservative" (needle-exchange activist), while others are likely to describe an important streak of social progressivism in the community. To locals, however, it is not confusing at all to describe River City as both liberal and conservative. The community is conservative in the sense of being traditionalistic, that is, a somewhat insular, family-focused place. As one gay rights activist describes it, "the River City ethos is pretty much 'mind your own business.'" The ACLU director characterizes the conservative side of the city's political culture in terms of "small-town politics. People tend to look locally for answers. It's tremendously parochial. People just don't believe in looking outside of River City to help them. You know, when there's a big opening in a major agency, the hiring process tends to happen in River City instead of having national searches. It's parochial and it's insular." More generally, the city can be understood as being "conservative in the working-class, conservative sort of way."

The liberal, or socially progressive, side of the city's traditional culture stems from its history as a bastion of both labor union power and civil rights developments. Unions are far less important than they once were, but the city and its people have a "huge union history," and that union heritage is still "worked into" the community's response to various social issues (gay rights activist). The city also has a legacy of being "somewhat of a leader in the area of civil rights," having developed one of the first fair housing laws in the nation (director of human relations).

Until 1989, River City had a hybrid version of the classic commission form of government. Although the city had a mayor, council members were elected at large and were given specialized responsibilities for committees in various areas of city administration. In 1989, the legislative structure was changed somewhat. Now, each of the nine council members represents one council district. City executive, administrative, and law enforcement powers are vested in the mayor, who is directly elected for a four-year term. The mayor's powers and responsibilities include preparing the annual operating budget and the capital improvement budget; appointing department directors, municipal court magistrates, and members of authority and commission boards; preparing and submitting legislative programs to the city council; and directing all long- and short-range planning for the city government.

South City. South City is a key distribution center. It sits at the crossroads of two major interstates, is served by six railroad trunk lines, and is just an overnight drive to 60 percent of the population of the United States. It is the location of one of the world's largest cargo airports and is the worldwide headquarters of a company specializing in distribution services. The city's economy, though focused on shipping and distribution, is nevertheless "diverse," according to the mayor, and includes tourism as an important component. There are efforts to refurbish and improve the downtown area to enhance its draw as a tourist center. Area leaders emphasize that they are striving for a "balanced industry mix which targets distribution, wholesale, biomedical, electronics/telecommunications, food processing, tourism, manufacturing, and corporate and divisional headquarters" (quoted from the county Web site).

But despite these efforts, South City is a declining city, manifested by low income rather than population loss. South City's median household income in 1989 was less than half that in Valley City and only about two-thirds that in Port City.

The city's placement among the conventional cities results partly from the strength of its religious forces. Virtually all interviewees volunteered information about how the community typifies the Bible Belt, and on-site observations verify that churches are remarkably plentiful. There is some disagreement about the political activism and importance of churches, however. The chief administrative officer notes that churches in the African American community have long been involved with public issues; historically, this has not been true of the white churches, although this is changing a bit. A county commissioner notes that, except for gambling and liquor issues, local pastors are politically uninvolved and suggests that religious leaders are reticent because they do not want to be too politicized. By contrast, the city council chairperson, who is herself an ordained minister, sees the church as being much more active and important in local affairs. She argues that "when the people of the religious community get involved, it gets the attention of the majority of the people in the community."

In addition to the strong presence of churches and the high level of church affiliation, South City lags far behind the unconventional communities with respect to the size and political activation of its gay community. The city ranks lowest among all ten study cities in the percentage of same-sex-partner households, and the level of organization and mobilization of the gay community is minimal; only relatively recently have gays begun to be more active in community affairs.

South City has a hybrid form of city government. It has a strong mayor as well as a chief administrative officer (CAO), an arrangement it adopted in the late 1960s. However, the mayor functions as the chief executive, is formally responsible for all operations of city government, and appoints directors of each functional division (with city council approval); the CAO functions as the chief operating officer. The city council is composed of thirteen members; seven are elected from traditional districts, and the remaining six are elected from two "superdistricts" (three members from each), each of which covers half the city.

Border City. Border City's downtown serves as the headquarters for a number of nationally known businesses, its economy benefits from the regional airport, and almost 20 percent of the region's manufacturing jobs—ranging from light manufacturing to steel and chemicals—are located in Border City. Despite these bright spots, Border City is in the economically declining category. It lost nearly 8 percent of its population between 1990 and 1998, and its median household income, at a little over $21,000, is third lowest among the study cities.

The city's economic development efforts have focused largely on strategies to draw more businesses to the downtown area. Border City has offered substantial tax incentives and is involved in a plethora of economic development projects, all of which are aimed at attracting or keeping middle- and upper-class interests and clientele in the downtown area. As a result, the downtown corridor has prospered at the expense of Border City's neighborhoods, which are segregated both economically and racially.

In many ways, Border City has the feel of a southern city. It is culturally conservative on economic, moral, and racial issues. The conservative culture of the city emanates from several sources. First, Border City is in a tricounty region known for its conservative politics and religious fervor. Second, Border City is home to a large Catholic population that is intrinsically conservative about many morality issues. Third, because of the interdependence of the inner-city and the suburban communities, many of the conservative suburban residents and communities are drawn into Border City's morality debates. Consequently, many of the morality issues are perceived as being relevant not only for Border City but also for the greater Border City area.

During the period of this study, Border City was governed under a classic council-manager form of government. The city council members were (and still are) elected at large. The mayor's position is ceremonial, awarded to the council member receiving the most votes in the election. Administration was exclusively in the hands of a professional city manager who was responsible for day-to-day operations. In 1998, the citizens of Border City voted to amend the city's charter to strengthen the position of the mayor while retaining the basic elements of the council-manager plan. Strong business groups viewed the weak mayoral system as a major handicap in terms of economic development issues, so they campaigned stridently for the amendments' success. The amendments to the charter, which took effect in 2001, give the mayor the power to appoint the city manager, subject to the approval of the city council.

Lake City. Lake City is by far the most economically distressed of all the study cities. Beginning in the early 1970s, the manufacturing industry that had been the mainstay of its economy went into a long decline that led to double-digit unemployment rates. City government was near bankruptcy on several occasions. By the late 1980s, industry restructuring and stabilization of one of the city's key companies began to produce a stable economy in the region. But it was not until the late 1990s that Lake City saw unemployment drop to single-digit levels; still, the unemployment rate in Lake City is double that in the surrounding suburbs. In 1990, the median family income in Lake City was less than $19,000. So many private-sector jobs have left the city that the largest employers are hospitals, educational institutions, and city government.

Recently, city government has initiated two strategies for redevelopment. The first is to build new housing in areas where demolition has occurred. The second is to attract entertainment industries into the central business district. This led to the opening of two casinos and the construction of new professional sports stadiums.

Lake City's categorization as a subculturally conventional city is based in part on its relatively high levels of church membership. Indeed, churches are very important in this community, and church leaders have political clout. Members of the clergy frequently endorse candidates and express their support or opposition for city issues from their pulpits. Additionally, the clergy may participate in negotiations that resolve political conflict, such as a prolonged teachers strike in the mid-1990s. Several individuals interviewed for this project listed the clergy rather than elected officials as the best representatives of the people of the city. But Lake City's conventional character is also reflected in the extremely low percentage of its population with a college education (less than 10 percent) and the very low proportion of same-sex-partner households.

In terms of governing institutions, the city has a combination of reformed and nonreformed elements. It has a strong mayoral system, but council members run in at-large elections that are ostensibly nonpartisan. More accurately, there is one-party dominance in this staunchly Democratic city.

Coastal City. Unlike the other four conventional cities, Coastal City is in good shape economically. Two elements are crucial to Coastal City's economy: tourism and the military. According to the city manager, tourism accounts for about one-fourth of its economy and the military for about one-third. Diversifying the economy is one of the big issues for this community. Although Coastal City has gained military-related employment in recent years, overall, the military is downsizing. And tourism has drawbacks in terms of fairly low wages for many jobs. So, the city manager indicates, "we're really stressing the 'other' category." The city has identified a series of target industries, such as telecommunications and other postindustrial service industries, that it is trying to attract. This strategy has been working. In 1998 alone, the average annual salary of jobs created through the city's economic development efforts was about $30,000, plus benefits. These new enterprises included a residential lending company that committed to building a $10 million headquarters to house 600 employees; a major car rental company's new call center; an information technology and engineering services firm that announced that it would locate in an upscale office building, adding 100 jobs; and a company that provides health care for Medicaid and Medicare recipients in several states, which will nearly triple its 300-person workforce.

Another important aspect of Coastal City's economic development is the city government's distinctively high-profile and aggressive involvement in various sports, recreational, and entertainment facilities, either as the sole proprietor or in public-private partnerships. The city recently built a $10.5 million sports complex, which its promotional brochure describes as "the nation's first municipal stadium built primarily for soccer," but it can also host a number of Junior Olympics events. The municipal amphitheater features big-name performers and draws large crowds from the region, thereby "returning more than $1.2 million to the city's operating budget." In addition to the two municipal golf courses now in existence, the city is building two more public golf courses. The city is also engaged in a "public-private partnership to build an upscale hotel and shopping complex."

Coastal City is strongly influenced by a suburban land use pattern and has a suburban mentality to go with it. The original city annexed outward, absorbing the entire county in which it sits in the early 1960s, growing dramatically in terms of both population and land area. Comments from interviewees suggest that people are still getting used to the idea that their city's population puts it in a category with other large urban areas; in fact, they are inclined to describe it as a suburban setting that does not have urban problems. Consistent with its traditional suburban character, Coastal City ranks relatively low with respect to the number of women in the workforce and the proportion of same-sex-partner households.

Some informants describe Coastal City as a relatively conservative place, but the more predominant depiction is of a community that, despite some pockets of conservatism, is more liberal and progressive than other places in this quite conservative state. There is evidence that the powerful Christian Communications Board and other institutions associated with the Christian right shape local politics by exerting their influence in various indirect ways. People in public positions and those who are active in local public affairs are very much aware of and sensitive to the likely reactions of these institutions. By the same token, knowledgeable observers point out that the general population of the community is "not particularly puritanical" and is not necessarily more religious than other communities. In fact, the proportion of the population that is affiliated with a church is relatively low. Hence, despite the looming presence of Christian right organizations, Coastal City's categorization as a conventional city has more to do with its household arrangements than with the religious dimension.

The city has a relatively standard council-manager form of government, with a city manager appointed by an eleven-member council. Seven of the members ostensibly represent districts, but only in the sense that they are required to reside in a designated district; in fact, all eleven members are elected at large in nonpartisan elections. The mayor is a member of the council, but in the late 1980s, the office was enhanced by having the mayor directly elected. The first mayor so elected in 1988 still serves in that position.

Beginning in 1994, there were efforts to change the city's form of government. In a nonbinding referendum held that year, 53 percent of the voters approved of a proposal sponsored by the city's council of neighborhood associations that called for actual district elections for seven of the eleven members of the city council and a redrawing of district lines to equalize population size. The wildly varying populations in the city's existing districts—one had less than 1,000 residents, while another had nearly 145,000—were part of the impetus for this proposal. The state legislature brokered a plan that required the redrawing of district boundaries to equalize population size, but it also required another local referendum before district elections could be instituted. The results of the 1996 election constituted a resounding endorsement of the status quo. By a two-to-one margin, voters opted for the existing at-large system.

With these brief introductions to the study cities in hand, as well as a theoretical map to guide us to relevant evidence concerning subcultural, institutional, and economic differences and intergovernmental contexts, it is time to turn to the stories of these cities' experiences with the five key morality issues: abortion, gambling, the sex industry, gay rights, and drug treatment innovations.

3
The Local Politics of Abortion

By the second half of the 1990s, one might have thought that the abortion issue would be largely irrelevant to local government officials, even though it continued to spark action at the federal and state levels. In *Planned Parenthood of Southeastern Pennsylvania v. Casey* (1992), the U.S. Supreme Court rendered a decision that, though leaving intact *Roe v. Wade*'s core principle of the legality of abortion, opened the door for states to limit access to abortion, such as by requiring abortion counseling and informed consent, waiting periods, and parental consent for unmarried minors. Scholars of morality policy and state politics have investigated the factors that account for variations in state governments' abortion policies in the wake of the *Casey* decision. That scholarship suggests that a policy's restrictiveness is shaped by a variety of factors, including public opinion about abortion (Goggin and Wlezien 1993), the extent of mobilization of pro-life and pro-choice interest groups (Cohen and Barrilleaux 1993), possibly the level of demand for abortion (Hansen 1993; but compare Cohen and Barrilleaux 1993), and the extent to which women constitute a politically mobilized force (Hansen 1993).

Even as the *Casey* decision encouraged continuing debate in state capitals, the federal government made a preemptive strike at the conflict surrounding abortion clinics. The federal Freedom of Access to Clinic Entrances Act (FACE), enacted by Congress in 1993 in response to increasing violence at abortion clinics, made it a federal crime, with stiff penalties, for individuals to block abortion clinic entrances, damage clinic property, or use violence or the threat of violence against women seeking abortion services. And in 1994, the Supreme Court ruled in *NOW v. Scheidler* that the Racketeer Influenced and Corrupt Organizations Act (RICO), with its crippling penalties for criminal enterprises, could be used to prosecute antiabortion efforts if they could be shown to be conspiracies to thwart abortion enterprises. These developments constituted substantial deterrents that were expected to stem violence at abortion clinics (O'Connor 1996). However, there was additional violence in the year or two after the passage of FACE. And although some of the abortion violence had abated by the late 1990s, incidents of violence or threatened violence continue to the present. According to the Web site of the National Abortion Rights Action League (NARAL 2001), "Since 1993, three doctors, two clinic employees, a clinic escort, and a security guard have been murdered."

The abortion issue remains an area of important local governmental action, for several reasons. For one thing, implementation of FACE means that local law enforcement agencies must decide what constitutes blockage of abortion clinic access and which antiabortion activities are worthy of arrest and prosecution. Because pro-life forces have developed a series of tactics meant to be intimidating to abortion clinic patrons or doctors without overtly violating FACE, and because antiabortion protest has moved to sites other than abortion clinics, local officials are forced to make decisions about the maintenance of order, decisions that are constrained by free speech rights. In addition, just as the abortion issue has been attached to a variety of other matters at the federal level, ranging from medical benefits for military personnel to the funding of family planning overseas, at the local level, the abortion issue has complicated decisions about the privatization of public hospitals and the provision of publicly funded health services for the poor.

Unlike studies of abortion politics at the state level, which focus primarily on policy making with respect to the restrictiveness of abortion, an examination of abortion politics at the local level must consider an array of governmental actions involving the handling of abortion activists at the street level as well as policy decisions concerning reproductive health services. This chapter presents stories of abortion-related decision making from the study cities or their home counties. In them, we find officials engaging in actions as diverse as large-scale arrests of abortion protesters, promulgation of policies that cater to abortion protesters, provision of local funds to support abortion for poor women, and efforts to disrupt such funding.

However, the purpose of this chapter is not to simply describe local officials' diverse handling of the abortion issue. The key goal is to account for this variation—to determine what factors shape local officials' actions with respect to abortion. Because these actions are more complex than official policy making with respect to abortion restrictiveness, straightforward factors such as the balance of power of pro-life and pro-choice forces and public opinion are unlikely to be satisfactory explanations. Consistent with the theme of the book, this chapter examines four explanatory possibilities: the influence of the local subculture, the role of institutional arrangements for governance, the impact of intergovernmental relationships, and the influence of economic development considerations. In addition, the possibility that the politics of race and ethnicity comes into play is explored. That is, communities with more substantial Hispanic populations might be more receptive to antiabortion forces because of the importance of Catholicism in those settings.

SUBCULTURAL EXPLANATION

A cultural explanation posits that, other things being equal, the policy stances of cities with conventional political cultures should be more favorable to anti-abortion forces, whereas cities with more unconventional political cultures should be less responsive to the pro-life point of view. Indeed, the list of individual elements that differentiate unconventional from conventional cities reads like a virtual summary of key factors that differentiate pro-life from pro-choice interests. Unconventional cities, with their highly educated populations, high numbers of women in the workforce, and relative lack of church affiliation, would be expected to be bastions of support for a "woman's right to choose" and hence of local action to sustain that policy position, while the reverse would be expected in conventional cities.

Study cities that vary in subcultural character but have similar institutional arrangements and economic development situations provide an excellent opportunity to explore the evidence for or against this expectation. To that end, this section compares and contrasts abortion policy in two prosperous communities with city manager forms of government—unconventional Hill City and conventional Coastal City.

Hill City: The Prototype of Pro-Choice Policy

Control of abortion clinic protest has not been an issue in recent years. This can be attributed to the city's response to dramatic events that took place in the late 1980s and early 1990s, when abortion clinic protest was prevalent, including major action by Operation Rescue, which brought national media attention to Hill City.

In 1989, 104 antiabortion protesters were arrested outside an abortion clinic for blocking the entrance. Among those arrested was a Roman Catholic nun who claimed that she was inappropriately subjected to a strip search by county jail authorities. Also jailed was Ron Issen, the leader of Hill City Rescue, who was heading up the protest action.

Meanwhile, one of the city's clinics sought an injunction that would bar protesters from blocking its entrance. A temporary injunction was granted by a district judge, but Issen's group continued to block the clinic entrance in violation of the injunction, and sixty-five protesters were arrested. After these arrests, a city spokesperson reported that a single Saturday of such protests cost the city and the county approximately $10,000 in overtime pay and vehicle costs. In December 1989, the first of several protesters arrested for blocking a clinic entrance was found guilty of trespassing, a misdemeanor, and was sentenced to five days in jail and a $1,000 fine. Ultimately, Issen and six other protesters were sentenced to thirty days in jail when they refused to pay fines for violating the injunction. After serving only nine days, Issen was released from the county jail by a state district judge on the condition that he obey the injunction and pay the fine.

In response to the continuing disruption, the director of one of the abortion clinics sued the abortion protesters in 1989. That same year, the county attorney adopted a more repressive strategy, filing criminal trespass charges against Issen's organization under RICO statutes. The attorney claimed that, based on his investigation, the purpose of the organization was to prepare and encourage its members to engage in criminal acts. The charges meant that, if convicted, Hill City Rescue could be fined $10,000 for each separate charge or double the amount of actual economic harm caused—by then, estimated to be $60,000 to $80,000. A Hill City police officer also sued Issen and another member of Hill City Rescue for injuries he incurred while on duty at a protest incident.

Both the abortion clinic director and the police officer won their lawsuits. In 1989, a jury assessed Hill City Rescue with nearly $600,000 in damages to the clinic, and within two weeks, a judge ordered Hill City Rescue to pay the police officer $750,000 in damages for the back injury he sustained. The clinic director has never seen a penny of the money, because Hill City Rescue claimed that it had no resources. But this, she says, is beside the point. The successful lawsuit, which included an injunction against the protesters, put an end to the protest activity at her clinic. In the face of these developments, Issen pulled his organization out of Hill City, alleging that it had lost the support of local churches. Nevertheless, the county ultimately won its case against Issen as well.

The clinic that had been the main focus of the protest activities has been largely protest free since winning its lawsuit, and the director of the other main abortion clinic in the city says that it has been the target of only "minimal" protest activity in recent years, "just a handful of the same people showing up on weekends." Although the aggressive action to stop the protests has made it a non-issue in recent years, the same is not true of other aspects of the abortion issue.

Since 1978, the city has paid for abortions for poor women through its funding of a medical assistance program that helps roughly 10,000 residents with limited incomes. About 1 percent of the program's spending is for abortion services, which are handled by a contract provider—Kapra Reproductive Services. In 1994, the city's funding of abortions became controversial when the city council agreed to a new five-year contract with Kapra that increased abortion funding from roughly $110,000 a year to more than $195,000 a year. The rationale for the increase in funding was a greater demand for services, coupled with higher service costs.

The decision to increase the funding for abortions for poor women was a very low-visibility one, apparently sandwiched into routine budget deliberations, and was not announced in advance. Although the city manager claims that the funding "has not been an issue," at least a few citizens attended the council meeting to criticize the city and to urge the city council to delay its vote, on the grounds that few people even knew that the city funded abortions. In addition, a spokesperson for Greater Hill City Right to Life criticized the city for not making its plans more public and was quoted in the local newspaper as claiming that "if more people had known about the contract, more would have signed up to speak in opposition." Nevertheless, the city approved the funding increase at a sparsely attended meeting. After the vote, one council member acknowledged that although it was a difficult decision, women had the right to make choices about their pregnancies, and the abortion option should not be available only to those with financial means.

The city's funding of abortions for poor women became a campaign issue in the 1996 elections. Council member Shannon announced that she would run for reelection in 1996 and indicated that she expected opposition from abortion opponents because of her support for increased abortion funding. In fact, Kristin Dale, who was opposed to the city's funding of abortion services, ran against Shannon. She was quoted in the local newspaper as stating, "I was born a Catholic. I was raised a Catholic, and there are a lot of people who have a fundamental belief about abortion. . . . You should not ask people to use taxpayer dollars for that." However, Shannon was reelected in 1996 in a close race.

The city's decision in late 1994 to increase funding for abortions had implications the following year, when the city turned its attention to the future of the city-owned hospital, which had fallen on financial hard times. In February 1995, the city manager indicated that the city was considering a contract with Hale Medical Center, a Roman Catholic facility that was interested in taking over management of the city-owned hospital. Hale Medical Center does not provide abortions, nor does it provide a number of other reproductive services, such as vasectomies, "morning-after" pills for rape victims, and the like. The city manager stressed that the performance standards in the contract would ensure that reproductive health services other than abortion would continue if the Catholic medical center took over the hospital. Abortions were not being performed at the city hospital anyway; they were performed by Kapra Reproductive Services, via referral from the city's health clinics. But Hale Medical Center was also interested in managing the clinics, and this raised concerns on the part of pro-choice forces, such as the local chapter of the National Organization for Women (NOW), that management changes would compromise the availability of abortion services for poor women. The city manager was quoted in the local paper as stating that any contract that included the clinics would "guarantee reproductive services."

The city put off making a decision about the health clinics, but it did reach an agreement with Hale to take over management of the city-owned hospital for thirty years. As promised, the contract that the city manager brought before the city council stated that reproductive services would be available in the hospital. In order to do this without violating church law, Hale officials agreed to treat reproductive services such as sterilization and the prescribing of contraceptives as private matters between the individual patient and the physician—thus taking the stand that the hospital allowed such services without providing them itself. It also agreed to set aside space in the hospital for the joint city-county public health department to provide reproductive information and counseling services, including information on abortion, and to compensate the city financially for providing such services. The city council unanimously approved the contract, and it was signed in October 1995. Hale officials believed that they had managed to walk the fine line between the city's demand that reproductive services be available and the Roman Catholic Church's restriction on the provision of such services. By the same token, this creative maneuvering allowed city officials to proceed with privatization of the hospital while avoiding a head-on confrontation concerning the touchy issue of religion and reproductive health services.

But the controversy did not end there. A number of conservative Catholics in Hill City anonymously complained to the Congregation for the Doctrine of Faith in Rome, the Roman Catholic entity that oversees compliance with church law. By the time the Congregation for the Doctrine of Faith determined (in March 1996) that Hale should wait until Vatican officials could rule on the matter, Hale had already signed the contract. During the next two years, Hale officials were faced with continuing pressure from the Vatican to stop sterilization and other contraceptive services at the hospital. Clearly, the Vatican did not accept that the contract arrangement provided a wall of separation between the hospital and the services provided there by others.

In order to help Hale deal with its problems with the Vatican, the city manager agreed to amend the contract, making the city directly responsible for sterilizations done at the hospital by having the nurses and surgical technicians involved in providing those services paid by the city. Even though these new provisions were intended to allow the disputed reproductive health services to continue, but in a way that was acceptable to the Vatican, spokespersons from Planned Parenthood and from the state's Family Planning Association were disturbed by the changes because their groups had not been included in the process of renegotiating the contract. The city manager acknowledges that, "occasionally the Vatican will continue to raise issues," and constant negotiation will probably be necessary.

Hill City clearly exhibits the strong pro-choice approach to abortion-related issues that we would expect in a city with an unconventional subculture. But the case of Coastal City shows a strongly contrasting approach in a place that is economically and institutionally similar but different in its subculture.

Coastal City: Tolerance of Antiabortion Protest

Coastal City has taken on the role of exporter of antiabortion protest to neighboring jurisdictions. Through the late 1990s, there are numerous reports of citizens from Coastal City participating in abortion clinic protests in neighboring communities, but there is little such protest in Coastal City itself, and there is no abortion clinic in the community. Nor is there any evidence that the absence of such a clinic and the relative absence of abortion protest inside Coastal City are attributable to actions taken by local government. Rather, the lack of both abortion clinics and abortion-related protest appears to be a function of the same phenomenon—the presence of a strong Christian right element and several high-profile antiabortion and Christian right organizations, which makes the climate uninviting for would-be abortion providers.

There are, in fact, three abortion clinics operating in the greater urban region in which Coastal City is located. With nearly 8,000 abortions performed in 1992, these clinics made the region the second most active for abortion in the state. Abortion services are therefore easily accessible for women in this community, and these clinics are also handy targets for protest by Coastal City residents. News coverage, as well as a brief telephone interview with a spokesperson for one of the clinics, suggests that they have been the focus of almost continuous protest activity for years.

At times, the protests at these neighboring clinics have been violent, such as when twenty-three shots were fired at one of them in January 1995. The local newspaper quoted a resident of Coastal City, who had just arrived at the clinic with his family to engage in their regular picketing, as saying, "It's just natural that this has evolved into a war. . . . And I think what he [the shooting suspect] did was justified. . . . A lot of people in the rescue movement are predicting violence due to FACE stopping peaceful forms of protest." At a rally outside the jail where the suspect was being held, an individual identified in the local newspaper as a resident of Coastal City held a sign calling the suspect a "prisoner of war"; another was quoted as saying, "I think he's right." This incident suggests that Coastal City not only is a regular supplier of antiabortion protesters to neighboring cities but also houses vociferous and even extremist views in this regard. At least one Coastal City resident was the subject of a federal probe directed at clinic violence in 1996.

In the late 1990s, plans to establish an abortion clinic in Coastal City quickly ran aground as a result of private rather than governmental decisions. In 1996, a building management company denied a lease to an out-of-state physician who wanted to use space in a professional building for an abortion clinic. The building manager explained that the lease had been denied because an abortion clinic would generate too much controversy and would be disruptive to the other occupants of the building. In the wake of what had happened at clinics in neighboring communities, this was an understatement. In fact, local abortion opponents were already poised to boycott the building, but they called off the planned action when they learned that the clinic would not be moving in.

The one form of abortion-related protest that has occurred within Coastal City is small-scale picketing at the homes of abortion providers who work in neighboring communities but live in Coastal City. According to police officials interviewed for this project, this is quite rare and involves only small numbers of protesters, no more than ten to fifteen people. In 1994, four protesters picketed outside the home of an abortion clinic doctor who was being protected by federal marshals because of threats he had received and because of the recent killings of an abortion provider and escort in a neighboring state. A police official notes that abortion clinic operators often have at least as much information as law enforcement about what is going on, and they sometimes alert the police if they believe protest activity is in the offing, so the police can plan for it. Officers who work in that area will institute high-visibility patrols and make sure that no one blocks the street. This action is not designed to squelch or deter antiabortion protest or send a signal that such protest is unwelcome. As long as protesters stay on the sidewalk and do not block the streets, the city's policy is to allow the protest, even if it occurs outside the home of an abortion provider. Despite the high potential for violence—which led the federal government to send marshals in at least one case—the city government here has reacted in a relatively passive way that is notably tolerant of abortion protest activity.

A comparison of events in Hill City and Coastal City reveals precisely the pattern that culturalist theory would predict. In unconventional Hill City, there is little in the way of abortion clinic protest, in part because local officials had already dealt with antiabortion activism very aggressively. Instead, Hill City officials have steadfastly pursued a policy course that maximizes access to abortion services, especially for the poor. Their commitment to increase funding for a city program that provides abortion services, the hasty manner in which

criticisms of that increase were brushed off, and their sustained efforts to ensure access to abortion and other reproductive health services, despite Vatican
objections, are all consistent with a strong pro-choice orientation and can be
viewed as unfavorable to pro-life forces.

By contrast, abortion politics in conventional Coastal City is a close reflection of the conservative, traditionalist character of that community's subculture. The near-total absence of abortion protest in this community does not
stem from repressive action on the part of local officials. Rather, it stems from
the fact that the community culture is so hostile to abortion that there are no
abortion clinics there. Instead, antiabortion activists from the community feed
a strong current of abortion protest activity in neighboring areas. When there
has been abortion protest within the community, targeting the homes of abortion providers, the city has not taken aggressive action to stop it.

Figure 3.1 (see p. 65) shows that the overall pattern of the study cities'
stance on abortion-related issues is highly consistent with a subcultural explanation. Four of the five unconventional cities have staked out a pro-choice
stance in one fashion or another, while none of the conventional cities have
done so. And three of the five conventional cities have adopted a policy stance
that is favorable toward antiabortion forces. This, combined with the more
pointed case comparisons outlined above, provides solid support for the conclusion that local policy on abortion is shaped by the local culture.

INSTITUTIONAL EXPLANATION

In addition to the importance of subculture in shaping local politics and policy
on abortion, it is possible that institutional arrangements matter. An institutional explanation posits that, other things being equal, cities with politicized
institutions, especially those with strong mayors, will politicize the abortion
issue. That is, they will reveal a pattern of responsiveness to the dominant cultural elements in the community. By contrast, cities with professionalized institutions, especially those with city managers, will depoliticize the abortion
controversy. That is, they will reveal a lack of responsiveness to pressures from
the local subculture. One way to explore this interpretation is to examine
groups of cities that have contrasting types of governing institutions but the
same subcultures and economic development situations. River City, Lake City,
and Border City, three subculturally conventional communities that are declining, offer a good example, given the strong mayoral form of government
in both Lake City and River City, contrasted with Border City's reform-style
city manager government.

River City's experience epitomizes the scenario of politicized governing arrangements yielding abortion-related action that is strongly responsive to the local subculture.

River City: Political Responsiveness in an Antiabortion Context

Abortion is far from a settled matter in this heavily Catholic city. The city appears to be one of a number of places across the country that are seedbeds of antiabortion activity, sometimes in the form of high profile, on-the-street activism in the community, replete with many out-of-state participants, and sometimes in the form of nationally focused activism. Regular and relatively vitriolic protest has occurred at Health Services for Women, an abortion clinic that has operated in the city for twenty-six years. According to both its director and the director of the local American Civil Liberties Union (ACLU), that clinic was the target of attacks in the 1980s by antiabortion protesters who threw tar, causing $25,000 in damage. They also broke into the office on the floor above, drilled holes through the floor, and poured smelly fish oil and water through the holes, causing extensive damage to the clinic. According to the ACLU director, there was "real harassment, including physical harassment of patients coming in. . . . The police knew about it and took no steps to stop them." As a result, the local ACLU interceded on the clinic's behalf to urge city officials to do a better job of providing security and safety.

By the late 1980s, local officials *were* taking stronger action against antiabortion protesters. In 1989, for example, more than fifty protesters were arrested when they blocked access to an abortion clinic in the city. The city also began stationing two uniformed police officers outside Health Services for Women every Saturday, when students from a Catholic university in an adjacent state come in to protest at the clinic. This has been going on for years, and the clinic's director reports a "good relationship with the police department."

A new direction in the city's handling of abortion protest is linked to construction and development changes in the commercial corridor where the clinic is located. In 1997, the street outside the clinic was torn up for construction work, and large cement barricades were placed between the street and the sidewalk. Hence, the space available for both protesters and patients outside the clinic's doors was restricted. The police officers assigned to the scene did their best to manage the situation by directing protesters to one spot or another, but this meant that, depending on which officers were on duty, there were different designated places where protesters were allowed to be. The protesters took objection to this and asked the city to come up with some rules about the matter.

In this case, the ACLU sided with the antiabortion protesters, who claimed that "some city police officers . . . were arbitrary and unreasonable in their edicts about who could protest where and when." After looking at hours of videotape, the ACLU concluded that the protesters had changed their tactics and were making "a concerted effort not to violate the law," but some police officers were arbitrarily moving the protesters farther away from the clinic. The ACLU went to the city and argued that there should be written guidelines to prevent ad hoc decision making by police officers.

The proposed guidelines developed by the city attorney in the summer of 1998 were appalling to the clinic. They would have allowed *six inches* between protesters and patients! According to the clinic director, this plays right into the hands of antiabortion protesters, whose primary tactic is to confront women approaching the clinic and, though obeying the letter of the law by walking with them rather than blocking their way, urge them, sometimes by screaming in their faces, not to go ahead with the abortion. The city attorney revised the proposed guidelines, and the final version substitutes for the stipulation of six inches some vague language that refers to a "reasonable distance" between protesters and other individuals. The clinic director is clearly disgusted with these guidelines, which she sees as doing nothing to resolve the volatile situation outside the clinic with a clear potential for violence.

In reaction, she wrote a detailed letter to the mayor, asking him to "please withdraw the guidelines before the [protesting] students returned in September." The mayor never responded, but three months later, the city attorney sent a letter disagreeing with the clinic director's evaluation of the guidelines and suggesting that the clinic sue for a buffer zone if it needed more protection. From the perspective of the ACLU director, the clinic would not "have a prayer of getting" a court to impose a buffer zone, because no need for such a zone could be demonstrated. Nevertheless, the ACLU director concedes, "If anything, they [city officials] have erred on the side of the First Amendment rights of the protesters." When asked why the city was so hospitable to protest activity in this case, he commented, "The mayor's a devout Catholic. That may well be part of it. I don't know that that's part of it."

The clinic director explains that she "did not go through the expense of suing for a buffer zone" because the clinic is planning to move anyway. The commercial corridor where the clinic is now located "is slated to be torn down in a couple of years." That corridor, which includes a roughly two- by five-block section of jewelry stores and other small businesses in the heart of the city's downtown shopping district, is the focal point of a retail redevelopment plan being pushed by the mayor—a plan that would raze a number of older buildings and bring in nationally known retailers. Several of the small businesses in the corridor have already sued the city over the disruption caused by the street reconstruction project, and others were threatening to sue over their displacement by the redevelopment project. Although it was never suggested by the clinic director, one must wonder whether city officials' interest in getting the clinic and other small businesses out of the corridor may have been the motivation behind their unwillingness to develop more rigorous guidelines concerning protest activity at the clinic. In effect, those protests helped accomplish something that was part of the city's plan—pushing the clinic out of the area.

Lake City: Abortion Nonpoliticized

Like River City, Lake City has a directly elected, high-profile mayor rather than a city manager. But abortion politics in Lake City does *not* exhibit the responsiveness to cultural pressures found in River City. Instead, there is no strong action on the abortion issue by local officials in Lake City. This may be due in part to the fact that subcultural forces, which are normally the source of anti-abortion sentiment in a conventional community, are somewhat less hostile to abortion here. For example, although the Catholic Church is officially opposed to abortion, some local elements of the church are more liberal on the issue. And according to one council member interviewed for this project, most members of the black community in this predominantly black city do not oppose abortion, because too many black people remember "abortions on the kitchen table." As a result, abortion is not a high-profile issue in the city.

State officials, however, are constantly trying to reduce access to abortion by introducing restrictions such as waiting periods. One council member participated as a plaintiff in an ACLU suit at the state level, protesting a requirement that women go to an abortion clinic to pick up information twenty-four hours before receiving an abortion. The law was changed so that the information packet could be mailed to the person. But despite this individual activism by a council member, there is no strong action on the issue by local officials. The police treat protests at abortion clinics like any other protest. They meet with both sides, set down guidelines and codes of conduct, and do not require a permit as long as people stay on public property and do not impede the flow of traffic or other people's movements. Protesters have to keep moving and stay off private property. There have been no major conflicts or policy-making incidents involving abortion in recent memory.

Even more damaging to an institutional explanation is the fact that the abortion issue was just as politicized in Border City as in River City, despite the prototypical professional city manager government in Border City.

Border City: Abortion Politics in a Reformed City

Border City is a fertile municipal context for frequent and ongoing abortion-related activity and demonstrations. The pro- and antiabortion camps are well armed with resources and strategies. On the antiabortion side are two greater Border City residents who are cofounders of a major antiabortion organization. Additionally, Border City, as a predominantly Catholic city, is largely antiabortion. The greater Border City area is also home to a state representative who is fervently antiabortion and is the primary author of most of the existing antiabortion legislation. On the pro-abortion side are three abortion clinics that operate within the greater Border City area. Planned Parenthood operates one of them; Women's Health Co-op is owned by a physician who is known for late-term abortions, and the Border City Women's Clinic also performs abortions.

Given the environment—three abortion clinics for antiabortion forces to target, and ample resources for pro-choice countermobilization—it is not surprising that there were violent and tumultuous protests in the late 1980s and early 1990s. In response, the city enacted an ordinance instituting penalties for trespassing on the land or facilities of abortion clinics. In recent years, however, "things have calmed down tremendously," according to the city prosecutor. The city ordinance may be part of the reason. In addition, a transformation has occurred in the tactics utilized by antiabortion groups. At the vanguard of these efforts is a local antiabortion organization that went through an important evolution from a more confrontational strategy to a quieter strategy of election organizing.

The transformed nature of Border City's abortion-related politics also stems from a change in the composition of the city council. One member notes that about a decade ago, there were four members who were stridently right-to-life, and they tended to keep the issue front and center among the mass public. By the time this council member was elected eight years ago, the "red-hot" nature of the issue had receded.

Consistent with these comments, there is evidence that abortion-related protests and demonstrations in Border City have become routine events, occurring with little fanfare or notice from political officials. For example, on July 11, 1997, a clinic was targeted for picketing. Representatives from Refuse and Resist, a pro-abortion organization, and from Operation Rescue, an antiabortion organization, were on hand to air their sentiments about the abortion issue. Police officers were on the scene to ensure that the protests were peaceful and law abiding, but they did not intervene or provide support for either group.

Although abortion protest and its management have become routine, local officials here continue to use policy-making venues to oppose abortion. In one case, Border County Commissioner Jeff Dover corresponded with five United

Methodist Church ministers who were aligned with the pro-choice Clergy for Reproductive Freedom in greater Border City. The letter requested that the ministers reconsider their support of legal abortion rights and also their support for the Planned Parenthood Association of Border City. Although Dover refrained from using official county stationery, he utilized his title of commissioner to buttress and authenticate his appeal. The response from one minister was that Dover had misinterpreted church doctrine, which clearly supports the legal right to an abortion.

However, Dover's efforts to undermine support for Planned Parenthood were only a prelude to subsequent county commission actions to block funding for organizations linked to abortion. The Border County Family Council is a countywide governmental agency that is a consortium of public agencies devoted to family and children's services, including Planned Parenthood. Following state government procedures, the Border County Family Council distributed child and family health grant monies to Planned Parenthood, as well as to other organizations in the consortium. In 1997, Richard Brant served as president of the Border County commissioners and president of the Border County Family Council's executive committee. In that capacity, he initiated a request that the Border County Family Council block $100,000 in grant money for Planned Parenthood. Although state law prohibits Planned Parenthood from using any state funds to cover abortion costs, Brant contended that the government should not have any relationship with an organization that performs abortions. Because Brant had no authority to make such a decision without the approval of the executive council, which had both pro-choice and antiabortion members, the state department of health stepped in and settled the conflict by agreeing to directly administer the grant to Planned Parenthood. Therefore, although Planned Parenthood remains a member of the consortium, Brant attained the symbolic victory of washing the Border County Family Council's hands of distributing funds to it.

In January 1999, abortion politics once again became high profile when antiabortion forces rallied at a city square that is a traditional gathering place in Border City. This provided a forum for elected officials who were so inclined to express their opposition to abortion. The overall tone of the January 1999 rally was religious rather than confrontational, with participants chanting the rosary, not political slogans, as they marched. However, several city council members participated, giving public voice to their opposition to abortion.

There is relatively little support in the foregoing triplet of cases for the institutional interpretation. As expected, River City, with its strong mayor, politicized the abortion issue and exhibited a pattern of action consistent with the political culture of that conventional community. But in Lake City, abortion is a nonissue, despite the existence of a strong mayor. And even though the institutional environment in Border City consists of a professional city government, the abortion issue there became at least as politicized as it did in River City. The instruments for politicization in the last case, however, included county officials as well as some city council members. This reminds us that even the most reformed of city governments may have to contend with highly politicized county officials who take a dominant role in areas of joint city-county action, such as public health.

But perhaps the institutional explanation will fare better in relatively prosperous unconventional cities, where the extent of responsiveness to pro-choice forces would be expected to depend on the degree to which governing institutions are politicized. In this regard, Western City, Valley City, Port City, and Hill City constitute an interesting quartet for comparison. Hill City, whose abortion politics has already been depicted, constitutes the reformed end of the continuum, with its pure form of city manager government; Western City and Port City represent the politicized end of the continuum, with their highly politicized mayoral governments; Valley City, with its combination of a city manager and a directly elected mayor, offers a middle ground, a hybrid case.

Consistent with an institutional interpretation, Western City has a history of high-profile, aggressive action that is responsive to pro-choice forces.

Western City: Aggressive Action against Pro-Life Protesters

In Western City, there is a history of high-profile conflict predating the study period; this set the stage for pro-life groups to view local officials as being largely hostile to them. In the late 1980s, Operation Rescue chose Western City as a target in its national clinic blockade campaign. Although local pro-life groups had emphasized peaceful protest, the Operation Rescue blockade at a Western City Planned Parenthood clinic turned violent when 300 antiabortion protesters rushed police lines and assaulted clients, eliciting a strong police response. In reaction to these disruptive, sometimes violent protest activities, Western City officials used aggressive strategies that included arrests, heavy sentences, financial penalties, and physical challenges to stymie pro-life groups. In addition, public officials made rhetorical attacks aimed at discrediting Operation Rescue, blaming it for undermining public order, linking the group with hate crimes, and questioning its real agenda.

Abortion conflict escalated again in 1993 when a major world leader visited Western City. This triggered intense mobilization of local and nonlocal pro-choice and pro-life activists. The anticipated arrival of thousands of pro-life groups, and Operation Rescue's threat to stop abortions in Western City during the leader's visit, prompted pro-choice groups to organize clinic defense teams and counterdemonstrations. Emphasizing the increased threat from the flood of nonlocal pro-life groups into Western City, local officials again adopted an aggressively hostile stance toward pro-life activities, and pro-choice groups succeeded in gaining a temporary restraining order against clinic blockades.

The high-profile protest events of the late 1980s and early 1990s, and the city's use of relatively harsh tactics to deal with them, left a legacy: pro-life activists believe that city officials are biased against them. In October 1994, a violent confrontation set the stage for pro-life activists to take the city to court over this alleged bias. The confrontation took place between the associate director of Planned Parenthood and an abortion protester (among others) in front of a Planned Parenthood clinic. Both were charged with assault, but within a month, all charges were dropped because the city attorney's office had reviewed a videotape of the confrontation and decided that the cases could not be proved beyond a reasonable doubt.

In response, the pro-life advocates sued the city in U.S. District Court, claiming that the city routinely deprived antiabortion protesters at the Western City Planned Parenthood clinic of their civil rights. They essentially charged that Western City treated the pro-life protesters unequally, pursuing complaints against them but ignoring their complaints against others. In addition to punitive damages, the protesters asked the judge to prohibit the city from enforcing the so-called policy of unequal protection in the future. This was an unusual lawsuit, in that it claimed that the city government had created the climate for altercations at abortion clinics. The lawyer defending the city denied that officials played favorites; argued that the city was protecting the rights of the clinic's neighbors to live a semipeaceful existence, as well as protecting clinic patrons from violence; and claimed that when protests degenerate into private conflicts, cities can impose "reasonable restraints" on the situation. In contrast, the pro-life activists argued that powerful city officials and a powerful organization (Planned Parenthood) were depriving peaceful protesters of their rights. In August 1997, the protesters lost their lawsuit against Western City.

In the years that followed, Western City officials continued their relatively strong tactics against antiabortion protest, although their efforts were sometimes constrained by legal concerns. Police officials have, on occasion, tried to remove antiabortion signs without just cause. For example, when antiabortion activists began holding up a sign on an overpass saying "Abortion Kills Children," Western City police officers tried on four occasions to make them stop, citing them for violating a city ordinance against posting signs on public property. Later, the city prosecutor had to throw out the charge because the sign was not actually attached to public property but was handheld.

Port City: A Fortress of Pro-Choice Advocacy

Although not as dramatic, Port City's history is also consistent with the institutional interpretation that a politicized, unconventional city will exhibit strong pro-choice action. One informant, who is the former chief of staff to three Port City mayors and now chairs the city's Fire Commission, says that Port City has been a "fortress" of pro-choice advocacy for years. All of the city's local government officials and political leaders, including Mayor Joseph Styxx, are unified and vigilant in their public opposition to abortion-related hate crimes and violence. When asked why the city's new and, by reputation, extremely conservative Roman Catholic archbishop had not yet taken a public stand supporting the antiabortion movement in a city where one in four residents is Catholic, this informant answered that the archbishop "knows that that is a battle he can never win here."

Given the longtime pro-choice stance of local officials here, it is not surprising that they took high-profile, aggressive action in response to the wave of violent attacks on abortion clinics that occurred nationwide in 1994. In August 1994, Port City's city council unanimously passed a resolution condemning the attacks. The resolution further called on law enforcement agencies to uphold laws protecting women's access to such clinics.

Six months later, in response to an outbreak of violence and murder at East Coast abortion clinics, Mayor Styxx issued an emergency directive ordering the Port City police department to plan tighter security at all abortion clinics throughout the city. The following month, arsonists set a tire ablaze outside the wall of a building housing two of Port City's abortion clinics. The fire caused only minor damage and no injuries. However, Mayor Styxx visited the arson scene and strongly condemned the action. He was quoted in a local newspaper as stating, "This kind of activity is totally unacceptable and something we will not tolerate in [Port City]." Federal agents with the U.S. attorney general's recently established Abortion Task Force arrived to investigate the arson and to work with local police and fire officials to determine whether it was part of a nationwide conspiracy and possibly linked to three similar attacks on clinics in a county just south of Port City.

So far, an institutional explanation works well for unconventional cities. As expected, the two that have the most politicized arrangements show strong evidence that elected officials respond in a way that is consistent with the presumably dominant pro-choice preferences in unconventional cities.

On institutional grounds, Valley City is a step away from these politicized cities, in that it has a hybrid form of city manager government. However, it also has a mayor, and the mayor has been a focal point for the city's handling of the abortion issue. Like the other unconventional cities described so far, this translates into a strong pro-choice stance. Indeed, Valley City has one of the more dramatic stories about the local politics of abortion, not because local officials chose to escalate the issue to high-profile status, but because of the city's need to respond to antiabortion forces that descended on it in the early 1990s.

Valley City: Mayoral Leadership for Pro-Choice Action

When Operation Rescue announced in 1992 that it would come to Valley City in July 1993 and stage a major protest event, it sparked an immediate governmental response. Contributing to that response was the fact that Planned Parenthood and a local health care provider claimed to have received threatening letters from Operation Rescue. Thus, the mayor and the city attorney immediately sought city council approval for three ordinances restricting Operation Rescue's activity, and they were successful in obtaining two of them. In August 1992, the city council adopted a so-called bubble law, making it a misdemeanor for demonstrators within a hundred feet of a clinic to come within eight feet of anyone who asked them to step back. Six months later, the city council approved an ordinance that barred protesters from picketing within 300 feet of targeted residences. One month before the scheduled protest by Operation Rescue, the mayor also proposed an emergency ordinance allowing the city to seek civil damages from demonstrators who broke the law and failed to disperse. This measure, which would have allowed the city to sue protesters or protest organizers for thousands of dollars in police costs and fines, was not passed by the city council.

A council member explains that the two main players in the bubble ordinance were the mayor and the city attorney. "They showed leadership: the mayor took the heat and the city attorney was fired up; the mayor handled the politics and the city attorney the law." It was a tough fight to get the bubble ordinance enacted, because all the council members received letters from the ACLU opposing it. According to the city attorney, the unsuccessful proposal for recovering civil damages from demonstrators had been initiated by him and proposed by the mayor as an emergency ordinance. Operation Rescue had threatened disruptions and destruction, which the city wanted to discourage; in addition, the protest would probably result in a lot of misdemeanors clogging the courts, so the city attorney came up with this proposal to raise money to cover the associated costs.

Apart from these developments, other events in the year prior to Operation Rescue's July 1993 appearance in Valley City demonstrated the community's pro-choice activism and offer some evidence of city officials' support for the pro-choice position. On the January anniversary of the *Roe v. Wade* decision, hundreds of abortion rights activists attended a pro-choice benefit in Valley City sponsored by the state's Abortion Rights Action League. In June 1992, the mayor had addressed a rally at a downtown federal building and was quoted in a local newspaper as stating that recent Supreme Court decisions that eroded *Roe v. Wade* were "a frontal attack on the rights of women in this country." Indeed, the mayor had made advocacy of a woman's right to choose a plank in her mayoral campaign.

In the three months leading up to Operation Rescue's event, police planned for the worst, envisioning that there might be as many as 20,000 protesters, although ultimately there were only 3,000. The department was mobilized, tents were set up at the jail, and there were extra deputies, officers, and buses for arrested demonstrators. The mayor, says the police chief, was strongly pro-choice and very active on this issue, and she, along with the city manager, was instrumental in preparing for the Operation Rescue protest.

As the date for Operation Rescue's kickoff rally loomed, the stage was set for a showdown. The mayor had vowed to keep the city's abortion clinics open "by whatever means necessary," according to a quote in a local newspaper. Valley City police took a lesson from a similar event in Wichita, Kansas, which was, according to Valley City's assistant police chief, to show strength at the outset so that the protesters would not take control of the situation. And that is what the police intended to do. Meanwhile, Planned Parenthood had trained hundreds of volunteers to help keep the clinics open, and a coalition of sixteen pro-choice groups urged their supporters to attend a pro-choice rally on July 10 at a downtown park.

On July 9, Operation Rescue opened its campaign with a relatively peaceful rally of about 250 at a local church, with about 300 noisy pro-choice demonstrators outside. One protester was arrested after he got into a shouting match with abortion rights supporters as police were trying to escort him through the crowd outside the church. On the second day of the campaign, nineteen people were arrested in conjunction with the antiabortion campaign, sixteen of whom were charged with picketing outside the home of a doctor. After the arrests, Operation Rescue changed its tactics, moving to more generalized picketing of a neighborhood that allegedly did not single out any physician's residence. Police allowed this form of demonstration, even though it occurred near a second doctor's home.

On the fourth day, police arrested thirty-seven Operation Rescue members for trespassing when they blocked the doors to a medical clinic. In subsequent days, police allowed Operation Rescue demonstrators to picket peacefully, even in front of doctors' homes, if they did not mention the doctor by name and kept walking. However, police arrested thirty-three antiabortion demonstrators and two abortion rights activists after Operation Rescue attempted to shut down a medical clinic in the city.

The following day, police made use of the city's new ordinance against targeted picketing, arresting four demonstrators who walked too close to a doctor's home and allegedly handed out leaflets naming the street where the doctor lived. As the campaign wound down to its final day, Operation Rescue blocked the doors to a Valley City medical clinic briefly before police arrested nineteen abortion opponents. These arrests brought the total to 129. Police officials estimated that the week of protests would cost the city from $500,000 to $2.5 million for officers' overtime, traffic control, emergency services, and jail and processing costs.

At the conclusion of the Operation Rescue campaign, many in the community were relieved, and still others were triumphant. The police chief noted that although Operation Rescue had had police "running in every direction," he believed that his department had planned better than Operation Rescue had, and police handling of the event had "killed their protest ability." In contrast, members of the local evangelical clergy were critical of city officials, the mayor in particular, even though the clergy had not supported the Operation Rescue event. When interviewed for this project, one prominent spokesperson for the evangelical churches explained that he thought the mayor was "spoiling for a fight," and he considered the city's bubble law and ban on targeting picketing unnecessary and counterproductive.

In 1994, smaller-scale abortion protest continued in Valley City, with protesters testing the city's resolve. Legal developments were unfolding in 1994 as well. A state supreme court ruling held that demonstrators could be barred from a public sidewalk in front of an abortion clinic to protect patient safety— a decision that Valley City's city attorney saw as concurring with the bubble zone ordinance. In June, however, the U.S. Supreme Court's decision in *Madsen v. Women's Health Center, Inc.* raised uncertainties about the constitutionality of Valley City's ordinances, especially the residential picketing ordinance. The Supreme Court struck down part of a Melbourne, Florida, injunction that banned protesters from approaching within 300 feet of the homes of clinic workers unless invited to do so, but it upheld a 36-foot protection zone around the clinic, saying that it was acceptable to restrict free speech within this zone. In July 1995, after studying the Supreme Court decision, the state supreme court again upheld a judge's order requiring demonstrators to stay across the street from an abortion clinic. However, a county judge ruled that the residential picketing law was an unconstitutional infringement on free speech rights, citing the U.S. Supreme Court's *Madsen* ruling.

Both the mayor and the city attorney announced plans to appeal this ruling. But one council member who opposed the original ordinance said that the city should adopt a narrower law that avoided infringing on free speech rights. He noted that home picketing was not limited to antiabortion groups; labor unions and antidrug groups used the tactic as well. The city council immediately suspended the ordinance, voted to appeal the court ruling against it, and adopted a weaker restriction while legal challenges were pending. The new ordinance prohibited only picketing that took place right in front of a particular residence. In February 1995, the state court of appeals upheld Valley City's 1993 ban on residential picketing within 300 feet of the homes of protest targets, and in October 1995, the U.S. Supreme Court let stand Valley City's restrictions on residential picketing, rejecting without comment a free speech appeal by sixteen demonstrators.

As these legal developments unfolded, violent incidents at Valley City clinics added impetus to the city's efforts to sustain its ordinances. Some pro-choice advocates said that harassment by protesters was getting much worse, citing a firebombing at a Valley City clinic. Although the firebomb did not ignite and no one was hurt, the FBI was investigating. The president of Valley City's chapter of NOW said that antiabortion activists demonstrated in front of one clinic every weekend, shouting at pregnant women, leaving threatening phone messages, and occasionally pushing clinic employees. Police increased patrols around abortion clinics and family planning centers and emphasized security at those locations at their daily briefings.

Tensions continued into the spring of 1995, when the state director of Operation Rescue announced that one or two abortion doctors in the Valley City area would be targeted. He was quoted in more than one local newspaper as claiming, "We're going to doctors' homes, we're going to expose them in their neighborhoods." Outside the church where the announcement was made, he was immediately surrounded by angry abortion rights demonstrators, who denounced him. In the wake of this incident, the Operation Rescue leader vowed to take the city to court, alleging that police had refused to arrest four participants in the rowdy protest. A local newspaper quoted him as saying, "What we're seeing in Valley City is what we believe is unequal enforcement of the laws." He complained that Valley City police were quick to respond harshly to the most insignificant complaints against antiabortion protesters while overlooking more blatant excesses by people demonstrating for abortion rights. Nothing came of that threat, but pro-life activism continued for years in Valley City.

The Institutional Interpretation: Assessing the Evidence

Earlier, we saw that a comparison of actions in two conventional cities showed no support for an institutional interpretation. Similarly, a comparison of actions in four unconventional cities reveals little evidence that the nature of local political institutions shapes the response. It is true that Port City, Western City, and Valley City each exhibit responsiveness to the pro-choice sentiments that are presumably prominent in those unconventional cities; at the very least, they take an aggressive posture against pro-life activism. The mayor's leadership role is especially clear in Port City but somewhat less apparent in Western City. Even in hybrid Valley City, where the mayor and city manager share power, the mayor has played a leading role in limiting the impact of antiabortion protest and maintaining the city's commitment, even in the face of constitutional challenges, to protect abortion clinics and their workers.

However, the institutional interpretation requires that there be a contrasting lack of responsiveness to pro-choice sentiments in the depoliticized setting of a city with a professionalized, city manager form of government, and this is not the case. Instead, Hill City's experience with local abortion politics is not much different from that of Valley, Western, or Port City. Although its experience with large-scale, disruptive antiabortion protest was largely over by 1994, it is clear that Hill City was as aggressive as any of the other three cities in repressing that activity when it occurred. And more recently, the city has taken aggressive actions to ensure that the availability of abortion services, especially for poor women, is not compromised by financial concerns or the complications of a Catholic health care provider assuming management of the public hospital. Much of this activity was handled by the city manager or city attorney—both consummate examples of reformed government professionalism. Nevertheless, the evidence from Hill City suggests that such individuals, who ultimately serve at the pleasure of an elected city council, show a high level of policy responsiveness to the pro-choice sentiments that would be expected to prevail in that unconventional city.

INTERGOVERNMENTAL EXPLANATION

As noted in chapter 2, the expected impact of state government on abortion politics and policy at the local level depends on the congruence between state-level action and predispositions in the communities at issue. With respect to abortion, two kinds of state policy action are particularly relevant. First, in the wake of the Supreme Court's decisions in *Webster v. Reproductive Health Services* (1989) and *Planned Parenthood of Southeastern Pennsylvania v. Casey*

Table 3.1 State Policy Context for Abortion Action

Study City	Indices of Restrictiveness of Home State's Abortion Policy		State-Level Clinic Protection Law, 2001
	1994	2001	
Unconventional			
Valley City	3	3	Yes
Hill City	1	2	No
Metro City	1	3	No
Port City	3	3	Yes
Western City	0	3	Yes
Conventional			
Border City	3	6	No
River City	4	7	No
South City	3	5	No
Lake City	3	6	Yes
Coastal City	2	5	No

Sources: The 1994 index of abortion restrictiveness is a count of the number of restrictions (out of five possible) listed in O'Conner (1996, 160–61); the 2001 index is a count of the number of restrictions (out of seven possible) reported by the National Abortion Rights Action League's state-by-state rankings of abortion laws (NARAL 2001). Information on the existence of a state-level clinic protection law is also from the NARAL (2001) state-by-state rankings.

(1992), states were empowered to enact a variety of restrictions on abortion. Many states chose to do just that, enacting measures such as parental consent for minors, mandatory waiting periods, restrictions on who can perform abortions, bans on abortion in public facilities or by public employees, and bans on "partial birth" abortion. Table 3.1 shows two summary measures of the restrictiveness of state abortion policy for each study city: one is a count of the number of restrictions (out of five possible) imposed by the state as of 1994, at the beginning of the study period; the other is a count of the number of restrictions (out of seven possible) imposed by the state as of 2001. The level of state abortion policy restrictiveness sets one important context for local-level action, in that it sends a strong message about the state's official degree of receptiveness to abortion (and, presumably, its support or lack thereof for local action unfavorable to pro-life activists). The table also indicates which study cities are located in states that have enacted laws ensuring and protecting access to abortion clinics. As of 2001, fourteen states had enacted such laws, which typically allow for a bubble zone to "protect patients and clinics from violence, harassment, and intimidation" (NARAL 2001). Such zones not only signify state support for local action to quell at least the most vitriolic of antiabortion activism but also provide a legal weapon for doing so.

Table 3.2 Typology of Local Action vis-à-vis State Government: Abortion

Status of State Policy	For Cities Predisposed to:	
	Protect Abortion Rights (Unconventional Culture)	Stay Neutral or Allow Pro-Life Activism (Conservative Culture)
Restrictive	*Compensatory action* Valley City (early years) Port City (early years) Hill City (clinic protection) Metro City (clinic protection)	*Legitimated action* **Border City** River City South City Lake City Coastal City
Permissive	*Legitimated action* Hill City Valley City (later years) Western City **Metro City** **Port City** (later years)	*Underutilization*

Cities in bold exhibit policy histories inconsistent with expectations shown in the framework.

Table 3.1 reveals considerable consistency between the local abortion policy context, as reflected by community subculture type, and state-level abortion policy. By and large, the unconventional cities are in states that scored lower on abortion restrictiveness in both years, and state-level clinic protection laws are much more common among the unconventional cities than the conventional ones. Two cities (Valley City and Port City) had state abortion policy contexts that were relatively restrictive by 1994 standards but less so by 2001 standards. Therefore, state-local relationships on abortion policy for these two cities are treated as different at the end of the decade than they were in mid-decade. Three study cities are in states where the policy stance with respect to abortion is mixed, in the sense that there is a highly restrictive abortion policy coupled with a state-level clinic protection law (Lake City) or there is a low level of restrictiveness on abortions but no clinic protection law (Hill City, Metro City); this complication must also be taken into account.

Based on the information in table 3.1, table 3.2 presents an analysis of the impact of the intergovernmental context on local abortion politics. Community culture serves as the key indicator of the abortion policy predispositions of the study cities. That is, we assume that in unconventional cities, popular pressure to restrict antiabortion activism and maximize access to abortion clinics is stronger, whereas in conventional cities, there is much greater tolerance of antiabortion activism or at least popular pressure that constrains local officials from repressing pro-life forces. And, as this chapter has already shown, that assumption is amply borne out. All study cities are placed in the typology according to their community culture and the character of their state's abortion policy, yielding a set of expectations about the category of state-local relationship.

The evidence from the cities' histories of abortion policy and politics during the study period is clearly consistent with these expectations. Valley City's adoption of aggressive ordinances to control disruptive abortion protest and its struggles to sustain them in the face of constitutional challenge exemplifies compensatory action, as does Port City's aggressive reaction to threats to abortion clinics. As the state policy context changed, coming more into line with Valley City's policy predilections, city officials have, under the banner of "legitimated action," been able to continue their aggressive action against antiabortion activists, despite a threatened lawsuit by pro-life activists. Hill City's mixed state context is also reflected in its local responses. The lack of a clinic protection law led Hill City to a compensatory action stance against disruptive abortion protest in its early years, but the state's relatively permissive stance toward abortion has allowed the city to proceed with a remarkable commitment to funding abortion services for poor women—a clear example of legitimated action. In contrast with Valley City's need to hurriedly develop ordinances to use in its battle against abortion protesters, Western City took aggressive action against protesters without the umbrella of such compensatory local ordinances, illustrating how the permissive state abortion context provided Western City with legitimated action. Only Metro City's pointedly neutral approach to the abortion issue and the absence of any evidence that change in the state policy context has affected Port City are inconsistent with the theoretically derived expectations.

Meanwhile, the histories of abortion politics in River City, South City, Lake City, and Coastal City are perfect examples of the "legitimated inaction" specified by the intergovernmental explanation. This is not to say that officials in these cities do nothing at all when there are disruptive incidents or threats to abortion clinics. However, the overall pattern is one of limited action, especially in comparison to cities that have taken more aggressive, high-profile action to constrain abortion clinic protest. The relatively passive approach of South City officials was especially evident when police failed to prepare for potential disruption at a scheduled protest in a visible location, and it is evidenced by the abortion clinic director who has given up calling local officials with regard to problems with protesters (see the appendix for South City's case narrative). Similarly, River City revised its low-key, hands-off approach to the continuing protest activity at its downtown abortion clinic only when pressed to promulgate a more official policy by antiabortion activists. By permitting

Table 3.3 Hispanic Population

Study City	% Hispanic
Coastal	4
Hill	31
Western	32
River	1
Border	1
Port	14
Valley	30
South	3
Metro	5
Lake	5

close contact between such activists and abortion clinic clients, the official policy only formalized the city's stance of inaction against abortion clinic protesters. The only case history that is somewhat at odds with the expectations
of legitimated inaction is Border City, where officials have been much more
aggressive in politicizing the abortion issue, but with respect to abortion funding rather than the handling of abortion protesters. With regard to the latter,
Border City very much fits the pattern of legitimated inaction.

ECONOMIC EXPLANATION

An economic development interpretation of local responses to abortion activism suggests that economically troubled cities would be more inclined to
take strong action against abortion protest or to otherwise squelch the abortion
issue because of concerns about damaging the city's image or jeopardizing already fragile developmental efforts. A review of these cities' policy histories,
however, reveals little evidence that such considerations are at work. In fact,
the declining cities were *less* active and *less* aggressive than the economically
advantaged cities in their attempts to constrain abortion-related activism.

There is very limited evidence of economic considerations of any kind fig-
uring into local abortion controversies in any of the cities. Valley City's aborted
effort to enact an ordinance that would have allowed the city to collect civil
damages from abortion protesters suggests some concern about the costs of
policing a major protest event, but like the other ordinances enacted at the time,
the main impetus was clearly the city's commitment to sustaining access to
abortion clinics.

One possible exception is River City. The city's handling of protests at a
downtown abortion clinic was responsive to pro-life protesters, who were em-

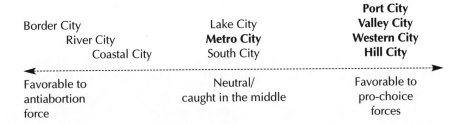

	Lake City	**Port City**
Border City		**Valley City**
River City	**Metro City**	**Western City**
Coastal City	South City	**Hill City**

Favorable to
antiabortion
force

Neutral/
caught in the middle

Favorable to
pro-choice
forces

Figure 3.1 Policy Stance toward Abortion, by Community Subculture Type

Cities in bold are unconventional.

powered to continue activity that, from the clinic's point of view, amounted to harassment of patients and constituted a continuing threat of violence. As speculated earlier, local officials may have had an ulterior motive for their reluctance to curb the protesters' activities—that is, encouraging the clinic and other small businesses in the area to move to make room for a retail redevelopment project—but this cannot be proved. If it is true, however, this suggests that economic imperatives can drive city policy making on morality issues in ways that are more complex and nuanced than originally expected. Cities with fragile economic development initiatives need not actively squelch abortion clinic protest that threatens those initiatives; in the short term, at least, they may be able to use that protest activity to their advantage.

ETHNICITY, RELIGION, AND THE ABORTION ISSUE

Although a consideration of racial and ethnic politics was not incorporated in the study design, questions can be raised about the possibility that the abortion issue would play out differently in cities with substantial Hispanic populations because of the importance of the Catholic Church. More specifically, it might be expected that local officials in these cities would be more receptive to antiabortion activism and less likely to push a pro-choice agenda.

As table 3.3 shows, three of the study cities do have substantial Hispanic populations—Valley City (30 percent), Hill City (31 percent), and Western City (32 percent); a fourth, Port City, has a higher-than-average percentage of Hispanics (14 percent). Examining the experiences of these four cities relative to the others allows an assessment of this alternative explanation.

The overall pattern of the study cities' stance on abortion (see figure 3.1) reveals evidence contrary to this proposed explanation. All four of the cities with more substantial Hispanic populations have policies that are highly favorable to pro-choice forces. All four cities also have unconventional subcultures, and their pro-choice abortion policy history is consistent with that, but not with this alternative explanation based on ethnicity. Hence, the evidence suggests that subculture trumps ethnicity, at least in the narrow sense examined here. The failure to find any evidence for this alternative explanation may stem in part from the fact that the research was not designed to test it. As a result, the possibility that unconventional cities with substantial Hispanic populations might be less hospitable to abortion clinics than are unconventional cities generally cannot be determined, because no such cities were selected. In addition, the alternative explanation may falter because its focus on the linkage among Hispanics, the Catholic Church, and the abortion issue ignores both the importance of the Catholic Church in some cities without substantial Hispanic populations (e.g., cities where Catholicism is dominant because of the presence of southern and eastern European ethnic groups) and the strong opposition to abortion from other churches, most notably evangelical Protestant churches.

CONCLUSION

Consistent with general expectations about the importance of culture in morality politics, this chapter shows that differences in community subculture are very important in shaping different responses to abortion-related controversies. The insights of the intergovernmental explanation are also important, especially in highlighting the various kinds of compensatory action that local officials take when state policy on abortion is at odds with local preferences. However, there is little support here for either an institutional or an economic explanation. This is not to say that local governing institutions do not matter. But at least for the core institutions considered here, institutional differences do not have the kind of patterned impact that was expected. The lack of evidence that economic considerations shape local abortion policy is consistent with the some analysts' view that economic considerations are almost by definition *not* a part of morality politics (Wald, Button, and Rienzo 1996, 1158). However, this may be specific to abortion policy rather than generally true of morality policy. The verdict awaits our inspection of other morality issues in the chapters that follow.

4
Morality Politics — Casino Style

GOVERNMENT-SPONSORED GAMBLING IN THE UNITED STATES: AN ECONOMIC PERSPECTIVE

In the past twenty-five years, there has been a startling transformation in the United States with respect to gambling, at least of the legalized variety. As of 1979, for example, only thirteen states had lotteries (*Statistical Abstract of the United States* 1980, 307); by 1999, thirty-eight states were operating lotteries (National Gambling Impact Study Commission 1999). As recently as 1990, legal casinos were operating in only two jurisdictions—Nevada and Atlantic City, New Jersey; by 1999, a variety of casino types had been legalized in twenty-eight states, ranging from conventional land-based private casinos to "nearly 100 riverboat and dockside casinos in six states and approximately 260 casinos on Indian reservations" (National Gambling Impact Study Commission 1999). In addition to lotteries and casinos, some thirty states have legalized pari-mutuel betting (*Statistical Abstract of the United States* 2000), primarily involving horse and dog racing. Finally, in a number of states, "convenience gambling" is made possible via the legalization (or the tolerance, in a legal gray area) of stand-alone electronic gambling devices such as slot machines and video poker in bars, convenience stores, and a variety of other locations (National Gambling Impact Study Commission 1999).

Studies of the adoption of lotteries and casino-enabling legislation at the state level have consistently offered four interconnected reasons for the startling growth in legalized gambling: a revenue rationale, a political expediency rationale, an economic development rational, and a competitive necessity rationale (Furlong 1998). That is, state officials presumably legalize lotteries and casinos because they need the revenue that gambling brings to state coffers (revenue rationale); because getting such revenue through lotteries and casino taxes is much less unpopular than increasing conventional taxes, since such taxes are "voluntarily" paid by those who choose to gamble (political expediency rationale); because casinos are expected to spark the development of tourism and associated jobs (economic development rationale); and because taking in revenue from out-of-state residents who purchase lottery tickets or visit the state's casinos is preferable to having one's own residents go out of state to spend money on gambling because in-state gambling is not legalized (competitive necessity rationale).

Many of these same considerations can be expected to apply to city officials' stance toward gambling in their communities. A number of writers have pointed out that casinos are especially attractive to industrial cities with struggling economies. In many such settings, casino gambling has been viewed as an attractive method to quickly transform the community into a tourist destination (Deitrick et al. 1999, 232). Putting the situation in less neutral terms, Goodman (1995, 32) argues that "local politicians and business leaders continue to tout the use of casinos as incubators of jobs and as generators of consumer dollars for local stores and other businesses." And gambling is an attractive economic development gambit for local officials on a variety of grounds. For one thing, gambling is a substantial and fast-growing component of the lucrative tourism business. Between 1990 and 1993, spending on all forms of legal gambling in the United States grew rapidly, and casino revenue grew at the especially impressive rate of 36 percent in the three-year period (Deitrick et al. 1999, 234).

In addition, gambling—especially casino gambling—is a politically attractive alternative to conventional tax increases on existing businesses and residents when governments desperately need new infusions of revenue. Just as states have found lotteries to be more politically palatable than tax levies, casinos are frequently viewed as a "low-cost political path to new taxes," because only the casino operator is "taxed" (Thompson 1997, 15). Furthermore, because these gambling establishments are invariably cast as enticements to tourists, the casino revenue that fuels local government's cash flow is envisioned as coming from outsiders rather than from community residents, and this too is politically attractive (Deitrick et al. 1999, 235).

CONSTRAINTS ON PRO-GAMBLING POLICY: INTERGOVERNMENTAL AND CULTURAL PERSPECTIVES

The foregoing arguments place economic considerations of one kind or another front and center in explaining some cities' aggressive efforts to legalize gambling. However, to understand the variation in city responses on this issue, it is also important to acknowledge several factors that serve as constraints on legalized gambling at the local level.

For one thing, local officials are powerfully constrained by state government policy with respect to gambling. Lotteries are established by state governments and are basically state-operated monopolies, and states have "become dependent on lottery sales as a source of revenue" (National Gambling Impact Study Commission 1999). For this reason, casino gambling is of primary interest to city officials. But the development of private casinos in major cities can, under some circumstances, also be a competitive threat to the state government's revenue base, such as when the state shares in revenue from Native American casinos. For example, the Mashantucket Pequot tribe, which operates the huge Foxwoods casino, for years paid $100 million annually to maintain exclusive rights to gaming in the state of Connecticut (Boger, Spears, Wolfe, and Lin 1999, 139). Casinos and pari-mutuel wagering, which are of interest to local governments, can also have a negative impact on the state's lottery revenues (Elliott and Navin 2002). Either because of perceived threats to the state's own gambling revenue or because of the strength of morality-based antigambling forces in the state legislature, a number of states have provisions designed to prevent the establishment of either gambling in general or casino gambling in particular.

Local political culture can also be viewed as a constraint on local officials' ability to foster legalized gambling in their communities. Studies of the status of gambling policy at the state level have shown the significance of some politicocultural factors. For example, the greater the prevalence of Protestant church membership and the higher the share of the state population that is Baptist, the less likely it is that a state has adopted a lottery (Wohlenberg 1992; Martin and Yandle 1990; Caudill, Ford, Mixon, and Peng 1995). Such findings underscore the extent to which population groups that oppose gambling on moral grounds serve as important constraints on officials' pursuit of a pro-gambling strategy. Consistent with this view of a sociocultural basis for the politics of gambling, published accounts of state- and local-level controversies over gambling feature active opposition by religious forces (Stafford 1998; Goode 1995). In 2002, religious opposition to gambling was elevated to the national level when a coalition of more than 200 religious leaders delivered an open letter to President Bush and Congress, urging action to deal with the negative consequences of gambling in the United States.

But beyond affiliation with a Protestant or, more specifically, a Baptist, church, church affiliation in general is a core element of conventional political culture. On cultural grounds, then, we might expect gambling to be more of a threat to the traditional moral values prevalent in conventional cities. Hence, we should expect that, other things being equal, gambling interests would be less favorably treated in conventional settings, whereas officials in unconventional settings would be freer to pursue a pro-gambling policy.

SUBCULTURAL EXPLANATION

The expectation that a community's subculture has an impact on its handling of gambling issues is amply illustrated by a comparison of Coastal City and Valley City, two relatively well-off communities with similar governing institutions but contrasting subcultures. Consider, for example, the intense hostility to gambling evidenced by officials in conventional Coastal City.

Coastal City: Antigambling Politics

Gambling casinos are not authorized by the legislature in this state, and Coastal City officials are quite content with this situation. The community, with its conventional, suburban values and the strong influence of high-profile Christian fundamentalist organizations, is generally "against gambling" on moral grounds, according to the city manager. In December 1994, a state legislator from a neighboring city sponsored legislation intended to make the concept of casino gambling more appealing by allowing cities with casinos to share their profits with neighboring cities. Officials from Coastal City were not enthusiastic about the proposal. A local newspaper, referring to the mayor, wrote, "She's not convinced that riverboat gambling is a good idea, or that regional cooperation is the way to go. . . . she has not seen enough information yet to convince her that the tax money generated by casino gambling is worth the risk."

Indeed, rather than putting pressure on the state legislature to allow casino gambling, Coastal City officials have enlisted state legislators' help in stamping out the fledgling effort of a local developer to circumvent the law against casino gambling. This sequence of events began in late 1998 when James Caldwell announced plans to start an offshore gambling business. Although state law bans casinos, a gambling establishment three miles offshore would be outside of the state's jurisdiction. The developer indicated that his plan was to refurbish one of the city's oldest marinas and take patrons on gambling cruises launched from there. He told a local newspaper reporter that he was already looking at a cruise boat for the purpose.

The reaction of civic leaders was immediate, negative, and reflective of both economic and moral considerations. Some were concerned that gambling would not square with the community's family-oriented tourism market. Others argued that legalized gambling was socially harmful and that the addiction and crime associated with it outweighed the economic benefits. Councilman Grigsby was quoted in the local newspaper as claiming that gambling "preys on people with weak wills and low-income residents." Meanwhile, it was clear that even if the offshore operation succeeded in skirting state law against gambling, the city still had the some power via its authority to grant or withhold business licenses.

Caldwell claims that the announcement of his plans for an offshore gambling enterprise was a red herring, designed to spark action from city officials who were giving him the runaround with respect to his real plans to redevelop the marina. In an interview for this project, he explains, "So I decided I would play the trump card and bring up an issue that would overshadow all the problems that everybody said I was creating. . . . I played the gambling trump card and quickly got on the planning commission agenda, because what they wanted to do was to have a planning commission hearing to stop the gambling boat." The strategy apparently worked, and Caldwell's case was placed on the planning commission's agenda in January 1999. The commission approved his plan for residential and commercial redevelopment of the marina but made its use conditional, barring him from utilizing the marina as a base for gambling.

It is not clear, however, whether the offshore gambling idea was really only a red herring. For one thing, the developer defends the substance of the proposal, arguing that what he had in mind was not a gambling operation that would involve "someone with their last five dollars pushing a grocery cart with their clothes in it and trying to get on a boat to go three miles offshore and gamble." Instead, he envisioned dinner cruises by reservation only; "it was a little higher scale than someone with their last five dollars." And he claims that a lot of people from outside the area approached him to say that if he got the permit to allow it, they would help him get a gambling boat there. He argues that there was and still is a potential market and lots of interest.

Red herring or no, city officials took the proposal for an offshore gambling operation very seriously. In December 1998, about a month after the developer's announcement of the gambling gambit and before his date with the planning commission, the city's vice-mayor signaled that although the city did not have the necessary legal powers to stop the gambling proposal, state officials would take up the fight. However, the city was not totally lacking in resources to push on the issue. City officials considered making changes in the zoning laws that would require operators of commercial passenger boats to get planning commission and city council approval for a permit, with that approval being contingent on a variety of conditions, such as the amount of off-street parking available at the dock area. A deputy city attorney argued, "This is not intended to stop Caldwell. It just allows the city council some measure of control." Others interpreted such regulations differently. The local newspaper, for example, noted, "City attorneys may have found a way to regulate or even ban offshore gambling from local docks by using the fine print of the zoning law."

When the state legislature convened a month later, action moved to that level as well. A legislator from Coastal City sponsored a law that would have made it illegal for boats to take on passengers in the state, go into international waters for purposes of gambling, and then return to the state. That legislation was acknowledged to be a response to Caldwell's proposal. Even though Caldwell had already dropped his gambling proposal and intended to proceed with only marina redevelopment, antigambling forces in the state legislature gathered their energies to ban what locals refer to as gambling "cruises to nowhere." In an effort to defeat this initiative, pro-gambling forces in the legislature added more extreme language in the hope that the measure would become so "preposterous" that even antigambling forces could not support it. The strategy appears to have worked. The proposed bill was defeated in the state house. But one legislative leader of the antigambling forces was quoted in the local newspaper as acknowledging that the bill was meant to "send a message" to Coastal City developer Caldwell, "and that message was received."

The story might have ended here, were it not for the appearance of an out-of-state video poker entrepreneur in Coastal City a little over a month later. In early April, John Atrin brought his casino boat to the city for repairs and signed a two-month lease for docking space in an estuary that Coastal City shares with a neighboring city. Atrin stated that he had brought his boat to Coastal City only because it was a good place to get repairs, but then he coyly added that he was always on the lookout for good locations to operate the boat.

In light of this event and the state legislature's failure to ban offshore gambling, the city's planning commission moved ahead with changes in the zoning laws that had been discussed after Caldwell's proposal of a gambling boat operation. In June 1999, the planning commission endorsed a proposal that would require cruise operators working out of marinas in the city to obtain a permit from the planning commission and city council; approval of such a permit would be contingent on traffic control considerations, nearby residents' concerns, architectural design issues, and the kind of activity planned.

In short, casino gambling is such anathema in Coastal City[1] that local officials have collaborated with state officials to keep it out. In stark contrast, casino-like gambling has long been legal in unconventional Valley City, and city officials have allowed an explosive expansion of it while raking in a share of the revenue. Only when extraordinary problems involving crime and other social ills became incontrovertible did city officials change their position, and then only to regulate gambling establishments more stringently while still allowing them to prosper.

Valley City: Addicted to Gambling

Valley City's gambling policy in the 1990s grew out of its long-standing experience with so-called card rooms, gambling establishments that had existed since the city's frontier days. For much of Valley City's history, these card rooms were generally places for social, low-stakes card playing. But by the 1970s, the city's nine card clubs, with a total of forty-five tables, had been linked with problems such as the cheating of customers and illegal campaign contributions, according to the police chief. In 1972, in an attempt to spruce up the city's image, the city council passed legislation designed to rid the city of card rooms: card room licenses were linked to owners (rather than businesses), and an owner could not sell or trade a license and could not incorporate. Hence, the license would expire when the owner either died or quit the business, and the card rooms were expected to gradually disappear.

However, the city council allowed the Gala Club to bypass these restrictions, largely because of the cozy relationship between local politicians and the club's owners, who provided campaign contributions to all and bought legitimacy with charitable and civic philanthropy. In 1974, the Gala Club incorporated, and in 1975, it was allowed to keep its license when it relocated from downtown (which was being redeveloped) to a new site in the city. The city council refused similar requests from other clubs wanting to incorporate and relocate. In 1979, the Gala Club was allowed to operate twenty-four hours a day, seven days a week, and in 1980, the betting limit was increased from $20 to $80. In 1982, the number of tables allowed at the club was doubled from twenty to forty. The Gala Club thereby became the largest casino in its half of the state.

Favorable treatment of the club continued in the 1980s, despite the police department's continuing opposition to gambling. In 1983, the betting limit was increased to $200, despite a report from the police chief warning that the increased stakes would lure professional gamblers from out of town and encourage cheating. In 1987, fourteen Gala Club employees, including members of its board of directors, were indicted for skimming $3.9 million and illegally laundering thousands of dollars in campaign contributions. Ultimately (in 1993), the owners were forced to give up control of the club after pleading guilty or no contest to felony charges of skimming from club profits, tax evasion, and illegal campaign contributions.

In light of the city's unsavory history with card rooms in the 1970s and 1980s, one might expect local officials to be less than enthusiastic about expanding these gambling venues. But revenue considerations altered the political landscape. By 1989, the city was facing a $24 million budget deficit; the recession of the early 1990s, coupled with continuing budgetary restrictions in the wake of a statewide tax-cutting measure, put substantial stresses on the city budget. According to a faculty member at an area university, the city's budget situation was further complicated by the fact that the liberal mayor was committed to getting through the fiscal crisis without cutting services.

In 1989, the city council allowed the Gala Club to introduce new Asian-style super-fast, high-stakes card games. These games proved so popular that the club added 300 new employees. During negotiations about adding the new games, the attorney for the Gala Club indicated that if the city wanted to levy a gross receipts tax on the club, it would not oppose the tax. Although the mayor claimed that the ideas of taxing the Gala Club and allowing it to play the new Asian games were not linked, she announced plans to study the implementation of a gross receipts tax only one day after the city council approved the new games. By 1992, the city had a gross receipts tax on card clubs in place.

In 1994, the Tropicana card club opened and soon became the Gala Club's chief rival. In fiscal year 1994–1995, these two clubs, along with one smaller club, provided Valley City with tax revenue of $7.5 million. In 1995, the city voted to more than double the number of tables allowed under its gambling ordinance—a moved widely interpreted as being driven by the city's reliance on the clubs for tax revenue. City officials wanted to circumvent a three-year state-imposed moratorium on card club expansion that was slated to take effect in 1996. Expansion of the city's card clubs was opposed by some members of the Vietnamese American community, who tried to convince the city council that the clubs' Asian games were targeting their community and wreaking havoc on it. But, according to one city council member interviewed for this project, the city's response was that certain people were going to gamble anyway, and it was better that they do so in legal, controlled settings within Valley City rather than in illegal, underground establishments or in nearby cities. Furthermore, proponents argued, it would be foolish to forgo the revenue that gambling provided for the city.

But in 1996, antigambling forces registered their first major victory when the city council voted to shift decision making about card club expansion from the council to the voters, thus removing control from public officials, some of whom had received campaign contributions from card club owners. Indeed, Valley City was among only a handful of cities that allowed card club expansion without a public vote. State law, which since 1984 had required voter participation, had exempted Valley City because its card clubs were already operating. Pressure to submit proposals for further gambling expansion to the voters came in part from two council members—one a newcomer, and the other a long-standing critic of gambling. According to the city attorney, both had political ambitions for higher elective office, and one was later elected to the district attorney's office. The ordinance, which would require a public vote on any expansion of gambling or any new gambling regulations in the city, was also supported by the police officers association, Vietnamese community activists, social workers, and a growing faction of high-tech business owners. The president of one of these high-tech businesses publicly blamed the card clubs for helping to foster a wave of high-tech crime. He claimed that his business had lost more than $1 million in a series of thefts and robberies in the past year, at least some of which was believed to be perpetrated by company employees who had been recruited at card clubs, where they had become financially vulnerable. In light of all this support for public control of gambling expansion, the majority of the council and even the mayor, who had been a strong advocate of card club expansion and the use of club-related taxes for city revenue, were forced to line up as supporters as well.

Antigambling forces followed up with efforts to impose more stringent regulations on card clubs. These efforts were given impetus by a newspaper exposé on alleged violations by the city's two main card clubs of a state law forbidding card rooms to link the fees gamblers were charged to the amounts they could bet, as well as alleged violations of the city's $200 betting limit. The district attorney's investigation of these alleged violations led to a superior court ruling against the card clubs, which were required to change their methods of assessing player fees—a requirement that would cost them a lot of money and cause the city to lose $1 million a year in taxes. Pressure to devise more stringent regulations on card clubs also came from the police chief, who argued that the city's ordinances were inadequate to the task, and from the state attorney general, who was pushing for a standard set of state regulations that would take oversight of card rooms out of the hands of local officials.

In Valley City, the push to revamp city-level regulation of card clubs temporarily stalled in 1998, when a majority of the council, which had traditionally been sympathetic to gambling, reasserted itself and outvoted the smaller faction that had previously forged a winning coalition to require voter approval of gambling expansion. In October 1998, the pro-gambling majority advocated a delay in instituting any new regulations, waiting to see what would emerge from state-level efforts to forge standard statewide regulations on card clubs.

For pro-gambling forces, however, the delay backfired. A new mayor was installed in 1999, and in stark contrast to the previous mayor, he strongly opposed card clubs. He urged that the police department, which historically had been highly critical of card rooms, be given jurisdiction over them. He also wanted to wean the city council from its dependence on card room tax revenue to fund favored projects such as recreational programs and other neighborhood services. Specifically, the new mayor suggested that card room tax revenue be sequestered from the general fund, so that nobody could count on it for ongoing services. Instead, it should be devoted to the capital improvements budget or treated as a windfall each year to be spent on incidental needs. With two new council members in place and other council members ready to rein in the seemingly ever-problematic card rooms, the new mayor's shift in policy stance took effect. By the end of 1999, there was a city-level Office of Gaming Control staffed by four full-time police officers who did background checks on card club operators and handled other administrative matters involving card room oversight. A separate vice unit in the police department did undercover investigations in the clubs. And the dwindling flow of tax revenue from card rooms was no longer being budgeted in a way that encouraged elected officials to rely on larger infusions of it.

ECONOMIC EXPLANATION

The preceding two cases illustrate the striking differences in gambling politics in two cities that differ on subcultural grounds. But the study cities in total do *not* yield the expected pattern of policy being more receptive to gambling interests in unconventional than in conventional cities. Instead, table 4.1 shows that Coastal City's hostility toward gambling is more the exception than the rule among conventional cities; meanwhile, Valley City's long-standing (and only recently tempered) enthusiasm for gambling activity is apparently not shared among unconventional cities more generally.

Why is there no strong subcultural pattern to gambling policy? The Valley City case reminds us that several economic considerations can be important. Even in a relatively prosperous city that was growing rather than declining by the latter half of the 1990s, the legacy of the city's reliance on gambling for revenue shaped its gambling policy making. Ultimately, another kind of economic consideration—concern that the city's high-tech industry was reacting negatively to the sleaziness and crime associated with gambling—was instrumental in making local officials in Valley City less receptive to gambling than they had been.

But if economic considerations can be relevant even in a prosperous community, they are presumably even more critical in cities with distressed, declining economies. The economic perspective on gambling policy suggests that economic imperatives can trump the socioculturally based morality considerations of a conventional setting, leading local officials to press state officials to legalize local gambling. The following case narratives for Lake City and

Table 4.1 Policy Stance toward Gambling, by Community Subculture Type, Economic Status, and Chief Executive Type

Conventional Cities

Declining
Lake City—determined and effective mayoral support (+++)
River City—mixed, wavering support (+)
Border City—nonsupport (–)
South City—determined but ineffective support (++)

Growing
Coastal City—hostility(– –)

Unconventional Cities

Declining
Metro City—tentative interest blocked by obstacles (+)

Growing
Western City—nonissue (0)
Port City—nonissue (0)
Hill City—disinterest/hostility (–)
Valley City—support to opposition (+++ to –)

Cities in italic have city managers rather than mayors.
+ indicates a policy stance receptive toward gambling (with more +s indicating more receptiveness).
0 indicates neutrality or no policy stance on gambling.
– indicates a policy stance hostile toward gambling (with more –s indicating more hostility).

South City, and the parallel case narrative for River City (see the appendix), show evidence that, to a greater or lesser extent, this was true in three of the four declining conventional cities.

Lake City: The Triumph of Economic Imperatives

In the mid-1970s, Lake City's declining economy had already created a budget crisis that led the mayor to support gambling, despite the fact that state law did not allow cities to have casinos. In 1976, the city council, following the mayor's lead, presented a proposal to voters to legalize gambling. Although religious groups varied somewhat in their level of hostility, the religious community mobilized opposition to the proposal. Ultimately, a substantial majority (59 percent) of the city's voters rejected the proposal for legalized gambling, and a similar proposal was defeated in a 1981 voter referendum.

The mayor, however, was a persistent advocate of gambling, and by the late 1980s, his continued support appears to have made inroads among the city's religious leaders. In 1988, he created a commission to study the potential effects of gambling on Lake City. Not surprisingly, his handpicked commission reported that gambling would be economically advantageous and recommended that Lake City build casinos.

Although local churches continued to oppose gambling and in fact formed a multidenominational group called the Alliance against Gambling, a key member of the pastors' coalition, the Reverend (and councilman) John Robbins, reversed his position in 1987. Robbins claimed that gambling was morally evil, but he recognized the economic needs of Lake City. Nevertheless, most of the religious community and the majority of Lake City voters still opposed gambling. To counter the mayor's increasingly aggressive promotion of gambling, these forces placed an initiative on the 1988 ballot that would ban gambling in the city, and it won handily. Meanwhile, at the state level, the prospects for casino gambling in Lake City were considered bleak. The legislature was unlikely to support it, and the governor was predicted to veto any bill that would expand gambling in the state.

Still, the mayor persisted in promoting gambling for Lake City. He approached the mayor of an adjoining jurisdiction about riverboat gambling in the water between the two cities, but that proposal was squelched when the state attorney general raised legal objections.

In 1992, economic pressures made gambling ripe for the agenda again. Faced with a $103 million deficit, the city was forced to take painful measures, such as wage and benefits cuts for city employees and increased bus fares for senior citizens and students. Gambling proponents noted that casinos would bring in $26 million a year in tax revenue for the city. To get around the obstacle posed by the state's ban on casino gambling, two local entrepreneurs suggested that the city take advantage of the fact that gambling is legal on Indian reservations in the state. The two entrepreneurs proposed donating 0.7 acre of land to a tribe to build a casino. This plan was supported (six to three) by city council members and forwarded to the U.S. Department of the Interior. Gambling proponents, organized as Citizens for Casino Gambling in Lake City, also pushed on another front, placing an initiative on the ballot in 1993 to overturn the city's 1988 ban on casino gambling and to give the city council the right to issue gambling permits if the state approved casino gambling. However, Lake City voters narrowly defeated this initiative.

Finally in 1994, after eighteen years of persistence, gambling advocates gained the support of Lake City voters. On the ballot were two gambling proposals: proposal B asked voters to support riverboat gambling, and proposal C asked them to support an Indian-run casino located on land within the city that would be donated by developers to Native Americans. Both proposals passed (by a three-to-two margin), effectively repealing the 1988 ban on gambling. The key difference from earlier votes was that by the spring of 1994, an adjoining city had opened casinos, and people were rushing across the river to gamble there.

Reacting to the successful vote, the city council immediately approved a resolution that the city create a committee to look into what would be needed in the way of casino regulation. Both the mayor and the city council wanted to get a jump start on the business of casinos, even though state approval was still required.

In response to Lake City's passage of proposals B and C and the interior secretary's approval of plans for a casino run by Native Americans on donated land, the governor created a panel to study the legalization of riverboat gambling and whether Native Americans should be permitted to operate off-reservation casinos. As the governor's commission deliberated, casino investors began wooing Lake City's mayor with offers, which included building an aquarium and a shopping mall, committing 50 to 65 percent of casino jobs to African American city residents, building a new firehouse for the city, reimbursing the city for providing fire protection for the casinos, and various offers of revenue sharing between the casinos and the city. The mayor negotiated vigorously to get a good deal for the city in exchange for the privilege of building casinos.

Although the governor's commission recommended that both off-reservation Native American casinos and other privately owned casinos be allowed in cities, as long as voters in those cities agreed, the governor, an opponent of gambling, turned down the proposed Native American–operated casino in Lake City and refused to expand gambling in the state. In the wake of the governor's decision, Lake City's mayor announced to the city council that he would launch a campaign to place a statewide voter initiative to legalize up to four casinos in Lake City on the November 1996 ballot. With large infusions of money from gambling interests and others who hoped to benefit from gambling, the required signatures were collected. The initiative passed, and the governor had sixty days to appoint a state gaming board to develop rules and monitor gaming in the state, especially in Lake City.

In the aftermath of the gambling vote, the mayor announced that casinos would have to be sited in locations other than the riverfront. He also revealed that the casinos would pay 18 percent of their gross revenue in taxes. Of this, the city would receive 55 percent to fund police services and economic development. The remaining 45 percent (of the 18 percent) would be given to the state for school aid.

With the passage of the proposition, which allowed up to three casinos in Lake City, the conflict over gambling shifted from whether it would be legal to who would control it and where it would operate. State officials, the mayor, and the city council jockeyed for position on the selection of casino operators, and there was controversy over whether to allow casinos on the riverfront. Native American tribes and African American investors asserted that the selection of casino operators was biased, and gambling opponents tried to repeal the proposition.

Ultimately, in April 1998, the city council voted to approve the $1.8 billion development agreements negotiated between the mayor and three casino investment groups. The successful vote was achieved only after intense discussion and controversy over the mayor's unilateral authority over casino negotiations, the immorality of gambling, and the lack of a minority casino investor. In August 1998, Lake City residents endorsed the mayor-supported proposal by voting for provisions that included the three development agreements and the refusal to reopen the bidding process to an aggrieved minority investor.

Because acquiring riverfront sites would require lengthy legal battles, two casinos opened at temporary locations in 1999 and 2000. At least one council member interviewed for this project wants the temporary casinos to become the permanent sites. But the long battle to have casinos operating in Lake City has finally been won.

Officials in another declining, conventional location, South City, have not been successful, but this is not for a lack of trying. The mayor, in particular, has been pushing for some time for the state to allow gambling in South City.

South City: Economic Imperatives in Process

South City is a community where, despite a conventional subculture, a majority of residents appear to favor gambling. The mayor is quick to point out that in 1992, local citizens' preference for gambling was demonstrated when more than 60 percent of voters endorsed the creation of a local commission whose mission would be to lobby for gambling. Gambling is not legal in the state, and the legislature has resolutely turned back efforts to change the constitution to allow gambling. In addition, even though the majority of South City residents favor gambling, the issue divides the community. In fact, the gambling issue is particularly salient both in this community and statewide among major voting groups, especially religious conservatives. The city council chairperson explains that the issue is linked to concerns about family values.

The push for gambling in this community stems in no small part from the fact that a casino operating in a neighboring state has been a tremendous success, yielding economic benefits for the state and local governments while drawing a large proportion of its clientele from the South City area. Counterbalancing this are antigambling forces, which include Christian right activists and the black church as well. In particular, Families for Responsible Living (FRL), which is active on obscenity issues, is also active in antigambling efforts. One of its key members, who now serves on the county commission, explains that "there are two issues that you can count on every pastor in South City and the county being activated about. While on other issues you have to beg and cajole for them to get involved and they are reticent because they don't want to be too politicized, on two they will come to you about. One is liquor and the other is gambling. . . . I don't understand it, I just take it and use it." Although the existence of successful out-of-state casinos bordering South City is a spur to action, it also constitutes an obstacle to getting the state legislature to change its position. Casino owners in the neighboring state lobby heavily in South City's state legislature to prevent the authorization of gambling there. The mayor claims, "There's been a ton of money in lobbying."

Despite the strong forces aligned against them, South City officials have made several attempts to introduce the gaming industry into the community. In the spring of 1994, the city council approved an ordinance that would allow the city's voters to decide in a referendum whether the city should sell a riverfront park to an American Indian tribe from another state to use for a casino. The referendum was never held, however, because the state election commissioner notified the county election commission that if it placed the proposal on the ballot, its members could be sanctioned.

In 1996, the state legislature grappled with a bill to allow a referendum on a statewide lottery; the bill also included a provision that would have given citizens of South City the opportunity to hold a referendum on casino gambling. But the majority of legislators clearly maintained that no other forms of gambling, even raffles or bingo, would be included in any vote on a state lottery. A frustrated state representative from the South City area was quoted by a local newspaper as claiming that "the legislature is fiddling while this state and South City's county is burning. Long before this takes effect all the attractive forms of wagering will be on our border."

The mayor has taken a clear stance in favor of gambling, but some of his own actions have undermined his position. It became known in the latter part of 1995 that he had become a member of the board of a gaming corporation headquartered elsewhere. Although the mayor claimed that there would be no conflict of interest, others believed that his membership on the board would impair his ability to be a strong spokesperson in favor of legalizing gambling. As an editorial in the local newspaper noted, the mayor would have to recuse himself from active support of gambling in order to avoid an appearance of conflict of interest.

Despite these many obstacles to casino gambling, South City has had reason to hope that it would at least be able to have a racetrack with pari-mutuel betting. The state legalized this one form of gambling in 1987 for any locality that endorsed it in a local referendum, and South City is one of only two places that have done so. South City's referendum on horse racing was approved in 1987, but in the years since, efforts to build a track have not succeeded, because potential track operators either lacked adequate financing or could not get approval from the state-level commission that regulates horse racing.

In 1996, the state legislature took both positive and negative action in terms of facilitating horse racing. It empowered would-be track operators to have betting via simulcasting of horse races being run elsewhere in the country, but it also placed a time limit on track development. By the spring of 1998, the state legislature had invoked that time limit, indicating that it would not reauthorize the state racing commission beyond June of that year, and without the commission, there could be no legal horse racing in the state. One track developer, whose preliminary request to build a track in South City had been approved by the racing commission, filed suit over the matter and got a favorable ruling from a county judge, but ultimately, the state appeals court overturned that decision. Although it struggled mightily to come up with a compromise bill acceptable to the governor—which would have required a reevaluation of the track developer's license obtained from the defunct racing commission, as well as a new South City referendum on horse racing—the state legislature failed to pass it. In the absence of a state regulating authority, and with no apparent willingness on the part of the legislature to reinstitute one, the push for a racetrack with pari-mutuel betting in South City stalled out.

INSTITUTIONAL EXPLANATION

The preceding cases illustrate that, although they may or may not ultimately prevail against state-level constraints, and although peculiar local circumstances may limit their support for gambling, local officials can and do ignore the moral objections that are a core part of the politics of a traditional, conventional city in favor of economic considerations if the city is a declining one. But how, then, are we to understand the case of Border City, which is also a declining city with a conventional subculture? Unlike South City and Lake City (and River City; see the appendix), Border City has shown no real interest in pursuing casino development.

Border City: Gambling as a Dead Issue

In Border City's state, the governor is firmly against casinos, and on a statewide basis, citizens also appear to be antigambling. A 1996 statewide initiative that would have allowed riverboat gambling in selected sites, including two casinos in Border City, failed to gain the necessary support. The initiative did, however, spark Border City officials to take anticipatory action. In an effort to circumvent any negative consequences from the passage of a referendum on gambling, city council members voted on temporary zoning measures to regulate the gambling industry. These measures included the requirement that riverboat casinos that hold 500 or more persons go through a permit process; be in a riverfront, commercial-enclosed industrial district; be directly associated with a marina; be more than 1,000 feet away from any church or school; and provide one off-street parking space for every 100 square feet of floor area used for assembly, dining, and gaming. Given the failure of the statewide referendum on gambling, this temporary ordinance was never implemented.

Institutional considerations may well be the crucial reason for the contrast between Border City and its three companions in the conventional, declining category. In Lake City and South City, a strong mayor emerged as the key political entrepreneur pushing for gambling, despite objections from church groups and other conservative forces. River City's mayor was also poised to play this role, and to the extent that he did, the city's policy exhibits support for expanded gambling, even though a complicated set of unique circumstances ultimately led the mayor to temper his full-blown support for gambling. But in Border City, the existence of the council-manager form of government means that the city lacks the type of local official that appears to be a crucial catalyst for overcoming moral objections to gambling.

One would expect officials in unconventional cities to be less constrained by the traditional morality concerns evident in cities with conventional subcultures. The Valley City case outlined earlier, with its highly permissive approach to high-stakes card clubs, is consistent with that expectation. However, the absence of a subcultural obstacle to gambling does not necessarily mean that city officials will eagerly pursue casinos or other gambling enterprises for their communities. The economic perspective on this issue suggests that city officials take a pro-gambling stance because of either revenue raising or economic development imperatives (or both), especially if legal gambling in a neighboring jurisdiction places the city at a competitive disadvantage. From this perspective, an unconventional city whose declining economy makes both imperatives relevant should be prime territory for legalized gambling, especially if it exists in nearby jurisdictions. Metro City presents just such a scenario. But as the following case shows, interest in legalized gambling may not translate into much action when the remaining obstacle—state government opposition—is coupled with idiosyncratic problems of other kinds.

Metro City: Obstacles to the Pursuit of Casinos

Metro City's home state adopted a lottery in the early 1990s, and the legislation enacting the lottery also banned casino gambling and pari-mutuel betting. In addition, the character of the games offered by the state lottery means that would-be gamblers are given the kind of continuous gambling experience that casinos might otherwise provide. Specifically, in 1995, state lottery officials introduced "quick cash" drawings, to be played in bars, restaurants, bowling alleys, and similar establishments, that provide players the opportunity to win up to a dozen times an hour.

Given these state-level obstacles to casino gambling, there have been only minor gestures of receptiveness to casino gambling by Metro City officials. In 1994, for example, the mayor met with executives from two major casino gambling companies that were interested in introducing casinos to Metro City. Although the mayor refused to comment publicly on the nature of the meeting, the casino executives described the mayor as noncommittal, indicating that no commitments had been made on either side. Interestingly, the mayor's sit-down with the gambling executives occurred just two months after the local newspaper broke a story about plans for a major casino on Indian land just across the state border, only a three-hour drive away for Metro Citians.

Four years later, a city council member convened an informal meeting to discuss the introduction of legalized casino gambling and pari-mutuel betting to a struggling downtown entertainment complex. The mayor was not invited to attend, but participants included four other city council members, a member of the chamber of commerce, the city's chief administrative officer, a member of the Metro City Redevelopment Authority, a member of the Metro City Convention and Visitors Bureau, and a former mayor. Again, nothing came of this preliminary session.

The need for a statewide vote to overturn the ban on gambling is one obvious obstacle to these local officials' tentative interest in bringing casinos to Metro City, but there are several others. One is that by 2000, Metro City's mayor was in the awkward position of being the target of a federal corruption probe, including queries about the financing of several out-of-town gambling trips he made to a casino resort in a nearby state. Under these circumstances, the mayor would not be a good champion for the introduction of gambling to Metro City.

In addition, Metro City officials would need to overcome the long tradition of illegal gambling in the community. For decades, the city has provided a receptive audience for an illegal numbers racket. The main "kingpin" for this illegal gambling operation, Stu Yates, served time in both federal and state prison but nevertheless made a fortune and invested his substantial profits in Metro City real estate, with the help of a former city councilman. The murder of Yates in 1995, and the fact that those who still play the numbers are a dwindling group of aging players, means that this form of illegal gambling is on the wane; by the same token, however, there is evidence that illegal sports betting operations have emerged to lure in younger generations of gamblers.

Finally, the experiences of Hill City and Western City offer test cases of an unconventional subculture matched with an economy that is secure. Although an unconventional subculture removes one potential obstacle to pro-gambling policy, cities that are relatively prosperous have little reason to pursue gambling.

Hill City: Hostility to Gambling

Hill City's home state does not permit casino gambling. Investors in gaming companies staged a major push in 1993 and 1995 to convince the legislature to allow casinos, but Hill City officials were not on the bandwagon. In the run-up to the 1995 campaign to legalize casinos, developers briefed Hill City council members on their proposal to bring a gambling casino to the city's downtown, claiming that it would create 4,000 jobs in the city, bring in as many as 10,000 daily visitors, and spur hotel development. The reaction of Hill City officials was less than receptive. The city council member serving as the ceremonial mayor, for example, explained that although there was interest in economic development, there were traffic flow and environmental issues, and he was not sure that casino gambling fit the public's vision of economic development. At least one council member was openly skeptical that the proposal constituted an appropriate economic development initiative.

The futility of the casino proposal for Hill City became clear in later years as the legislature resolutely refused to authorize casino gambling. The legislature had just enacted a state lottery in 1993, and although lottery ticket sales were showing healthy growth, casinos were viewed as a potential competitor for gambling dollars. Rather than moving in the direction of welcoming casino gambling, state officials were trying to stem the proliferation of electronic gaming devices (EGDs) in bars, pool rooms, bingo halls, and other establishments. The EGDs skirted the state's prohibition on games of chance that paid more than $5 in prizes. Local officials, including the county attorney, were part of the push against EGDs. In 1996, for example, the county attorney responded to complaints from citizens and sent investigators to check EGDs in various establishments in Hill City, including the newly opened Let It Ride Entertainment, which relied solely on EGDs for its business. Subsequently, he notified business owners that although the machines themselves were not illegal, the prize amounts his investigators were finding were illegal. He asked business owners to comply voluntarily, with the threat of prosecution if they did not. As a result, Let It Ride Entertainment closed one week after it opened.

It is important to note that Hill City's opposition to gambling appears to have little or nothing to do with morality. Rather, it is based on local officials' conceptions of the strengths of the local economy, the substantive character of economic development plans in the community, and the lack of fit between each of those and the gaming industry. Western City exhibits very similar dynamics.

Western City: Gambling as a Nonissue

In 1990, Western City's state legislature authorized casino gambling in three small communities, all of which were historic places, and two of which were less than thirty-five miles from Western City. After only three years, casino gambling in the three towns had exploded into a hugely profitable business, with sixteen casinos and profits of nearly a quarter of a billion dollars generated. The majority of the casinos' patrons come from Western City.

Despite this, there is no evidence that Western City officials have any interest in bringing casinos to their community. This may be because at least some tourist dollars already spill over into Western City—that is, gamblers in the nearby casinos are drawn into the larger orbit of Western City activities. More likely, it is also because of the problems the casinos have brought to the communities that welcomed them. Law enforcement resources there have been severely taxed, with an increase in the number of arrests for driving under the influence, drugs, and other crimes. And social problems stemming from gambling addiction began to get media attention in the mid-1990s. Furthermore, consistent with the vision of Western City as a high-tech, postindustrial city, a Western City–based multimedia company announced in 1997 that it would buy an existing online gambling company and within two months provide gambling over the Internet.

As would be expected, then, neither Western nor Hill City officials have pursued casino gambling, even though the communities' unconventional subcultures mean that they are freer from moral pressures than a conventional community would be. Rather, gambling has been eschewed either because the

Table 4.2 Typology of Local Action vis-à-vis State Government: Gambling

Status of State Policy on Casinos	For Cities Predisposed to:	
	Have Casinos (Declining Cities)	Not Have Casinos (Growing Cities)
Restrictive[a]	*Compensatory action* Lake City (later years) River City South City Valley City (later years)[b] **Metro City** **Border City**	*Legitimated action* Hill City Coastal City Western City
Permissive	*Legitimated action* Lake City (early years) Valley City (early years)[b]	*Underutilization*

Cities in bold exhibit policy histories inconsistent with expectations shown in the framework. Port City is omitted because of the negligible information about gambling politics there; apparently, gambling has not been an issue for a very long time.

[a]Restrictive means that no local casinos are permitted or, as in Western City's case, that casinos are allowed in only a few cities other than the study city.

[b]Valley City is included as a city with a predisposition for legal gambling, even though it is not a declining city, on the basis of the unique elements of its history with gambling and its reliance on gambling revenue.

character of gambling enterprises does not fit the city's upscale vision of what economic development means (Hill City) or because the existence of nearby casinos brings all the spillover tourism benefits the city wants, without the problems of casino gambling (Western City).

INTERGOVERNMENTAL EXPLANATION

For many of the study cities, intergovernmental context is an important factor in understanding local action on gambling. In contrast with abortion, state policy on gambling is more often at odds with the predispositions of local officials, especially those who want casinos in their communities, and as this chapter has shown, these local predispositions are based largely on economic imperatives rather than sociocultural considerations.

Taking all this into account, table 4.2 presents the intergovernmental typology developed in chapter 2, but adapted to gambling policy. Although the expectations about the nature of state-local relationships are not borne out in every case, most of the study cities exhibit evidence consistent with the typology. Most notably, in four of the six cases in which local officials' desire to have casinos clashed with restrictive state policy, officials engaged in "compensatory action" in the form of campaigning in various ways to change state policy (or, in Valley City's case, aggressively expanding the city's casinos to preempt an expected moratorium on expansion). Of these, only Lake City has achieved that goal, allowing it to move full speed ahead on casino development ("legitimated action"). Valley City, which in its early years allowed the liberal establishment of card rooms under its exemption from state restrictions ("legitimated action"), has been only partially successful in protecting its card rooms from regulatory crackdowns. In contrast, those cities that have economic (or, in Coastal City's case, economic and subcultural) reasons for eschewing casino gambling have found it easier to do so when state policy is restrictive. If anything, the "legitimated inaction" that is predicted here understates the aggressive action against gambling that officials in Hill City and Coastal City have taken in consort with state officials.

CONCLUSION

Table 4.1 summarizes what the case histories show relative to the institutional, cultural, and economic explanations. The bottom line is that the economic explanation is paramount in accounting for these cities' stance toward gambling. Officials in four of the five declining cities are receptive to gambling, while officials in four of the five growing cities are either disinterested or hostile; that economically based pattern is the opposite of what a purely subcultural explanation would suggest, especially for conventional cities. This pattern, coupled with details from the cases, clearly indicates that economic considerations trump subcultural morality considerations in the realm of gambling policy.

This is not to say that sociocultural forces representing the "politics of sin" are lacking or that gambling should not be considered a morality policy issue. Indeed, if it were not for the opposition from religious groups, it would not be possible to conclude that money trumps morality, for there would be nothing to trump. In many of these communities, there has been church-based opposition to gambling along precisely the lines that a morality politics perspective would suggest. But this aspect of conventional subculture does not deter public officials from pursuing gambling casinos, especially when a declining local economy, competition from a successful neighboring gambling operation, or both push the economic development imperative to the center of attention. Indeed, some of the cases even show the softening or crumbling of opposition from religious leaders under the pressure of economic considerations.

The institutional explanation plays a minor role here, but there is evidence that strong mayors are crucial in the transformation of casinos from moral anathema to economic salvation. In cities lacking a strong mayor, there is a vacuum in the type of executive leadership needed to legitimize casinos. At the local level, therefore, casino gambling is a morality issue driven by economic considerations, fostered by strong elected leadership, and constrained more by state government than by subcultural forces.

5
Local Government and the Sex Industry

Although the major U.S. cities in the first decade of the twenty-first century can hardly be described as outposts of Puritanism, they are and have long been the locus of conflict and control efforts with regard to sexually explicit businesses, behavior, and information. In part, this involves local government's stance with respect to businesses that sell sexually explicit books, magazines, videos, and pornographic devices or adult entertainment businesses such as nude dancing establishments. It also involves governmental policy with respect to prostitution.

There are, of course, a number of differences among these issues. One difference has to do with the kinds of officials typically involved. For example, local police, along with the elected officials that give them policy direction, are key actors in city government's response to prostitution. In addition to these officials, city attorneys and county-level prosecutors are key actors in controversies over nude dancing establishments and the purveyors of allegedly obscene material because of the legal and constitutional issues involved in prosecuting individuals for obscenity or devising new policies to restrict sexually explicit expression. There are also differences with respect to the legal status and the popular acceptability of the activity in question. With the exception of a few rural counties in Nevada, prostitution is not legal anywhere in the United States, and on the rare occasion when such an idea is floated elsewhere, it goes nowhere (Weitzer 2000, 160–61). By contrast, pornographic books and movies are readily available and are constitutionally protected. To ban such items, prosecutors must show that the item in question meets the legal standards for obscenity. In *Miller v. California* (1973), the Supreme Court stipulated that in order to find an item obscene, it must be shown that the *average* person, applying *community* standards, would find the work as a whole to depict sexual conduct in a patently offensive manner and that the work as a whole lacks serious literary, artistic, political, or scientific value (Daynes 1998, 223).

Despite these notable differences, prostitution, pornography, and adult entertainment businesses are considered together here. Each involves some element of what Weitzer (2000) calls "sex for sale," and each has frequently sparked community controversy on the grounds that the activity in question is indecent—that is, an affront to moral values with respect to sexual behavior. Admittedly, in contemporary discourse, the morality aspect of these issues has been somewhat submerged. Based on intensive observation of antiprostitution efforts in two cities, Weitzer (2000, 166–69) found that neighborhood residents who mobilize against prostitution claim to be concerned mostly with the "environmental effects," such as disorderly conduct, public health risks, merchants' loss of business, and neighborhood decline rather than the immorality of prostitution per se. Similarly, some opposition to X-rated theaters or stores selling sexually explicit material is said to be based on "quality-of-life" considerations in the neighborhood and concerns about property values rather than the morality of pornographic entertainment. Although these other elements of the issue must be acknowledged, the morality aspect is undeniable. Weitzer (2000, 169–70) noted that "many activists harbor strong moral objections [to prostitution] but are careful not to express them out of fear of hurting their cause," because such moral concerns might be viewed as "puritanistic"; conversely, he found that some activists explicitly voiced their moral objections. Furthermore, many of the allegedly "environmental" objections to prostitution and to sexually explicit businesses, including decline of property values and lack of investor interest in the neighborhood, are indirect manifestations of the moralistic side of this issue. If individuals are less interested in buying property in an area harboring sexually explicit businesses or prostitution, it is at least partly because such activities are viewed as unsavory, deviant, and hence not appropriate for "decent" residents or customers to be exposed to.

But what do local governments do with respect to prostitution and sexually explicit businesses? In his study of local government's handling of prostitution in St. Paul, Minnesota, from 1865 to 1883, Best (1998, 125–26) argues that there are three fundamental ways that government can deal with vice or the social control of deviant activity: prohibition, regulation, and prevention. Prohibition involves bringing sanctions against those engaging in acts that have been legally barred. Regulation involves efforts to control the circumstances under which deviant activity is carried out. A key to the distinction between regulation and prohibition is that with prohibition, the assumption is that enforcement of a ban can lead to eradication of an undesirable activity. With regulation, the assumption is that the undesirable activity cannot be eradicated completely, so it must be managed to minimize its negative effects. Finally, prevention involves efforts to stop deviant acts from occurring by blocking either the motivation or the opportunity for such activity.

With respect to prostitution, it may seem that, except for Nevada, where brothels are legal, state and local governments in the United States have adopted the prohibition strategy. Best (1998) shows, however, that even where prostitution is officially illegal, the strategy of regulation rather than prohibition may be at work. In post–Civil War St. Paul, city government enforced the laws against prostitution in a way that gave brothel prostitution a measure of legitimacy. Every month, the operator ("madam") of each of the city's brothels was arrested, found guilty in police court, assessed a set fine, and allowed to return to the running of her brothel until the following month. This policy allowed local officials, who assumed that prostitution was "inevitable," to keep a rein on it. Operators of brothels where robberies, assaults, and drunken behavior occurred were handled more severely and run out of business; streetwalkers who plied their trade openly would likewise be treated harshly, while those who kept orderly brothels were allowed to conduct business with only the monthly check-in at police court. Characterizing policy with respect to prostitution in U.S. cities in the contemporary period, Miller, Romenesko, and Wondolkowski (1993, 313) suggest that a regulatory strategy is still very common, in that "periodic crackdowns on prostitution and related vice are followed by periods of relative inattention"; visible prostitutes (i.e., streetwalkers) are arrested and prosecuted, while prostitution in other settings is allowed to continue, as evidenced by telephone book advertising for "purchasable sex services."

These characterizations, which are offered in the form of broad generalizations, suggest that local governments typically use some form of regulatory strategy to deal with prostitution. But presumably not all local governments fit this characterization. Some might eschew a regulatory approach in favor of prohibition, which would be characterized by more aggressive and sustained efforts to crack down on prostitution or attention to sophisticated, off-the-streets sex services in addition to streetwalkers. Still other cities might use a prevention strategy instead of (or in addition to) regulation or prohibition. For example, a number of cities have targeted the customers of prostitutes ("johns") with programs designed not only to shame them into avoiding prostitutes in the future but also to educate them about the health risks and other personal costs of having sex with prostitutes (Weitzer 2000, 171). Another form of prevention strategy involves programs designed to provide women with alternatives to prostitution. In Portland, Oregon, for example, city and county government grants have been awarded to the Council for Prostitution Alternatives, which counsels prostitutes about the degrading aspects of sex work and provides services to help them transition to a different life (Davis 2000).

Government policy with respect to pornography and sexually explicit businesses can also be placed into the typology of prohibition, regulation, and prevention. As with prostitution, the regulation category is the broadest and presumably the most inclusive, encompassing a wide array of control efforts that city governments undertake. Most notably, local governments can use their power to regulate land use to limit sexually explicit businesses to designated areas. Local governments can also use their police powers to regulate sexually explicit businesses by devising licensing requirements or ordinances to restrict alcohol from being served where there is topless dancing, to prohibit juveniles from being employed as nude dancers, to require that operators of such establishments have no criminal record, and so forth. As the cases in this chapter show, the creativity with which sexually explicit businesses attempt to get around such restrictions frequently leaves local governments scrambling for ever-more-creative ordinances to close the loopholes.

As with prostitution, cities that take a more aggressive and sustained approach toward the eradication of sexually explicit businesses choose a prohibition strategy. That strategy is somewhat more problematic when pornography and sexually explicit businesses rather than prostitution are the target, because of the free speech issues noted earlier, but in principle, cities might be able to regulate such businesses so aggressively that they are functionally barred from the community.

The prevention category may be an empty one when sexually explicit businesses are the issue. In the abstract, one might envision some sort of prevention efforts, such as incentive programs explicitly designed to encourage entrepreneurs of X-rated businesses to turn to other ventures. In practice, however, city approaches to sexually explicit businesses rarely fit this category.

Characterizing a city's strategy with respect to the business of sex thus entails consideration of both policies and enforcement activity with respect to prostitution and X-rated businesses. To complicate things further, a city could have a mix of strategies for dealing with these issues. For example, while using a predominantly regulatory framework with respect to prostitution, a city might add an element of prevention strategy in the form of a program to provide prostitutes with information about alternatives. Indeed, because the prevention strategy is so seldom used for any of the "decency" issues considered here, even an emergent element of prevention in an otherwise regulatory regime constitutes an interesting hybrid.

PROHIBITION, REGULATION, AND PREVENTION

With these complications in mind, cities' dominant approaches to prostitution and to sexually explicit businesses and information can be placed along a continuum ranging from the most restrictive prohibition-oriented approach to the permissive-within-limits approach of a regulatory regime to the least punitive prevention strategy. As the following three case histories show, cities at different points along this continuum are taking dramatically different action with respect to the issue of "sex for sale." Consider, for example, the striking contrasts among Border City, which epitomizes a prohibition strategy, Hill City, which epitomizes typical regulatory policy, and Port City, which has moved the furthest in the direction of a prevention policy.

Border City: Prohibition Epitomized

Since the 1970s, Border City and Border County have had a tradition of aggressive law enforcement and prosecution in the area of pornography and obscenity. As a result of this approach, there are very few pornographic outlets in Border County. Not surprisingly, prostitution seems to have disappeared as well, or at least it is such a low-visibility practice that it does not emerge as an issue.

Crucial to an understanding of Border City's war on pornography is Samuel Landow, who served first as a prosecutor, then as a judge, and now as sheriff of Border County. Led by the conviction that pornography is an evil activity that would not find a home in Border City, Landow has used the powers of his various offices to root out, prosecute, and render stiff penalties for obscenity.

Border City's war on pornography has centered primarily around numerous legal battles with Frank Lofton, a high-profile entrepreneur of sexually explicit enterprises. In the 1970s, Lofton and his partner were tried on obscenity charges related to their strip club in Border City. They were convicted but were freed on appeal. After their release, they agreed to leave Border City in return for having the charges dropped. However, some local officials contend that Lofton has never forgiven Landow for arresting him and for making Border City a staunchly antipornography city.

In the spring of 1997, this history came back to haunt local officials when Lofton returned to the city with the intent of once again selling sexually explicit material. When word of Lofton's intended return was made public, Border County prosecutor John Doe indicated that he did not intend to stand in Lofton's way but would prosecute Lofton if he broke the law. But Doe was not the target of Lofton's return. In an interview, the city prosecutor explained, "I think Frank Lofton is back in Border City because of a personal grudge with Samuel Landow. I think he wants to get back for what happened [decades earlier, when he was prosecuted on obscenity charges here]. Even though the conviction was ultimately reversed, he still wants to make a personal statement. . . . If he could have, he would have wanted to open his shop right across from the jailhouse where Samuel Landow is, now that he is sheriff. But this is as close as he can get."

Lofton's first gesture was to show up at a downtown city square to distribute pornographic material, apparently with the explicit intent of baiting local authorities. In statements to the news media, he threatened to open a local store if he were not arrested. City and county officials chose to react by monitoring Lofton's activities at the city square to see whether he broke any laws, ranging from blocking the sidewalk to pandering pornography. In fact, his publicity stunt attracted a large crowd—but only a couple of antipornography protesters—and Lofton was not arrested. The Border County prosecutor's office was, however, reviewing the content of the material he had distributed to determine whether it could be called obscene.

Within three weeks, county prosecutor Doe decided that he would not prosecute Lofton for distributing pornographic material at the square. Claiming that law enforcement resources were finite and that attention to Lofton would simply foster publicity that would help his financial interests, Doe concluded that Lofton's short visit did not warrant further attention.

Upping the ante, Lofton announced that he would make good on his threat to open a store in Border City. In response, a city council member proposed an ordinance that would restrict sexually oriented businesses in all but a few sites zoned for heavy commercial use. Meanwhile, Sheriff Landow appeared at a press conference and introduced a relative of Lofton's who denounced Lofton's activities and called for a war against pornography.

The idea of deterring Lofton with a new zoning ordinance failed because he astutely chose to buy an existing downtown bookstore that was already selling some sexually explicit material. Still, city officials attempted a last-minute maneuver to keep Lofton from operating his business. Only hours before the scheduled opening of Lofton's store, the city council held an emergency meeting to amend the city's temporary law governing sexually oriented businesses. As adopted in 1996, the law pertained primarily to bookstores that also showed videos and films in the store. However, the new law would require licenses for all bookstores that sold significant amounts of sexually explicit merchandise, thus requiring Lofton to obtain a license to operate his business. Ultimately, Lofton opened his store with only minimal protest by local decency activists.

However, the saga of Border City's involvement with Lofton was revisited within a few months. Spurred by rumors that Lofton planned to sell adult videos in his downtown store, the city council called another emergency meeting to fine-tune the law requiring licenses for adult bookstores. As a result of the council's action, sexually explicit videotapes, compact discs, and other non-printed materials would be counted as part of the significant or substantial amount of sexually explicit merchandise on which the licensing requirement was based.

In January 1998, the city council approved permanent changes to the temporary licensing and zoning laws that had been passed in 1996. Under the new legislation, adult businesses could locate only in areas of the city zoned for heavy or medium manufacturing. Nudity would be prohibited in these businesses, and the city attorney would have the authority to bring civil actions to enforce the new laws. After the city council's enactment of these new ordinances, Border City police raided Lofton's downtown store and seized business records. Two of the store's employees were charged with operating a sexually oriented business without a license. Additionally, Lofton and his partner were charged with disseminating material that is harmful to juveniles, pandering obscenity, engaging in a pattern of corrupt activity, and conspiracy. A Border County grand jury returned a fifteen-count indictment involving the videos sold at Lofton's downtown store. Ultimately, Lofton's lawyers accepted a plea bargain, which included guilty pleas from store personnel on two counts of pandering obscenity and Lofton's agreement never to sell sexually explicit videos in Border County; in exchange, prosecutors dropped all charges against Lofton and his partner, who could have spent up to twenty-four years in prison if convicted.

City and county officials have also moved aggressively against other purveyors of sexually explicit material. In 1994, for example, Border City police officers charged the owners and employees of the Purple Pig Bookstore with pandering obscenity because the store's videotape rentals included an Italian film that featured sexual torture and other objectionable material. A national coalition of museums, film societies, arts organizations, film directors, and actors filed a legal brief supporting the bookstore's fight against the obscenity charges. Ultimately, the case was settled by a plea bargain, under which the store was fined $500.

Hill City: Regulation Epitomized

Hill City's city manager explains that prostitution, adult entertainment businesses, and the like are not usually the subject of controversy, because city government has done "a pretty good job with [regulating] it" via zoning laws. The city has long-standing ordinances regulating nude dancing and other sexually explicit businesses. The police chief explains that in the 1980s and 1990s, the city dealt with these types of businesses by restricting them to certain sectors of the city.

Nevertheless, prostitution and pornography have been active issues in recent years. In the Hill City neighborhood along Jefferson Avenue, prostitution has long been a source of complaints by residents. In the mid-1990s, the problem became more acute when commercial redevelopment and gentrification of the area just north of the neighborhood caused prostitutes to move operations closer to residential Jefferson Avenue. In November 1996, police officers, responding to complaints from residents, organized a sting operation that led to the arrest of more than a hundred people. In addition, the police department, with the input of a community-oriented police officer assigned to the neighborhood, applied for a state grant to get better lighting and sidewalks and a federal grant to devise a more durable approach to problems in the area.

In the spring of 1997, the city was awarded the federal grant, which was slated to be used to expand crime prevention activities in the Jefferson Avenue neighborhood. An activist in the neighborhood association applauded the grant, noting that although the sting operations provided temporary relief, the grant offered the hope of a long-term solution. Nevertheless, the sting operations continued that spring and summer, and by October, another major sting operation generated a record number of arrests.

Meanwhile, an adult theater located in the same area had been the focus of complaints and problem-solving efforts for some time. A former city council member who had pushed to get the theater converted to another use was quoted in the local newspaper as saying, "That intersection . . . on that hilltop should be the grand gateway to the city of Hill City. Instead, we have a crapped-out porno theater." In 1998, a potential buyer wanted to convert it to a revival theater, but the owner's asking price was well above its appraised value, and the deal was put on hold while the prospective buyer tried to get the city to subsidize the purchase.

At about the same time, the district attorney adopted an innovative legal strategy to deal with the theater. He filed a public nuisance lawsuit against the theater on the grounds that it served as a site for prostitution. Prior to filing the lawsuit, the district attorney had collaborated with the Hill City police department, which provided undercover officers for prostitution sting operations at the theater.

Meanwhile, the buyer went ahead with the purchase of the theater, without any financial backing from the city. According to the district attorney, this purchase made the public nuisance lawsuit moot. The new owner indicated that, despite his initial intention to convert the theater to another use, he would continue to operate it as an X-rated movie theater for the foreseeable future. However, under the city's regulations, adult enterprises that were in existence when the city revised its zoning regulations were allowed to continue operating only as long as they had the same owner and use. Any new owner had to abide by the new regulations. Thus, the new owner could not operate an X-rated theater. Ultimately, the building was renovated for use by an Internet and computer networking services company.

The most complicated of this trio of cases is Port City. Although it retains some elements of the regulatory strategy, it has gone further than any of the other study cities to incorporate a more lenient, prevention-oriented approach, especially with regard to prostitution.

Port City: Regulation-Prevention Hybrid

Prostitution had long been a problem in several of the city's most distressed neighborhoods, and the police dealt with it mainly as a law enforcement issue. Few, if any, health, social services, or rehabilitation programs were available to prostitutes, and the police did little to protect prostitutes from violent abuse by pimps and johns. But in the early 1990s, a liberal-progressive majority assumed control of the city council and began to pursue initiatives that were widely viewed as responsive to the demands of increasingly well-organized advocates of the decriminalization of prostitution, the idea of prostitutes as victims, and sex workers' civil rights. In 1993, the city council passed and the mayor signed a resolution creating a task force to look into the social and legal problems behind prostitution in Port City and to find new ways to cope with those problems. The task force included representatives from the mayor's office, neighborhood groups, law enforcement agencies, public health and social services agencies, city departments and commissions, women's rights advocates, and prostitute rights groups. Before long, all six neighborhood representatives resigned from the task force in protest, claiming that their concerns about the negative impact of prostitution on neighborhood safety and quality of life were being ignored.

In March 1996, the task force submitted its report to the city council advocating the decriminalization of prostitution, more police focus on crimes committed against prostitutes, licensing of massage parlors and escort services by the city's health department rather than by the police, and greater city funding of shelter and substance abuse programs for prostitutes. The prostitution task force's report was highly controversial. Newly elected liberal mayor Billy Green rejected the decriminalization proposal outright, and a local newspaper editorial ridiculed it as a document that "seemed to fall off the edge of Earth." Shortly after releasing its report, the task force disbanded, and its most controversial recommendations faded into collective memory, with no major local government actions taken to implement them.

However, at least one of the report's less controversial recommendations would be taken seriously two years later. In December 1998, the city's police chief, with support from the district attorney's office, created a new full-time investigative unit in the police department to deal exclusively with crimes against prostitutes. Officers of the unit worked closely with a nonprofit group run by former prostitutes that helps women and girls leave the trade. The head of the new unit was quoted in the local newspaper as saying, "We used to just look at this from a very narrow law enforcement perspective. What we've realized is that we can't just make more arrests and think that will solve any of the problems." The new unit was praised by the district attorney, advocates for sex workers, and some prostitutes themselves.

Another important innovation, implemented even before the task force's report, explicitly added a prevention strategy to the city's policy with respect to prostitution. In March 1995, a consortium of Port City government agencies (including the district attorney's office, health department, and police department) and nonprofit community organizations launched the First Offender's Program (FOP) as a new approach to prostitution offenses. Under FOP (also known as the "school for johns"), first-time arrested solicitors of prostitutes are offered relief from criminal prosecution if they agree to pay a fine and attend classes designed by former prostitutes to educate johns about the dangerous lives prostitutes lead, the destructive impact of prostitution on women, and the risk of sexually transmitted diseases. The fines are used to pay for program staff and provide counseling and health services to the city's prostitutes. This collaborative multiagency program was initiated by the head of the police department's vice squad and a former prostitute who is now a director of a nonprofit organization that provides prostitutes with peer education, job training, and mentorship to encourage them to leave the profession. According to a variety of news reports and the district attorney's Web site, the program was created "to shift local government's approach to prostitution offenses" and was based on the belief shared by all participants that "the root issues of prostitution are sexual exploitation, abuse, addiction, and violence."

Port City's foray into innovative and prevention-oriented policies concerning prostitution does not mean that conventional regulation has been completely abandoned. In fact, the city exhibited a regulatory policy of containment in the late 1980s when a concentration of brothels fronting as massage parlors became problematic for the distressed, inner-city Abner neighborhood. Over the years, the police had experienced considerable frustration in regulating these massage parlors and closing down those that engaged in prostitution. Often, on-paper changes in ownership would allow owners to dodge license revocation proceedings. In the spring of 1998, the city council member representing the Abner neighborhood proposed a permanent moratorium on new massage parlors, with the exception of therapeutic massage establishments, which would be exempt. With the imprimatur of the planning commission, the moratorium on new massage parlors in Abner was adopted unanimously by the city council and signed by the mayor. As enacted, the law also includes "good neighbor" standards that restrict business hours and the use of neon lights and sidewalk barkers by all new massage parlors anywhere in the neighborhood.

Similarly, Port City has a regulatory approach to strip clubs, X-rated theaters, and other adult entertainment businesses—albeit a relatively permissive version of regulation. The police department, which issues and regulates operating permits for adult entertainment businesses, has generally avoided monitoring strip clubs and X-rated theaters. The last time the police entered a strip club to make arrests for lewd behavior was in the late 1970s. This hands-off approach was partly a response to the perception that court decisions made prosecution of lewd behavior in private clubs very difficult and partly because of the city's culture of tolerance, secularism, and sexual liberation.

The community's culture of tolerance and law enforcement's permissive approach were tested in the 1990s when adult entertainment entrepreneurs trying to expand their operations in the West Beach district were met with opposition from well-organized resident groups and historical preservationists. Yet the outcome of several controversies suggests that a relatively permissive approach has been sustained, despite resident opposition. In 1997, for example, West Beach merchants and residents opposed the city's issuance of permits to new establishments such as those proposed by the Adult Fun Corporation, which is owned by an out-of-town, ex-con, multimillionaire "porn king" who has more than eighty adult-oriented businesses in fourteen states. Once the new club owners satisfied the requirements, however, they were given temporary operating permits; in response to continuing concerns by West Beach merchants, the permit board simply imposed the condition that there could be no nudity at the establishments. In 2000, an upscale club that had never applied for an adult entertainment license sparked protest from leaders of the West Beach neighborhood association, who claimed that the club's topless dancers were engaging in lap dancing. The owner had twice been admonished by the police for allowing lap dancing, but they had simply informed the owner of municipal code requirements that exotic dancers stay at least six feet away from the closest customer and perform on a stage at least eighteen inches high. Despite these brushes with the law and the neighborhood association's complaints, the permit board decided that the club was a legitimate restaurant and bar operation that did not need an adult entertainment permit to stay open.

SUBCULTURAL EXPLANATION

In addition to exemplifying three different policy stances on the sex trade, the three preceding case histories are also tempting pieces of evidence in support of a cultural explanation for which type of stance a city will adopt. Consistent with the understanding of community subculture that was laid out earlier, we might expect cities with conventional subcultures to be the least tolerant of pornography, prostitution, and other elements of the sex industry as a result of substantial pressures for a prohibitionist approach; at the other extreme, a more permissive stance featuring a looser version of the regulatory approach and perhaps even some elements of a prevention strategy would be expected to emerge in unconventional communities.

However, the evidence overall is disappointing with respect to a subcultural explanation of city differences. Consider, for example, the similar stances toward prostitution and adult entertainment in unconventional Valley City and conventional South City. Despite subcultural differences, both cities' policies are nearly as restrictive toward pornography and sexually explicit businesses as Border City's are, although Valley City's efforts have been more successful than South City's.

South City: The Frustrations of Ineffective Prohibition

South City has a history of high-profile and heavily politicized crusades against pornography and sex-oriented businesses dating at least to the 1970s, when J. Crandall, then an assistant U.S. attorney, prosecuted a large number of obscenity cases in the city. The chairperson of the city council describes the community as "basically a Christian city" with a "commitment to morality," and the police chief accounts for the high level of concern about sexually explicit businesses by noting that the city is in the Bible Belt and that there are "churches on every corner in South City."

Furthermore, the city is the locus of at least two well-organized antipornography citizens groups—Citizens for Decency and Families for Responsible Living (FRL). FRL is a conservative Christian group, established in 1980, that has been active in efforts against abortion and homosexuality as well as pornography. Mary Matthews, an FRL board member, served as a county commissioner in South City's home county. Citizens for Decency was established in 1992 by a mother and former health care industry professional who is also affiliated with FRL.

Not surprisingly, then, public officials have been heavily involved in efforts to squelch sexually explicit businesses. These efforts have often failed, however, and these failures have sparked renewed pressure from decency activists.

One front in the war against sex-related businesses involves hourly rate motels. In response to complaints from residents of a predominantly African American neighborhood where a number of these motels had sprung up, the city council voted in April 1994 for a six-month moratorium on motels with seventy-five or fewer rooms; the moratorium was later extended for the rest of the year. The city had already passed an ordinance in 1991 that put limitations on the operation of a variety of sexually oriented businesses, including such motels, but enforcement of that ordinance was on hold while a federal appeals court heard a legal challenge to it.

In October 1994, Mayor Gradison laid out a plan to deal with the growth of sexually oriented businesses generally and hourly rate motels in particular. A key part of his plan was an effort to get the federal appeals court to lift its injunction against enforcement of the city's 1991 ordinance, which banned sexually oriented businesses from locating within 1,500 feet of churches, parks, schools, residences, and other adult businesses and allowed the city to close down any such business that was not in conformance with the distance requirements. The court had balked on the latter provision because it conflicted with the city's charter, so the mayor was proposing a charter amendment. In addition, the mayor's package of proposals included a change in the city's zoning laws that would place hourly rate motels in an industrial rather than adult entertainment category, the adoption of a new special-use permit requirement for such motels, and strict enforcement of all existing city codes as they apply to sex-oriented businesses.

The mayor's proposals were endorsed by several council members, most notably the one representing the district where most hourly rate motels were locating. But in the years since, the moratorium on building motels has been lifted, and instead of relying on ordinances such as the one challenged in federal court, the city uses an indirect method of control. As the city council chairwoman explains, if someone proposes to build a motel, the city asks whether there are plans for it to be an hourly rate motel. No one admits this, of course, and the denial is documented. If a motel is later found to be functioning as an hourly rate establishment, the city believes that this documentation gives it the authority to close the business down.

But hourly rate motels are not the only problem. South City has also had to deal with complaints about topless clubs operating in the community. According to the city council's chairwoman, these establishments were objectionable to churches and other groups in the community, and the police reported that underage patrons were frequenting the clubs and a variety of illegal activities were going on there.

The city's efforts to rein in the topless clubs were initially handled by the South City Alcohol Commission (SAC), which issues permits for the sale of beer. These efforts were not very effective in either stopping objectionable activity at existing topless clubs or preventing the establishment of new ones. In early 1994, for example, SAC issued a beer permit to a new topless club over objections from Citizens for Decency activists. Within a month, five of the city's topless clubs were fined for violating city ordinances. The owners of the clubs, including the new one, appeared before SAC with promises that they would no longer allow dancers to be completely nude or to perform simulated sex acts and lap dancing. But later in 1994, the city again fined several topless clubs, based on evidence brought by police officers of dancers performing completely nude.

In addition to this track record of ineffective deterrence of topless clubs, the city faced bad news in 1994 when a federal judge ruled against its 1992 ordinance that banned topless performances. The judge found that the ordinance was unconstitutional on the grounds that it was overly vague and selectively applied to topless clubs; in addition, it was equivalent to a 1983 ordinance that had been subject to a preliminary injunction. As a result, the city was found to be in contempt of court and had to pay some of the plaintiffs' fees.

Despite these setbacks, many city officials forged ahead with efforts to curb sexually oriented businesses. The city council member who had sponsored the failed topless dancing ordinance indicated that she intended to devise a new one that would pass constitutional tests, and the SAC warned topless clubs that, despite the court's ruling, it would aggressively enforce other ordinances barring sexual contact and nudity in businesses selling alcohol.

The ineffectiveness of South City's various regulatory strategies led to a change in approach in 1995. This new approach involved a high-profile effort to use litigation to actually drive such establishments out of businesses rather than merely regulating their activity. Early in the year, District Attorney John Piscotta named J. Crandall as a special prosecutor for purposes of an initiative to close down all eight topless clubs then operating in the city. Crandall, as noted earlier, had been a notable antiobscenity crusader when he served as assistant U.S. attorney in the 1970s, and he was now in private practice in South City.

In July 1996, the district attorney's office organized a high-profile raid on all the city's topless clubs, culminating what was said to be an eighteen-month investigation of the clubs and their alleged involvement in prostitution, drug use, racketeering, obscenity, and other illegal activities. The raid was the opening salvo in a new strategy of using the civil forfeiture provisions of the federal Racketeer Influenced and Corrupt Organizations (RICO) statute in an attempt to seize the clubs and close them down permanently. District Attorney

Piscotta explained this new approach by claiming, "It appeared to us the only way we could have an impact . . . you don't have to get into all the First Amendment arguments—obscenity and this, that and the other."

However, questions arose about Crandall's appointment and the financing of the war on topless clubs. Piscotta acknowledged that Catharine Collum of Citizens for Decency had brought up the possibility of using Crandall and that the money to pay the special prosecutor had been collected by her organization. In this state, the law permits privately financed payment of prosecutors to represent the government in certain cases. But the local newspaper criticized the district attorney's office for "falling under the influence" of a citizens group, and things got worse when it became known that most of the $56,000 collected to pay Crandall had come from members of the evangelical church where he worships. Less than two weeks later, the district attorney announced that he was resigning, and county commissioner Jay Hawkins was appointed to fill the post.

Meanwhile, the topless clubs that had been closed down in the raid were allowed to reopen as a result of a decision by a federal judge, who questioned the legal sufficiency of the documents on which their closure was based. Once they reopened, the topless clubs continued the practices that had decency activists in the community outraged, and the city's police department and alcohol commission continued their seemingly futile round of regulatory efforts.

Very quickly, the newly installed district attorney took up the crusade against topless clubs. In December 1996, county sheriff's deputies raided several clubs and served employees and management with warrants on criminal charges, including prostitution and contributing to the delinquency of a minor. Hawkins also made it clear that, like his predecessor, he intended to file public nuisance petitions designed to close down the clubs through forfeiture actions. He also reiterated that, despite the controversy, Crandall would remain the special prosecutor for the cases. By February 1997, nearly 200 indictments for obscenity, indecency, and prostitution had been served by the county grand jury.

Six months later, the financial scale of the crusade against the topless clubs and its interconnections with an out-of-town decency organization were becoming apparent. Special prosecutor Crandall revealed that the private contributions to fund his operation had grown to over $300,000, including $100,000 from Citizens for Decency that had been funneled to it by a Cincinnati-based organization. Ultimately, the crusade was dealt a crushing blow the following spring when a criminal court judge disqualified Crandall and the rest of the district attorney's staff from prosecuting a topless club owner, calling the criminal indictments they had brought tainted. The judge stated that the huge sums of money donated by private groups to fund the special prosecutor's operation gave him a substantial financial interest in the case. When a state appeals court upheld the decision a year later, the crusade officially hit a dead end. Putting the best face on the fiasco, an assistant district attorney was quoted in the local newspaper as saying, "I think we knew in the beginning that what we were doing was unique. Nothing like this had ever been tried in any jurisdiction. And we're kind of testing the waters to see exactly what the law does and doesn't allow."

Valley City: Aggressive Regulation with an International Twist

Like South City, Valley City's approach to prostitution, pornography, and the like has long been one of aggressive regulation, bordering on prohibition. With respect to sexually explicit bookstores, the city adopted a policy in the 1980s that effectively removed all those that were operating in downtown Valley City and severely limited their location elsewhere in the city. At the time, adult bookstores were viewed as incompatible with downtown redevelopment efforts, especially since solicitation of prostitution was allegedly going on in those businesses. According to the city attorney, the city got around potential legal problems by adopting a set of ordinances specifying that the store owners would be given a reasonable amount of time to make enough money to cover their investments; then they would be expected to relocate. Legally, the city could issue injunctions to close down the bookstores over a certain time frame, as long as there were "adequate theoretical possibilities" where they could relocate. The city also adopted an ordinance limiting the location of adult bookstores to commercial-retail zoning districts outside the downtown area and prohibiting such stores from locating within 200 feet of each other or of residences or within 500 feet of schools. Since regional shopping centers were not willing to lease to them, adult bookstores had to relocate in unincorporated pockets of the county.

By the mid-1990s, prostitution surfaced as an issue in Valley City because of the limited success of traditional regulatory policies, such as staging crackdowns in response to complaints from affected neighborhoods. City officials responded to constituents' pressure by adopting a shaming strategy that other cities have tried—that is, placing the names of men arrested for soliciting sexual acts in news releases. As one city council member acknowledged in a local newspaper story, "It takes two, you know. Pimps bring in the prostitutes, but it takes johns to make it work." However, the local newspapers balked at printing the names of the arrested men, and the city attorney also feared lawsuits if the city released their names. Hence, this innovation was short-circuited.

Meanwhile, sparked in part by the belief that international crime rings were operating prostitution enterprises in Valley City and in part by the desire to fight innovative forms of prostitution enterprises with enhanced law enforcement attention, city officials pushed ahead with more aggressive enforcement strategies. Valley City had a couple of sensational prostitution cases involving Asian gangs with alleged links to the international sex-slave trade and Russian prostitution rings. By the mid-1990s, a network of as many as ten Asian brothels had become established in the community, allegedly part of an organized, multimillion-dollar international business. These brothels catered to the many Asian newcomers in the area, including businessmen working temporarily in high-tech companies. They eluded police by playing a cat-and-mouse game with vice officers, moving often to escape detection. In the fall of 1997, Valley City police cooperated with the U.S. Immigration and Naturalization Service and Canadian law enforcement officials in the arrest of a madam and five sex workers suspected of participating in an international sex-slave ring that imported young women from Southeast Asia to Valley City and other North American cities. No evidence to substantiate the brothel's involvement in an international sex-trade ring was ever presented, and under a plea agreement, the madam ultimately pleaded no contest to one count of pimping.

In 1995, after a yearlong investigation, Valley City police had made arrests in connection with a major Russian prostitution ring that operated under the guise of escort services in the region. And in June 1998, Valley City police capped a five-month investigation with the arrests of two people who were allegedly operating a large-scale prostitution ring employing more than 100 male and female prostitutes in the metropolitan area, which had become a target for prostitution because of its high volume of business travelers. None of the alleged prostitutes was arrested in the case, because authorities were interested primarily in the head of the organization.

Valley City's enforcement efforts thus extend well beyond the typical regulatory approach in most cities, consisting of periodic crackdowns on streetwalkers when neighbors get upset. Instead, a much more aggressive approach involving substantial undercover work and collaboration with national and international law enforcement authorities has targeted sophisticated brothel operations that presumably would be largely invisible to local residents. In addition, the city has become much more aggressive with respect to brothels that attempt to function under the guise of "relaxation" centers. Because the city heavily regulates massage parlors, unlicensed facilities such as tanning salons, relaxation centers, and hot towel salons began to be used as fronts for prostitution. Using evidence obtained from undercover police investigations, the city had gotten court orders to close down seven or eight of these salons.

With their quite different subcultures yet similar approaches to sexually explicit businesses, the South City and Valley City cases do not support a sub-

Figure 5.1 Policy Stance toward the Sex Industry, by Community Subculture
Type

Cities in bold are conventional; those in italic are unconventional.

cultural interpretation. In addition to the counterevidence from this pairing of
cities, the subcultural explanation is limited by the fact that, as a set, conventional cities are not that much more restrictive of the sex industry than are unconventional cities.

Foreshadowing the other case histories to come, figure 5.1 shows the
placement of all ten cities along the continuum from the most restrictive prohibitionist approach to the most permissive prevention-oriented approach. It is
true that the extremes of the policy continuum are anchored by a conventional
city at the most restrictive end and an unconventional city at the most permissive end. But apart from these extremes, unconventional and conventional
cities are different only in that two of the remaining four conventional cities
have regulatory regimes aggressive enough to verge on prohibition, while only
one of the remaining four unconventional cities is more restrictive than a
straight-ahead regulatory regime.

Feminist Mobilization on Decency Issues

There is a slight twist to the subcultural explanation that should be considered.
Feminist opposition to pornography and the mobilization of feminist groups
with respect to pornography and sexually explicit businesses in general have
been important parts of the history of the decency issue. Indeed, one of the best-
known case studies of the local politics of decency features high-profile feminist mobilization in Indianapolis and Minneapolis in the 1980s that led to the
enactment of radical city ordinances against pornography, which were ultimately struck down by the courts (Downs 1989). In the same vein, a recent
analysis of state-level enforcement of obscenity laws finds that enforcement is
much stronger in states where women are more politically empowered (Smith
2001). To the extent that heightened female empowerment is an element of

unconventional subculture, all this could be taken to mean that our expectations about subculture and the decency issue should be reversed or at least tempered. That is, perhaps we should expect unconventional cities to be hostile to the sex industry because of feminist activism rather than relatively permissive and tolerant. This would make unconventional and conventional cities appear to be similarly situated on this issue, except that in conventional cities, the opposition to sexually explicit businesses would likely stem from religious groups or other elements of traditional culture rather than from feminist activism.

There is, however, scant support for this interpretation in the case study evidence. In four of the five unconventional cities, there are a number of opponents of the sex industry, but none are organized women's groups or individuals with a feminist agenda. The only evidence of the involvement of women's organizations comes from Port City, where groups pushed for the decriminalization of prostitution and sex workers' civil rights—an exception that certainly does *not* show hostility to the sex industry.

Indeed, there is scant evidence of any women's organizations mobilized in opposition to pornography or sexually explicit businesses in any of the study cities. Perhaps the key exception to this is South City's experience, which features two organizations with female leadership and a decency agenda. It is important to note, however, that neither of these organizations can be described as women's organizations per se. Rather, they are conservative, family-values organizations. For at least one of them, opposition to the sex industry runs side by side with opposition to gambling and other issues.

In short, despite the intellectual importance of feminists on the issues of pornography, prostitution, and the sex industry, as well as the local mobilization by feminists in some well-known cases, the case studies in this book do not yield evidence that feminist opposition drives decency politics at the local level. For the same reason, there are no grounds for concluding that the disappointing performance of the subculture explanation is due to the complicating effects of that component of unconventional subculture that reflects enhanced involvement of women. However, the failure of this alternative explanation may stem from the fact that the research, including the selection of study cities and foci for fieldwork observation, was not designed to test this hypothesis.

INSTITUTIONAL EXPLANATION

The preceding section shows that variation in the study cities' handling of the sex industry is not strongly patterned according to subculture. However, it is possible that the significance of city subculture is not apparent until the role of

Table 5.1 Policy Stance toward the Sex Industry, by Community Subculture
Type and Chief Executive Type

Unconventional, Mayor	Unconventional, City Manager
Western City—regulation	Valley City—regulation verging on prohibition
Metro City—regulation	Hill City—regulation
Port City—regulation-prevention hybrid	

Conventional, Mayor	Conventional, City Manager
South City—semiprohibition	Coastal City—regulation verging on prohibition
Lake City—regulation	Border City—prohibition
River City—regulation, some prevention	

local political institutions is taken into account. That is, if political institutions
mediate between the demands of the citizenry and policy outcomes, then we
might expect subcultural contrasts on decency issues to be apparent among
cities with highly politicized chief executives (i.e., directly elected mayors
rather than city managers), and perhaps the responsiveness-fostering institution of district elections (rather than ward elections) functions in the same way
to enhance pressure on city officials. By contrast, among cities with the muted
politics of reformed government (i.e., city managers and at-large elections), we
might expect city subculture to make less of a difference in the city's stance on
decency issues. Table 5.1 shows that the evidence from the study cities overall does not support these expectations, at least with respect to the mediating
effect of chief executive type. Three cities fit the scenario that should generate the most restrictive stance with respect to the sex industry—a conventional
subculture coupled with a politicized chief executive (lower left-hand cell of
the table). But there are as many differences *within* this group of three cities as
there are *between* this trio and the pair of conventional cities with city managers rather than mayors. And there is certainly no pattern showing a more restrictive approach when mayors have political incentives to be in the moral
vanguard in conventional settings. Nor is there a pattern to suggest that mayors in unconventional settings are especially attuned to progressive forces demanding innovative, prevention-oriented approaches. Only one of the three
cities in this scenario (Port City; upper left-hand cell of the table) shows the
emergence of a prevention-oriented approach.

A closer look at Western City's experience suggests two important reasons
why taking the type of chief executive into account does not yield the expected
pattern of results. As the following case narrative shows, even in an uncon-

ventional city, the citizenry is often up in arms about sexually explicit businesses because of quality-of-life issues. And because those problems are often manifested at the neighborhood level, institutional arrangements with respect to the city council may be more important than those involving the chief executive. In short, city council responsiveness to neighborhood-level concerns related to the sex industry constitutes an important part of decency politics and policy making, even in unconventional settings.

Western City: Regulation as Responsiveness

Pornography, prostitution, and other sex-related issues have been highly salient in Western City in recent years, with citizens demanding amelioration of quality-of-life problems stemming from sex-related businesses impinging on neighborhoods. The city's response has typically been one of policy changes designed to make its regulatory approach to such matters more effective.

Controversy over adult entertainment businesses reached a high level in 1996, with the opening of a so-called pop shop in a residential neighborhood. Pop shops are nude dancing establishments that evade regulatory oversight by not serving alcohol. Triggered by complaints from citizens, the city council ordered a fifteen-month study of adult businesses and imposed a moratorium on new strip clubs and adult movie theaters, video stores, and bookshops near neighborhoods and schools. The study found that such businesses create public health threats, reduce property values, and increase traffic, crime, and noise.

In May 1998, after input at open meetings and over the objections of the American Civil Liberties Union (ACLU), the city council made the moratorium on new adult businesses permanent, but only in selected districts. This cut the possible sites for new adult businesses from eighty-nine to sixty-nine but did not affect the twenty-one adult-oriented businesses already in operation. In other districts, the ordinance maintained the city's existing policy of requiring adult businesses to be 500 feet from residences and schools and extended the distance requirement to amusement parks and arts, learning, daycare, and children's indoor play centers. Because the ordinance concentrated the allowable sites for new adult businesses in industrial zones, it was opposed by a councilwoman from a Hispanic area of Western City with many such zones, who was quoted in the local newspaper as complaining, "We don't want to be a wasteland for what everybody else doesn't want." Nevertheless, the ordinance was approved over her objections, with promises from fellow council members that they would study the impact on her area in the future.

Prostitution has also been a highly salient issue in Western City, sparked in part by the usual complaints from residents in areas where prostitution is

visible and in part by concerns that a neighboring city's crackdown on prostitution could lead prostitutes and johns to descend on Western City in even
larger numbers if something were not done. Western City's response has been
three-pronged. In 1995, the city began a nuisance abatement program designed
to deal with properties being used for prostitution, as well as other problems
such as noise from bars and gang activity at certain locations. Under this approach, citizen complaints trigger a process that can lead to the citation of the
property owner and, in some circumstances, city seizure of the nuisance property. For example, in the fall of 1996, the city seized and shut down six motels in one neighborhood on the grounds that they were nuisance properties
being used for prostitution and drug dealing. In 1997, in response to objections
from neighborhood leaders that the process for making a complaint was too
cumbersome, the city council voted to expand the definition of a nuisance,
tighten the process for issuing citations, and strengthen penalties. Despite concerns from mortgage lenders and bar and liquor store owners, who were fear-
ful of property seizures, the city council enacted the new nuisance ordinance
by a vote of twelve to one.

Western City has long used and continues to use sting operations and other
conventional tactics to target law enforcement resources at locations where
prostitution is especially problematic. Such stings, conducted by the Western
City police department's vice squad, were repeatedly focused along Coloran
Avenue, where streetwalkers plied their trade, and they were used to arrest
johns as well as prostitutes. The episodic nature of these stings and their apparent ineffectiveness are evident by the fact that virtually the same locations
targeted in 1995 and 1996 were still having prostitution problems and attracting more sting operations in 1999.

Western City's use of public health measures to punish both prostitutes and
their clients has been more controversial. A city council member and former
police officer worked with the city attorney to draft legislation that would be
a more effective deterrent to prostitution, and in December 1994, the city council unanimously approved this tougher law. It increased fines for prostitution
violations and, more important, required that both prostitutes and johns be
tested for HIV and sexually transmitted diseases (STDs) at their own expense;
it also gave police the authority to keep johns in jail until they were cured of
their STDs. Previously, these requirements had extended only to prostitutes,
not their customers. The ACLU opposed the ordinance, charging that it forced
people to be tested before they were charged with a crime.

In short, Western City's approach to decency issues of all kinds involves
regulatory policies that assume the continuing existence of various objectionable activities and attempt to manage the circumstances under which those

Table 5.2 Policy Stance toward the Sex Industry, by Community Subculture Type and Council Election Type

Unconventional, District	Unconventional, At-Large
Metro City—regulation Western City—regulation Valley City—regulation verging on prohibition	Hill City—regulation Port City—regulation-prevention hybrid

Conventional, District	Conventional, At-Large
South City—semiprohibition River City—regulation, some prevention	Border City—prohibition Lake City—regulation Coastal City—regulation verging on prohibition

activities occur. A local newspaper editorial explicitly acknowledged this with respect to the city's new zoning restrictions on adult entertainment, noting that the city "is not trying to eliminate the adult-entertainment industry, which has a constitutional right to exist. It is merely moving sensibly to head off future neighborhood conflicts of the type that have erupted in Chaneyville and other suburban communities." And although prostitution does not enjoy the same constitutional protections that pornography and adult entertainment businesses do, the city's approach to prostitution is also regulatory, featuring periodic stings in chronic prostitution zones, the use of nuisance laws to weed out prostitution where it creates problems for neighbors, and mandatory HIV testing, which limits the consequences of prostitution from a public health point of view and imposes an additional penalty on those who are arrested.

Western City's experience directs us to the possibility that a more restrictive approach to the sex industry is more likely where there are district-elected officials to champion the concerns of citizens who object to the neighborhood-specific spillover effects of sexually explicit businesses. However, across all ten cities, there is very little evidence of such a pattern (see table 5.2). Three of the five cities with district elections have a relatively restrictive stance at least verging on prohibition, but the only full-blown case of prohibition is at-large Border City; at-large Coastal City verges on prohibition as well. As with the character of the chief executive, city council election type does not appear to account for patterns of city response to the sex industry.

Lake City's experience provides one important reason why the institutional explanation, even when expanded to encompass type of council election, is of limited utility for understanding the politics of city response to the sex industry.

Lake City: Tuning up a Failing Regulatory Policy

Nearly half of the approximately 100 officially licensed adult entertainment establishments in this state are located in Lake City. Lake City relies primarily on zoning ordinances dating from decades ago to control the location of new adult entertainment establishments, which are limited to industrial zones. However, preexisting establishments located in residential neighborhoods were exempted from those ordinances and have been allowed to continue operating ever since. Consequently, many adult entertainment establishments are located on boulevards adjacent to residential neighborhoods.

These establishments are a source of conflict. Most of the controversy involves the nuisance problems associated with these establishments that spill out into the adjoining residential areas. For example, residents complain about noise as drunken people leave the establishments and head for their cars parked on side streets or mill around in parking lots next to people's homes. People have also reported finding condoms and drug paraphernalia on their lawns and in their driveways.

Motels that permit pimps to rent rooms that are used all day by several prostitutes and their customers also pose a problem for neighborhood residents. Although these motels are located in strip commercial areas, they adjoin homes located on side streets. Prostitutes pace up and down in plain sight, and there are reports of children being accosted by prostitutes and of neighborhood residents engaging in vigilante justice, such as slashing the tires of cars parked in areas frequented by prostitutes.

As a matter of policy, topless dancing is legal in Lake City, and both topless dancing establishments and dancers are licensed by the Department of Consumer Affairs. However, lap dancing or touching of customers by dancers is illegal. Prostitution is illegal as well. Motels and hotels are required to keep guest registers and to limit the guests entertained in the rooms to those who are registered. The police have the authority to check business establishments to see that they have the proper licenses, and they do this routinely.

But the enforcement of these licensing laws and of city and zoning ordinances governing adult entertainment businesses has been a problem in Lake City. For years, there has been a recognized need to improve the monitoring of illegal activities in adult businesses, to increase the enforcement of laws against prostitution, and to reduce the undue friendliness between police officers assigned to precinct-level vice units (referred to as "morality units") and the business owners they were supposed to be monitoring. To that end, the police department began to centralize its vice activities and replace these morality units. The transition started in 1993, with the creation of a specialized police task force that handled vice issues on a centralized basis and showed great performance statistics. When a new police chief was appointed in 1998, he immediately established the current centralized vice section, with mayoral approval, and the precinct-based units were disbanded, although officers in precincts still roust prostitutes off street corners, check on licenses, and respond to citizen complaints about adult entertainment establishments. According to several sources, the existence of a centralized unit to handle vice issues is an important ingredient in the police department's policy to monitor adult entertainment in the city.

The department of consumer affairs has also come under attack for its underenforcement of licensing regulations with respect to adult entertainment businesses. In the summer of 1996, this led the city council to hold a special public hearing on the regulation of topless bars and adult entertainment establishments. Attendees included a community representative and representatives from the city's law, consumer affairs, and police departments. At the meeting, videotapes showing illegal contact between customers and dancers at some of the city's topless clubs were shown. The tapes were provided by the "video posse," a group that includes citizens, the county sheriff's department, and law-abiding club owners who enter topless establishments undercover and secretly videotape events occurring there. (The club owners participate because they believe that those establishments that permit illegal touching between dancers and customers put the law-abiding businesses at a competitive disadvantage.) Based on the videotapes, the council was convinced that illegal contact was occurring at some of the topless clubs. At the same meeting, officials were given evidence that little action had been taken by the consumer affairs department against establishments with as many as 100 violations. Although the issues of property rights and due process were mentioned as reasons for not revoking licenses or for allowing clubs to keep operating while they appealed attempts to suspend their licenses, council members were concerned that businesses could flagrantly violate the law.

It is important to note, however, that adult entertainment is a $65 million business in Lake City. This fact could account for owners' ability to fight legal challenges to their license renewals and would also cause the mayor's office to be careful about antagonizing businesses that pay taxes, particularly during lean times in the 1970s and 1980s.

In response to the revelations at the special hearing, the city council requested and the mayor created a citizens advisory council on adult entertainment, which operated for nearly two years. Its recommendations were instrumental in nudging the police department to create a centralized vice unit. In addition, in the immediate aftermath of the public hearing, the director of consumer affairs retired and was replaced by a more aggressive manager. In the two years prior to the old director's departure, his department had held only one license revocation hearing; in 1998, when the new director took over, fourteen owners of adult entertainment businesses were given notice that their licenses would not be renewed. The new director was quoted in the local news-paper as saying that in previous years, "inspections were put away in a file and never looked at again. We're trying to make an effort now." Finally, because questions had been raised about the flow of information between the police department and agencies that could use that information to monitor and regulate adult entertainment businesses, a policy change made it mandatory for the consumer affairs department to be notified by the police of any license violations that came to their attention.

The use of zoning regulations to contain sexually explicit businesses has been less controversial, perhaps because the zoning board of appeals (ZBA) appears to be very responsive to the concerns of neighborhood residents. In 1997, for example, when the owner of the Glitz Club attempted to expand the business, the ZBA turned the application down because the owner had a horrid record that included the sale of alcohol to minors and lap dancing.

Zoning continues to be the primary tool used to limit the growth of adult businesses in Lake City. In the late 1990s, Lake City made its zoning regulations even more stringent by prohibiting X-rated businesses on radial trunk roads leading into the city. This seems to have been motivated by a desire to present what a city council member calls a more "wholesome" appearance to suburbanites driving into the city to visit the casinos and the stadiums being developed by Lake City. It also appears to have been motivated by fears that, with new casinos opening, license applications for new adult entertainment businesses would increase.

It is clear that there are neighborhood-level concerns about sexually explicit businesses in Lake City, just as there are in Western City; it is also clear that city officials have been less prohibitionist in their stance toward these businesses than neighborhood residents would like. But the case shows that, in several respects, the existence of at-large rather than district council elections in Lake City does *not* account for this limited responsiveness. There are, in fact, both centralized institutions and decentralized, neighborhood-level institutions in Lake City that are relevant to this issue. Ironically, the more centralized institutions have been more responsive to neighborhood residents' concerns, such as when the at-large city council took the department of consumer affairs to task for its underenforcement of regulations. Furthermore, the police department replaced a precinct-level approach to vice control with a more centralized vice section because of concerns about the failure of the precinct units to satisfy neighborhood residents. It is somewhat ironic that a centralized governance institution would be more responsive to neighborhood residents (but perhaps in this situation, the precinct-level response was misplaced—focusing on adult businesses rather than residents). This case also shows that the institutional arrangements affecting a city's stance toward the sex industry are complex, encompassing not only the chief executive and city council but also the character of the police department and the nature of leadership in bureaucratic organizations such as the licensing department and zoning board.

ECONOMIC EXPLANATION

Why does the subculture explanation fail to account for the cities' responses to sexually explicit businesses, even when institutional differences are considered? Important hints are already evident in the economic factors uncovered in the cases examined so far, such as the possibility that Lake City's weak version of regulation stems from the unwillingness of a financially distressed city to come down too harshly on a lucrative industry. A more dramatic illustration is provided in the story of Coastal City's approach to these businesses.

Coastal City: Tourism Pushes Regulation toward Prohibition

According to city attorneys interviewed for this project, Coastal City was historically a place where people from several nearby states came to "bet on the horses, to gamble, and to drink." The town had a reputation as a wide open, wild place, and this, in addition to the area's natural attractions, is how it got started as a resort destination. "Because of the tourism and the importance of the restaurant and bar business . . . it's a much more tolerant community toward some of those sorts of things" than other midwestern towns might be, says the city manager. This characterization suggests that the community would also be relatively permissive with respect to adult entertainment, pornography, and other aspects of the "sex business." But instead, recent developments surrounding these interrelated topics suggest that the city is not permissive—in fact, it has been relatively aggressive in attempting to stamp out these activities. At least one city attorney attributes this in part to the presence of powerful religious institutions in the community; another emphasizes that it is a suburban-type city that does not have a core urban area, "and you have a family atmosphere throughout the community." In any case, this local government's policy stance is clearly linked to the city's contemporary strategy of marketing its resort area as a family-oriented place. When framed in this way, good morals make for good business. Hence, morality issues in this study city are closely intertwined with economic issues.

Prior to the 1990s, the city's zoning ordinance already included restrictions on adult bookstores. Such stores were prohibited within 500 feet of any apartment or residential district, single- or multiple-family dwelling, church, park, or school. In 1993, an additional restriction was placed on adult bookstores in response to reports that they were having "peep shows" and allowing all sorts of sexual activity, as well as concerns about the associated "health problems." The new restriction prevented adult bookstores from having closed booths or cubicles for viewing X-rated videos. An outright ban on peep shows would, of course, be on shaky constitutional ground. But city attorneys argued that by "taking the doors off" the peep shows, they were able to prevent sexual activity in the bookstores.

While the city was using zoning restrictions to deal with the adult bookstore problem, the district attorney's office was taking action to treat their sale of sexual devices as an obscenity issue. In October 1993, the deputy district attorney, allegedly in response to citizen complaints, arranged for detectives to purchase sexual devices in local stores and set up a three-citizen panel to determine whether there was probable cause to take action against the stores. In the spring of 1994, that panel found that there was probable cause, leading the district attorney's office to raid six stores and seize thousands of dollars worth of merchandise. To prosecute the individual owners under obscenity statutes, there had to be a showing that the material in question violates established community standards; to do this, a second panel of nine citizens was established in August 1994. By a seven-to-two vote, that panel determined that the merchandise was obscene, and on the basis of that determination, five of the six business owners entered guilty pleas, including one who was facing felony charges because he had already been convicted of selling pornographic items; as part of the plea agreement, he was forced to sell his stores. The others pleaded guilty to misdemeanor charges in January 1995, and charges against the sixth store owner were dropped in May 1995, at the request of prosecutors, after the judge ruled that police had made an illegal search of the store.

But controversy emerged over the composition of the nine-member panel that had determined that the merchandise was obscene. Initially, the district attorney's office was critiqued by some local lawyers for keeping the panel members' identity a secret. In response to a Freedom of Information Act request by two local newspapers, the names of the individuals on the panel were revealed in early October 1994, and it became clear that they were far from a cross section of the community. Eight of the nine were white Protestants and, according to a local newspaper, included "five members of the same

Methodist church and a former city councilman who led an anti-smut campaign in the 1970s." A police official recalls that "there were some local attorneys who felt that the district attorney handpicked the people to view [the merchandise] and didn't get a cross section of the community, and we were kind of fudgin' on that."

In this case, the linkage between morality policy enforcement and the city's determination to sustain a family-oriented image for its resort area is particularly clear. One of the individuals who served on the district attorney's obscenity panel stated that the deputy district attorney told the panel that officials periodically crack down on sexually explicit material in the city. He was quoted in the local newspaper as explaining, "It's not the hope of wiping out pornography completely in [Coastal City], but the message was: We need to keep this under control so it doesn't spread all over the [resort area]."

In a similar vein, the city adopted an ordinance in 1996 governing the display of lewd merchandise in stores. An attorney in the city attorney's office says that they "affectionately refer to it" as the "dirty T-shirt" ordinance. A number of beachfront store owners were displaying "lewd, lascivious, or, at a minimum, in-poor-taste T-shirts that a lot of other businesses didn't feel should be displayed where juveniles could see them." City officials had been hearing complaints about this for years from both business owners and residents, but no one wanted to make an issue of it until the summer of 1995, when it really started to be "what a lot of business owners considered to be an epidemic" of "lewder and lewder" merchandise. Many business owners wanted a voluntary agreement among themselves not to display the offensive merchandise, but others continued to do so, and residents increasingly registered objections.

The city attorney's office believed that any attempt to ban the sale of such merchandise altogether would be an unconstitutional infringement on First Amendment rights. So they tackled the problem from the standpoint of protecting juveniles. Hence, the ordinance they devised restricts the display of "merchandise which graphically depicts or describes sexual activities or organs in an indecent manner" to areas where juveniles walking into a store could not see it. The city attorneys report that the new ordinance has been "excellent" in practice. Police officials working in the area verify that compliance has been good.

Finally, the city has taken an aggressive approach to squelch an innovative effort to get around existing regulations on nude dancing. The ordinance adopted in June 1999 prohibits live exhibitions or performances in private viewing areas. It was developed in response to "lingerie modeling" enterprises that were actually fronts for sexual entertainment. A female member of the city council contacted the police department about the problem in the spring of 1999 after getting complaints from residents about sexually explicit clubs opening in their area.

The city has had an ordinance against public nudity for a much longer time, and there are also laws preventing intimate touching in public. According to city attorneys, Coastal City requires that exotic dancers wear "bathing suits, very skimpy bathing suits, but bathing suits nonetheless" rather than going topless. The lingerie modeling operations were an attempt to circumvent these ordinances. A customer would come in and request that a certain girl model for him; they would go into a private cubicle, and the modeling would turn into other things, such as nudity. But because it was not in public, it was nearly impossible for police officers to enforce laws against it. So, city attorneys explain, what we basically did was, "we took the doors off." Modeling would not be prevented, but it would not be allowed in private settings.

There was no controversy involved in passing this ordinance; only the owners of these establishments had any objection to it. As expected, the owner of one lingerie modeling businesses filed suit challenging the constitutionality of the ordinance. In September 1999, a local judge held a hearing on a request for a temporary injunction. In defending the ordinance, an assistant city attorney argued that, unlike "nudity for artistic expression," erotic dancing for commercial purposes "is not protected by the First Amendment because it does not express a message." When the judge turned down the request for a temporary injunction and indicated that he would likely dismiss the case before it got to a hearing for a permanent injunction, the owner agreed to close the business.

The Coastal City case underscores the importance of economic considerations in driving local responses to the sex industry; similar considerations were evident in the Valley City case, presented earlier. In both cases, relatively prosperous cities found prostitution, lewd businesses, or other elements of the sex industry to be threatening either to the city's family-oriented, tourist-based economy (Coastal City) or to downtown renovation and high-tech businesses (Valley City). Thus, although conventional Coastal City and unconventional Valley City differ on subcultural grounds, the economic development imperatives they share yield similar policy stances with respect to the sex industry. In short, an important reason that the subcultural explanation fails to account for the pattern of local government action on these issues is that economic considerations can override subculturally defined responses.

But an economics-based explanation of local responses to the sex industry is complicated. For one thing, it is not a simple matter of more prosperous cities being less permissive of the sex industry and declining cities, because they are more desperate and less capable of being choosy about the industries they foster, being more permissive. Consider, for example, the multiple ways in which economic considerations come into play in two declining cities: Metro City and River City.

Metro City: Ineffective Regulation

Metro City has engaged in several efforts to shut down or relocate adult book-stores and lingerie modeling shops, and the means of achieving these objectives have generally been either zoning regulation or liquor licensing. These actions have largely been discretionary on the part of Metro City government, targeting specific establishments in particular neighborhoods, as opposed to general responses encompassing an entire industry. But Metro City's efforts in this regard are often clumsy and ineffective.

In October 1993, for example, the city council passed an ordinance designed to regulate lingerie modeling studios—establishments that consist largely of women disrobing in front of men in small rooms. Because no alcohol is served, the only regulations that must be adhered to are obtaining a regular business license and complying with zoning codes. But council members claimed that such studios breed illegal activities, so they passed a new ordinance that limited hours of operation, required extensive background checks on owners and employees, and gave police the authority to search the establishment without having to show cause. The existing studios were given sixty days to comply.

The new ordinance was quickly challenged by a lingerie modeling establishment, and the state supreme court ultimately struck it down, stating that the city had failed to properly document its reasons for enacting the ordinance. The court noted that although vice squad officers testified that there is a connection between lingerie modeling studios and prostitution, no evidence was presented that the police had alerted the city to this connection.

Meanwhile, Mayor Joe Lipton had fallen back on regular zoning rules to squelch a new lingering modeling studio. In January 1996, he denied a business license for a studio that wanted to open across the street from two multimillion-dollar festival attractions in downtown Metro City. The mayor based his decision on the city's zoning code, which requires a 1,000-foot buffer from public spaces where children may be present.

The city's efforts to eliminate other sexually explicit businesses have also had mixed results. In May 1995, for example, Metro City's vice squad raided six adult novelty stores after residents complained that the stores were selling illegal pornographic devices. More than a dozen store owners and employees were arrested in the raid, and all were charged with distributing obscene material and being a public nuisance. The arrests were made on the basis of a 1968 state law that forbids the sale or distribution of any device intended primarily to stimulate the human genitals. That law had been enacted specifically in response to the proliferation of sleazy bookstores in Metro City. Quoted in the local newspaper, the commander of Metro City's vice and narcotics unit says, "We don't want to be policing these stores, but we're going to deal with those items that the state believes affect a citizen's quality of life." Although the jurors convicted the adult video store owner on all eighteen obscenity charges, they did so reluctantly, citing an archaic law that left them no choice but to render a guilty verdict.

In another section of Metro City, neighborhood residents and community leaders organized pickets in front of a new adult entertainment store in an attempt to shut it down. As many as sixty-five protesters, including the local councilman and representatives of neighborhood groups, churches, and businesses, appeared nightly. Fearing that the store would encourage criminal activity and project the wrong message to children, protesters called for Metro City officials to adopt a special ordinance to ban such businesses from operating near places of worship and to require community notification of the intention to open such a store, similar to a county ordinance adopted in response to a controversy involving the same chain of adult stores. The city council complied and unanimously approved an ordinance to limit the location of adult-oriented shops and nightclubs. Existing laws had restricted adult businesses to Metro City's industrial and commercial areas, but the new ordinance restricts new adult businesses to areas zoned for heavy commercial use. In addition, the new law prohibits an adult business from locating within 1,000 feet of religious institutions or schools.

The new ordinance received its first test in early 1997, when some adult video store owners threatened to sue the city because their application for a building permit to construct their ninth store in Metro City had been rejected. Community leaders in the middle-class neighborhood where the new store would be located objected strongly and turned to the city for help in keeping it out of their neighborhood. Although city officials maintained that the owners had failed to file an application for a building permit before the new adult entertainment ordinance took effect, they were eventually overruled by the county superior court, and in the end, the new store was allowed to operate in its preferred location.

Metro City officials have also tried to use the city's liquor licensing powers to regulate adult businesses and clubs. However, recent events illustrate how ineffective this strategy has been. In 1998, the city successfully revoked the liquor license of one adult entertainment establishment in response to concerns raised by neighborhood residents. A more contentious case involved efforts by community leaders, residents, and politicians to close an adult entertainment club (Rizzo's) in a low- to moderate-income neighborhood that was trying to revitalize its business district, which had been plagued by prostitution and drugs for many years. A special hearing before Metro City's licensing review board was held to determine whether Rizzo's should be allowed to continue to sell liquor. Despite more than ten hours of testimony by community leaders, residents, and elected officials, the board recommended that the license be renewed, and the decision on renewal passed to Mayor Lipton. Neighborhood leaders were furious and complained that the city's case had been poorly presented and that the licensing review board was confused about its own procedures. In May 1999, Mayor Lipton ignored the board's recommendation and revoked the club's liquor license. Two days later, the club owner won an injunction in county court that prohibited the city from revoking Rizzo's liquor license.

Similarly, in November 1999, federal prosecutors charged the Platinum Connection, a Metro City adult entertainment establishment, and its owners with racketeering; the specific charges included providing prostitutes for customers, bribing Metro City police officers, money laundering, credit card fraud, loan sharking, and having ties to organized crime. Less than a week after the federal indictment, Mayor Lipton revoked the strip club's liquor license, but the club's attorneys were able to persuade a county superior court judge to overturn the mayor's decision. The judge ruled that the mayor's highly publicized move to suspend the club's liquor license was not an appropriate use of his emergency powers. The mayor had acted before the city's licensing review board could meet to determine whether the club's liquor license should be revoked. When the board met a few days later, it voted unanimously to revoke the Platinum Connection's liquor license after hearing more than five hours of testimony from city attorneys about alleged violations at the club. Mayor Lipton then revoked the club's liquor license. However, because of a county court ruling, the city is prohibited from enforcing the license revocation until after the club owners' federal trial is completed.

About half of the forty or so strip clubs in the Metro City region are located within the city limits. They are stable and profitable businesses that their owners claim are vital to the city's huge convention industry, which brings in hundreds of millions of dollars every year. According to a local newspaper account, the twenty-four licensed nude dance clubs in the city constitute less than 5 percent of the establishments that pay liquor-by-the-drink taxes, but they are the source of about 10 percent of the liquor taxes collected. One council member explicitly acknowledges that the current mayoral administration does not want to shut down the adult entertainment industry because of the belief that it is an important component in making Metro City a convention destination.

Although the nude dance clubs have been linked with some notorious crimes over the past several years, an analysis of Metro City police department records indicates that crime at and near these clubs is not nearly as bad as it is often portrayed. The local newspaper quotes one Metro City police official as saying that "the number of incidents requiring police intervention at nude dance clubs is 'peanuts' considering the number of patrons they serve."

River City: Regulation Laced with Prohibition and Prevention

Morality issues in the form of pornography controversies, prostitution crackdowns, and other sex business–related conflicts have been comparatively rare in this city in recent years. The director of the city's ACLU characterizes the city as "permissive" on such matters, as does the director of the city's human relations department. The relative quiet on this front may stem from the fact that nearly two decades ago, a public-private group called the River City Cultural Foundation cleared adult entertainment businesses out of the downtown area by buying them out over a period of years. In their place are facilities for the arts, such as the theater and the symphony.

The city has a full array of ordinances banning or regulating sexually explicit activity or business—all enacted in the 1980s—including one banning intersexual massage, one prohibiting the dissemination of sexually explicit materials to minors, one banning the display of obscene materials in public places, and one that makes any action or solicitation that results in sexual acts (actual or simulated) a nuisance. In recent years, River City has rarely enforced these ordinances. One exception occurred in February 2000 when a nightclub manager, two employees, and several others were arrested and prosecuted on charges of prostitution, promoting prostitution, obscene performance, and conspiracy after an undercover police investigation yielded evidence of stripping and lap dancing.

But River City seldom has problems with sex-related businesses or major controversies involving adult entertainment. When it does, it typically involves either prostitution-related controversies or the city's continuing effort to clear adult businesses out of the main redevelopment area. With respect to the latter, the city recently concluded an expensive four-year battle with the owner of an X-rated theater. The Palace Theater was the last remaining business in a rundown area that is the focus of a $40 million redevelopment plan. Beginning in 1997, the urban renewal authority initiated efforts to seize the theater, along with other properties in the area, through eminent domain. The theater owner, Greg Andre, was the only business owner in the area to resist eminent domain proceedings. His lawyer argued that the city's restrictive zoning laws meant that the theater would be unable to find a suitable place to relocate.

City officials characterized their actions as an appropriate use of eminent domain and explained that the city had been trying to refurbish this rundown area for nearly a decade. Urban blight plagues the area, with its bars, vacant

storefronts, and drug activity, and residents have complained about the theater frequently over the years. But Andre and his attorneys went to court to
resist, arguing that the attempted taking of the theater was actually an effort
to squelch X-rated entertainment. Referring to city officials as "self-appointed
guardians of the public morals," one of Andre's attorneys was quoted in the
local newspaper as saying, "The politicians fall all over themselves to be the
first guy to hate pornography. . . . You don't have to go to an adult theater if
you don't like it." Andre's lawyers subpoenaed the mayor and two city council members with the intent of grilling them under oath about public statements
they have made indicating their hostility to pornography.

The dispute is thus a blend of morality and development considerations.
The existence of businesses that were perceived as sleazy, such as rowdy bars
and this X-rated theater, clearly contributed to the initial definition of the area
as blighted and in need of redevelopment. And the mayor's designation of an
art gallery owner to bring new cultural and arts enterprises into the area illustrates the substitution of an officially sanctioned set of aesthetics for a set of
preexisting activities viewed as distasteful and problematic.

By late 2001, the cost of the city's eminent domain fight with the Palace
Theater owner was more than $1 million, or nearly four times the property's
assessed value. In 2002, a municipal court ruled in favor of the city, empowering the urban renewal authority to acquire the property and proceed with its
plans to clear out the area and introduce a cultural milieu completely different
from that of the old neighborhood.

Although prostitution is typically dealt with through routine enforcement
action, there are occasions when it becomes a more high-profile issue, spark-
ing higher levels of enforcement and new programs. Typically, the district attorney's office handles approximately 150 to 200 prostitution cases a year, most
of which originate in River City rather than elsewhere in the county. The male
offenders arrested for soliciting prostitution usually do not go to criminal court;
rather, they are charged with minor offenses that are handled in municipal
court, resulting in nothing more than fines. Likewise, women engaging in prostitution are typically handled with a minimalist approach; prostitution charges
are usually reduced to trivial charges at the initial court hearing. But in recent
years, there has been a noticeable upturn in governmental action with respect
to prostitution in River City and the county in which it is located. This came
directly on the heels of an awkward incident involving a police officer's participation in prostitution.

In June 1998, Jane Smith, who was assigned to the Carney neighborhood
as a community-oriented police officer, was arrested on charges of prostitution.
Some nine months earlier, two fellow police officers had become suspicious

when they overheard Smith describing herself and quoting prices on her cell phone. The officers reported their suspicions to the police chief, who ordered an investigation. It was discovered that Smith had an ad in the adult classified section of a free weekly newspaper that read "Lunchtime Treat, Mon & Tues," with her cell phone number listed. Smith was arrested by an undercover investigator after she accepted money in exchange for the promise of one hour of sex services. Interestingly, the same free weekly paper had many other similar advertisements of sex for sale.

In the wake of her arrest, it was clear that because of her status as a police officer, Smith's case would be handled differently from other prostitution cases. The district attorney acknowledged that prostitution charges are frequently reduced to more minor charges at a preliminary hearing. But in this case, the local newspaper quoted him as saying, "We'll have to take a long, hard look . . . because here you have a person who was in a position of responsibility to the public." Meanwhile, Smith also faced disciplinary action from the police department for conduct unbecoming an officer and violation of the ethics code. Within one day, after a thirty-minute hearing, the police chief decided to fire Smith. In the spring of the following year, a jury convicted Smith of prostitution. The judge, however, imposed a relatively light sentence—fining her $1,000 when she could have been sentenced to one year in jail—in part because she had already been penalized by losing her job as a police officer.

The blasé attitude of local officials concerning the numerous ads for sexual services that appear regularly in local weeklies, the occasional complaints from some residents about police inattention to prostitution problems in their neighborhoods, and the district attorney's acknowledgment that charges in routine prostitution cases are frequently reduced from misdemeanors suggest the relatively accepting attitude toward prostitution that is typical of a regulatory approach. But for a police officer to engage in such activity was a threat to this status quo. The visibility of her arrest brought public attention to an activity that can most easily be allowed to continue when there is little or no public acknowledgment that it exists.

But Officer Smith's case raised the public profile of prostitution in the city, and it may not be a coincidence that within one month of her sentencing, the city adopted a new program to discourage prostitution in general. The program, popularly referred to as "john school," was announced in March 1999 and was expected to start operations within three months. The previous month, River City had sent two police officials and a prosecutor to San Francisco to get information on that city's program, which involves the creation of a special court in which those arrested for the first time for solicitation are lectured by prostitutes and a prosecutor on the adverse consequences of prostitution, from venereal disease to legal implications. Each individual sentenced pays $500 for diversion to the program, and some of this money is slated to develop programs to help prostitutes find alternatives.

Taken together, the Metro City and River City cases provide a variety of insights about the nuanced ways in which economic considerations can affect declining cities' handling of decency issues. The Metro City case shows that some sexually explicit businesses are treated permissively because of economic considerations. Because the city's lucrative strip clubs not only pay substantial liquor taxes but also are perceived as being crucial assets to the city's convention industry, the mayor was unwilling to crack down on them; by contrast, a proposed lingerie modeling studio was viewed as a problem because of its proximity to popular showcase attractions in the downtown development area and thus was denied a business license. Similarly in River City, prostitution in the form of various call-girl services was subjected to minimalist law enforcement (except when a police officer was involved). However, an X-rated theater that stood in the way of a high-profile redevelopment project was subjected to a full-blown displacement effort by city officials who were willing to spend considerable sums and exert all their legal powers to quash its existence.

These two cases suggest that declining cities, like more prosperous ones, will take a strongly prohibitionist stance against sexually explicit businesses *when those businesses directly threaten an economic development project;* other sexually explicit businesses that are not perceived as a threat to economic development are treated more leniently. Figure 5.2 suggests that an economic explanation of city responses to the sex industry cannot be based on a simplistic differentiation of declining and growing cities. Again, except for the two extreme cases, both types of cities are represented at most other points along the continuum.

In short, economic considerations come into play in both declining and growing cities, and economic considerations can work in more than one direction—sometimes leading to a relatively permissive regulatory stance, and sometimes leading to a more restrictive stance. Even in a single city, different elements of the sex business can evoke different responses. Thus, the economic explanation of city action with respect to the sex industry is complex and highly nuanced. Rather than yielding a straightforward pattern, economic considerations function to upset the pattern of responses that might have been expected on subcultural grounds. Economic considerations are important elements in decision making about the sex industry in many of the study cities; as a result, they play a spoiler role with respect to other explanations.

	South City	Lake City		
	Coastal City	Western City	**River City**	
Border City	Valley City	Hill City		Port City
		Metro City		

◄---►

Prohibition   Regulation   Prevention

Figure 5.2 Policy Stance toward the Sex Industry, by Economic Status

Cities in bold are declining.

INTERGOVERNMENTAL EXPLANATION

In contrast with a number of the other morality issues considered in this volume, intergovernmental relations are not, in principle, a fertile ground for explaining city differences with respect to the sex industry. This is not to say that states and the federal government are uninvolved or irrelevant to local governments in this policy area. In particular, federal and state court decisions frame what city governments can do with respect to prosecutions related to obscene materials, nude dancing, and the like. This is amply illustrated in the case details. For example, Metro City's lingerie modeling ordinance was declared unconstitutional by the state supreme court, and River City was constrained by a state supreme court ruling that another city's ordinance requiring nude dancers to wear G-strings and pasties was unconstitutional under the First Amendment. Then, of course, there are South City's difficulties in devising ordinances against topless clubs that can pass muster in federal court. In addition, state legislatures have enacted laws on the subject, such as the requirement in South City's home state that sexually explicit material be placed in racks above the reach of children or have wrapping that covers all questionable images, and that same state's 1994 legislation banning public nudity and public sex acts.

But in the ways that matter most, the federal and state policy contexts are relatively similar across the ten study cities. Prostitution, for example, is against state law (as well as being prohibited by local ordinance) in all these places. Likewise, the standards set by the U.S. Supreme Court for prosecuting obscenity cases apply in all the states and their localities.[1] State courts have issued rulings striking down some local governments' efforts to constrain the sex industry, such as Metro City's lingerie modeling ordinance. But this cannot be taken to mean that there is a clash between state and local sex industry pol-

icy in this state. In other cases during the same period, the supreme court in
Metro City's state was supportive of local efforts to crack down on sexually
explicit businesses, such as when it upheld a 1993 suburban Metro City ordinance that instituted lighting requirements, distance requirements between
patrons and dancers, and other specific regulations for nude dancing establishments. Likewise, the court upheld another local ordinance in 1997 that prohibits the sale of alcohol in nude dance clubs. As in the other study cities, there
was a mix of favorable and unfavorable rulings in Metro City. In short, there
is no clear evidence that states' policies regarding the sex industry differ in the
way that they differ with respect to abortion. Without clear-cut variation in either the state or federal policy context, the intergovernmental explanation becomes irrelevant.

CONCLUSION

Local governments' stance toward the sex industry appears to be driven more
by economic considerations than by any of the other factors considered here.
The intergovernmental policy context is largely the same across cities, the subcultural differences that seem so important in other policy areas do not matter
as much for this issue, and although there is anecdotal evidence of the importance of a variety of governing institutions, none of the evidence examined here
substantiates the expected impact systematically across the study cities. The
economic explanation is very important, but it appears to be much more nuanced than might have been expected. Rather than clearly differentiating sex
industry politics in declining cities from that in economically robust cities, the
evidence is consistent with Peterson's (1981) much-debated contention that all
cities face economic development imperatives. However, the evidence also
shows that those imperatives can mean either a harsh or a tolerant stance toward sex-oriented businesses, depending on the specifics of the business and
their perceived implications for the city's economic development initiatives.

6

Gays, Rights, and Local Morality Politics

Elaine B. Sharp, Susan Clarke, and Marjorie Sarbaugh-Thompson

The story of gay and lesbian politics and policy making in the United States can be told from the perspective of the states and even the federal government. Gay and lesbian activists have targeted the federal government to try to get civil rights laws passed that include sexual orientation as a protected category, and the federal government has been the venue for a variety of other issues involving gays and lesbians, most notably the government's responses to the AIDS epidemic and gays in the military (McFeeley 2000). Taking the role of the Supreme Court into account, the federal government becomes an even more important venue, because the Court has issued a number of rulings that are crucial to gays and lesbians. For example, in its 1986 *Bowers v. Hardwick* decision, the Court found that adult homosexuals have no constitutional right to private consensual sex, thus upholding various states' laws against sodomy; the 1996 *Romer v. Evans* decision invalidated Colorado's Amendment 2, which stipulated that no state law could give protections to homosexuals (Leonard 2000).

As these cases show, the states have been even more of a hotbed for issues involving gays and lesbians than has the federal government. State legislatures and state courts have been an important battleground in the movement for legal recognition of same-sex marriage, with many state legislatures banning the practice. The Vermont Supreme Court declared that state's ban on same-sex marriage unconstitutional, and the Vermont legislature responded with a statute allowing "civil unions," which entail the same benefits and responsibilities as marriage for same-sex couples (Chambers 2000). More recently, the Massachusetts Supreme Court ruled that same-sex couples are entitled to be married. A few states have amended their civil rights legislation to include sexual orientation as a category protected from discrimination, while voters in other states have attempted to use the initiative process to enact provisions that would bar special protections for gays (Witt and McCorkle 1997). Meanwhile, state courts have had to make decisions about child custody and adoption in the context of lesbian and gay parents (Polikoff 2000).

Though states and the federal government are important venues for gay politics and policy making, local governments are at least as important. Local governments have been especially active in the proliferation of policies banning discrimination on the basis of sexual orientation. Such policies banning discrimination in government employment, which are often created through executive order, were on the books in twelve states and fifty-three localities by the mid-1990s. The more aggressive policy of banning discrimination on the basis of sexual orientation in private-sector employment had been adopted by nine states and more than eighty cities or counties by 1995 (Klawitter and Hammer 1999).

Above and beyond these antidiscrimination policies, local governments have been at the cutting edge of domestic partnership policies that allow same-sex couples to enjoy some of the benefits of marriage. One form of domestic partnership policy specifies that a particular benefit, most commonly health insurance coverage, be provided to partners of gay or lesbian employees in the same way that the benefit is provided to spouses of married employees. Another form of domestic partnership policy involves a registration system whereby unmarried same-sex couples can officially declare their partnership status and have that status receive official recognition (Chambers 2000, 299). By the early 1990s, the movement for domestic partner benefits had picked up considerable steam: "At least one municipality or county in over half the states adopted some form of domestic partner registration, and some provided benefits to their employees' partners" (Chambers 2000, 301).

In addition to their role in adopting these policy innovations, local governments are crucial settings for gay and lesbian activism more broadly. As Bailey (1999) argues, urban space is culturally defined, and identities find expression in urban settings. This has been particularly true for gays and lesbians. In many cases, the expression of gay identity creates the potential for conflict between gays and local government, such as when local officials are faced with the task of managing gay pride parades and other gay identity-celebrating events or must decide whether to enforce laws (e.g., laws against lewd behavior in public) in a way that disproportionately impacts gays.

There is enormous variation in city governments' handling of these matters. Some cities have enthusiastically supported gay pride events and adopted not only antidiscrimination provisions but also more controversial measures, such as domestic partner benefits; some have implemented even more provocative pro-gay policies. In many other cities, officials may be willing to support gay pride events, but efforts to use the city's regulatory powers to formally extend gay rights falter; in still other cities, the gay agenda may be met with overt hostility from public officials.

The emergent literature that attempts to account for differences in local governments' handling of gay issues typically focuses on a single gay rights policy rather than local governments' response to gays overall. Although these studies' independent variables do not necessarily reflect the explanatory approaches highlighted in this book, these analyses provide evidence of the statistical significance of variables that are relevant to the cultural, institutional, and economic explanations used here. For example, in their pioneering study of 125 cities and counties with policies banning discrimination on the basis of sexual orientation and 125 cities and counties without such policies, Button, Rienzo, and Wald (1997) found that subculture-defining variables such as educational attainment, the pervasiveness of nonfamily households, the prevalence of church adherence generally, and adherence to evangelical Protestant denominations more particularly differentiated cities with gay rights policies from those without; they also found that economic status variables such as population change and per capita income were important predictors of which cities would have gay rights policies. Other studies provide some corroboration and some conflicting evidence. Dorris's (1999) study of 102 cities with and 100 cities without ordinances barring discrimination in public employment based on sexual orientation found no significant explanatory role for either per capita income or extent of conservative religious affiliation, but it did corroborate the importance of education. Meanwhile, Klawitter and Hammer's (1999) study of all large counties in the United States showed that economic indicators, such as income and unemployment rate, and subcultural indicators, such as percentage of the population in nonfamily households and percentage of conservative Protestants, are not significant predictors of whether a county has adopted a policy barring discrimination in private employment based on sexual orientation.

Although these studies contribute to our understanding of the politics of gay rights at the local level, they are limited in a number of ways. For one thing, each tends to focus on a single gay rights policy, thus obscuring the larger picture of a jurisdiction's response to gay activism. The conflicting findings generated by this set of studies are also problematic. In addition, the methodology requires reliance on inferences about the importance of various factors in shaping a city government's decisions about gay rights policy. By contrast, this chapter presents case histories of contemporary governmental responses to gays in the study cities. These case histories are stories that deserve to be told, not only because they are inherently interesting but also because they provide contextually rich evidence concerning local governments' responses to a wide array of gay and lesbian issues. Furthermore, the interviews and documentary material often allow us to use direct evidence rather than statistical inference to discern the role of cultural, economic, institutional, and intergovernmental factors in shaping gay politics and policy making at the local level.

SUBCULTURAL EXPLANATION

Viewed solely from the perspective of the adoption of public policies beneficial to gays, there is striking evidence that unconventional cities are much more amenable to gays than are conventional cities. Table 6.1 shows the status of nondiscrimination provisions and domestic partner benefits (as well as the percentage of black residents, discussed later) in the study cities, revealing a striking subcultural contrast. Three of the five unconventional cities have amended their human rights ordinances to add sexual orientation to the other categories (e.g., race, religion) that are protected broadly against discrimination in employment, housing, and public accommodation; both of the other unconventional cities have at least partial nondiscrimination provisions (e.g., covering city employment or choice of subcontractors). By contrast, only two of the conventional cities have broad nondiscrimination ordinances that include gays, and one has a nondiscrimination provision limited to city employment.

The differences are even more marked with respect to the more controversial policy of providing domestic partner benefits. All but one of the unconventional cities have domestic partner benefits in place; in two cases, such benefits were reenacted after voters repealed the initial adoption through ballot initiatives. The only unconventional city without domestic partner benefits is Hill City, which adopted them in 1993 but has been unable to overcome their rollback via ballot initiative the next year. By contrast, only one of the conventional cities has enacted domestic partner benefits.

But this bare-bones scorecard of the status of gay-related policy does not capture the full flavor of the contrast between conventional and unconventional cities. A clear illustration of the importance of political subculture can be found in a comparison of South City and Metro City—two declining cities in the South that have similar political institutions (i.e., directly elected and visible mayors and city councils elected primarily from districts) and state settings that are equally hostile to gays, but different subcultures.

Metro City

Several estimates describe Metro City as having a comparatively large concentration of gays, and local newspapers claim that Metro City is "a Mecca for gay men and women" with "one of the country's most thriving and open gay

Table 6.1 Status of Key Gay Rights Legislative Provisions, by Community Sub-culture Type and Racial Composition

Study Cities	Nondiscrimination Ordinance		Domestic Partner Benefits	% Black
	Full	Partial[a]		
Unconventional				
Hill City	X		Adopted in 1993; voided by ballot initiative in 1994	11
Valley City		X	Adopted in 1997	4
Western City	X		Adopted in 1996	12
Port City	X		Adopted in 1989; voided by ballot initiative in 1989; readopted in 1990	9
Metro City		X	Adopted in 1993; overturned by state court; readopted in 1996	62
Conventional				
Border City[b]				44
Lake City	X			83
River City	X		Adopted in 1999	28
South City				62
Coastal City		X		4

[a]Nondiscrimination provisions apply only to city employment or to the city's selection of subcontractors.

[b]Border CIty changed its human rights ordinance in 1992 to include sexual orientation as a protected category, but the ordinance was overturned by voter initiative in 1993.

communities." In each of the past few years, more than 300,000 people have attended the city's annual gay pride celebration, which includes appearances by many local political officials.

Gays have also emerged as a potent force in Metro City politics. According to gay activists, 15 to 20 percent of registered voters are gay, and gay organizations are very active in local elections. One gay civil rights group has held voter registration drives and distributes a voters' guide that ranks all candidates for Metro City offices according to their positions on civil rights issues. Some candidates, including Metro City's current mayor, have received endorsements and campaign contributions from the gay rights group. As early as 1972, the mayor appointed an openly gay man to the city's community relations committee. In 1986, the city council, with little controversy, adopted a ban on discrimination against municipal workers on the basis of sexual orientation.

More recent efforts to provide domestic partner benefits for gays have pitted Metro City leaders against state government officials. In November 1991, Metro City councilwoman Jane Anderson announced her intention to introduce an ordinance that would provide health insurance and other benefits to city employees and their live-in partners, both gay and straight. The Anderson ordinance was endorsed by a study committee appointed by Metro City mayor Bill Johnson in 1990, in fulfillment of a campaign promise he had made to the gay and lesbian community.

After eighteen months of negotiation and study, and after Anderson agreed to remove a provision that would have extended pension benefits to domestic partners, the city council's finance committee cleared the measure for floor consideration in June 1993. The pension provision had galvanized opponents, including Metro City's chairman of the firefighters' pension board. Metro City's finance department estimated that the benefits provisions would cost the city about $2.3 million annually and would increase the portion paid by city employees by $800,000.

Anderson's proposal was divided into two separate ordinances. The first, which would create a registry whereby couples could officially record their status as domestic partners, passed by a vote of fourteen to two. Councilman Denton Jones, who opposed the provision, immediately challenged the program and called for a referendum to ask Metro City voters to approve it. The second measure, which would permit city employees to enroll their registered partners in the city's health, dental, and life insurance programs, passed by a narrow margin of nine to seven.

Mayor Johnson vetoed the ordinance that would have granted health and insurance benefits to city employees' registered domestic partners. His spokesman was quoted in the local paper as explaining that the mayor had vetoed the ordinance because "there are questions about whether the city has the power to enact legislation governing domestic relations under the state's Home Rule Act." The mayor did, however, sign the ordinance establishing a domestic partner registry.

Within a few days, more than forty lesbian and gay organizations had mobilized to coordinate a weekend of protest actions. In a closed-door meeting with gay and lesbian activists that weekend, Mayor Johnson explained that he could not sign the benefits ordinance because of the serious financial implications. But he promised the activists that a benefits package would be enacted before he left office at the end of the year. Some advocates suggested that the mayor may have been misled by overzealous high-ranking city employees who were opposed to the domestic partner ordinance. Councilwoman Anderson, sponsor of the ordinance, noted that although the city's finance department had estimated the cost at $2.3 million, figures from other cities with similar programs indicated that the cost would be well below $100,000.

In a day of heated protest and bitter debate, the city council voted nine to seven to override the mayor's veto of the benefits ordinance, but that was three votes shy of the number needed. Immediately after, Anderson introduced legislation nearly identical to that vetoed by the mayor, although the new proposal included provisions for funding the additional benefits. The council also voted down a proposal by Councilman Jones that would have put the matter before Metro City citizens in a public referendum.

In the days following the council's actions, tensions mounted in Metro City. Six activists were arrested outside a downtown gay bar for circulating petitions supporting benefits for domestic partners. One gay resident awoke one morning to find that the gay rainbow flag hanging from his porch had been torched. The executive director of the state's American Civil Liberties Union (ACLU) expressed concern that the city was "using arrests to harass and intimidate those who are working to pass the legislation on domestic partnership benefits."

After holding the proposed new ordinance in committee for several weeks, the city council passed it by the narrowest of margins, with the council president casting the tie-breaking vote. As he had promised, Mayor Johnson signed the ordinance into law. A senior assistant in the city attorney's office noted that she had been "very surprised" by the mayor's veto of the first ordinance and revealed that the mayor had received "tons of calls" from right-wing groups urging him to veto it. She added that "after the veto, the mayor was inundated with requests from the community to reintroduce and sign the ordinance. The fact that the ordinance was reintroduced and signed within a month strongly suggests that the gay community was able to muster a great deal of political pressure to achieve this outcome. It typically takes a much longer time period for vetoed ordinances to wend their way back through the process to successful adoption."

Ten days later, two conservative groups sued the city, asking county superior court judge Irving Bristol to grant a restraining order to block the ordinance's implementation on the grounds that the registry, the benefits program, and the 1986 ordinance prohibiting discrimination based on sexual orientation all violated the state constitution and the Home Rule Act. Judge Bristol denied the restraining order because he could find no emergency. Nevertheless, the two groups filed suit, hoping to overturn Metro City's domestic partner ordinance. According to one city official familiar with the case, the briefs filed were very nasty in tone, playing heavily on the rhetoric of the Christian right, making claims that domestic partners were not what the Bible teaches and that the diseases those types of people were likely to acquire (i.e., AIDS) "would cost the city millions of dollars."

In early November, the state's insurance commissioner and attorney general delayed the approval of health insurance coverage for the domestic partners of Metro City employees. The timing could not have been worse, as the city was in the midst of its health care enrollment period for new coverage, which would take effect January 1. According to one Metro City gay rights activist, "this action appears to be a deliberate tactic on the attorney general's part to thwart the will of the city." The following month, the attorney general issued an opinion that the registry and the benefits ordinances were both illegal under state law and the state constitution, citing the city's lack of authority to define unmarried partners as dependents under state insurance laws. Based on that ruling, the state's insurance commissioner declined to approve a plan submitted by an insurance provider to offer coverage to domestic partners. In April 1994, the domestic partner benefits program was declared unconstitutional in county superior court when Judge Bristol agreed with the attorney general and the insurance commissioner that Metro City cannot change the legal definition of a domestic relationship such as marriage.

The city appealed this decision to the state supreme court, and in October 1994, Metro City lawyers argued their case. Joining the city in support of its motion were the ACLU, the Lambda Legal Defense and Education Fund, and the AFL-CIO. In March 1995, the court issued a mixed ruling, upholding the domestic registry and nondiscrimination ordinances but striking down the benefits ordinance.

Following this ruling, Metro City council members rewrote the ordinance in September 1996, replacing the term "family" with "dependents." According to one Metro City official, it took about a year to rewrite the ordinance because Councilwoman Anderson needed that long to round up the votes needed to secure its passage. During this time, Metro City's law department did some additional research on the cost implications of enacting such an ordinance, which showed that, based on similar ordinances enacted elsewhere, there would be essentially no additional costs or liabilities to the city for extending benefits to domestic partners.

In the fall of 1996, the rewritten ordinance was approved by a close vote and signed into law by new mayor Joe Lipton. Immediately, the same organization that had sued the city three years earlier announced that it was ready to mount another legal challenge. That lawsuit went all the way to the state supreme court, which in November 1997 upheld Metro City's domestic partner ordinance. The battle for domestic partner benefits continued, however, when the state insurance commissioner again refused to approve an insurance policy that would provide coverage. Metro City filed suit against the insurance commissioner in March 1999, and in June, the city's lawsuit survived its first test when superior court judge Katherine Grigsby refused the insurance commissioner's request to dismiss the lawsuit and allowed Metro City councilwoman Debra Cotton, the state's first openly gay elected official, to join the suit. Cotton maintained that the commissioner's actions were preventing her from enrolling her partner of eleven years in the city's health benefits program. On September 22, Judge Grigsby issued a strongly worded ruling in favor of Metro City and ordered the state insurance commissioner to approve the city's plan. A few days later, city officials and the Lambda Legal Defense and Education Fund held a celebration in city hall for the new domestic partner benefits ordinance.

Although Metro City eventually succeeded in extending domestic partner benefits, it took nearly a decade to accomplish, during which time other gay rights issues were squeezed off the agenda. Immediately after the institutionalization of domestic partner benefits, however, efforts were under way to move that agenda forward. In 1996, the mayor had issued an administrative order requiring that all bid documents and city contracts contain a nondiscrimination disclaimer pertaining to sexual orientation. By the end of the 1990s, Metro City officials were considering how the city might craft legislation that would transform this administrative order into a full-blown city ordinance banning private contractors from discriminating on the basis of sexual orientation. Consideration of an even more dramatic step—requiring city contractors to provide benefits to the domestic partners of their employees as a condition for doing business with the city—was one of Mayor Lipton's campaign promises. Although he has been slow to follow through on this commitment, gay activists credit this mayoral administration with blazing the trail for other local governments to follow. In short, Metro City epitomizes an unconventional setting where the gay rights agenda has prospered.

South City

In South City, by contrast, efforts to push a gay rights agenda have been virtually nonexistent, even though issues involving gays have been contested at the state level. In 1989, the state enacted a sodomy law "which applies only to people of the same gender," and between 1989 and 1994, twenty-five individuals were prosecuted under it. In 1993, the constitutionality of that law was challenged by a group of five gays, and in 1996, an appeals court panel upheld a circuit court judge's 1995 ruling that the sodomy law was unconstitutional. Also in 1996, there was an effort to ban homosexual marriages in the state.

Although some gay and lesbian organizations are active in South City, the evidence suggests that these organizations are relatively new to the community and relatively fragmented, with schisms within and between groups; in addition, their level of political mobilization is minimal. Only by the end of the 1990s had a more politically minded coalition formed, one with an issue agenda that included a nondiscrimination ordinance. This new coalition is trying to define goals and set priorities in a way that will be satisfying to the diverse elements of the gay community. However, this group was still at the beginning stages of mobilization in 1999.

The apolitical stance that gay organizations have taken so far is reflected in the mayor's comment that although he was reelected for the third time in 1999, it was the first time that gays in the community had contacted him and asked him about his stance on gay issues. Gay pride events in the city are organized by leaders of the gay community, who have explicitly rejected an aggressive, politicized approach. In fact, they decided that the march and rally held in 1992 were too political and that something more uplifting was called for; subsequently, they have opted for a parade and a festival instead. Gay, lesbian, bisexual, and transgendered activists hold celebratory parades each June that attract increasing numbers of participants, but there have been no counterprotests or other controversies. City officials have not participated in these events, but they do accommodate them. However, the city has a policy of freely accommodating all requests for permits for rallies and parades (including one for the Ku Klux Klan—no questions asked).

Despite this apparent accommodation, in many ways, the South City context was still quite hostile to gays in general and to gay rights in particular in the latter 1990s. The strongly religious character of the community is one part of this context. South City is also the home of a nationally prominent spokesperson for a controversial approach that tries to convert gay men from homosexuality.

By the fall of 1998, gay and lesbian organizations were beginning to host events that had a more political flavor. To commemorate National Coming Out Day, gays and lesbians gathered at a picnic and forum at which various speakers discussed sexual orientation and the gay civil rights agenda, which had previously been viewed as inappropriate topics for public discussion in South City. One speaker emphasized the harassment and employment discrimination that gays face in the Bible Belt. The following weekend, an organizational meeting of the South City Lesbian and Gay Coalition for Justice was held at a local church, where participants discussed becoming a political force in the county and spoke out against the religious right. The organizer of the South City Fairness Coalition of Gays and Lesbians was quoted in the local paper as saying that he hoped "the coalition can count on liberal and progressive churches as a springboard in much the same way the Religious Right has relied on fundamentalist churches in its grassroots political strategy."

The case histories of these two cities underscore the difference that political subculture makes. In Metro City (unconventional culture), where gays are a politically potent force, officials are pushing hard and successfully to enact gay rights policies in the face of substantial opposition, primarily from outside forces (i.e., state officials); meanwhile, in South City (conventional culture), where gays are politically insignificant, city officials have provided nothing more than tolerance of gay pride events.

INSTITUTIONAL EXPLANATION

Coupled with the overall results in table 6.1, the contrasts in the Metro and South City cases suggest that a community's subculture has a substantial impact on the character of gay politics and policy. But what about the impact of local governing institutions? To the extent that there is variable responsiveness to gays among the unconventional cities, is it because those with more politicized governing institutions, such as Metro City's directly elected mayor, are more vulnerable to politically mobilized segments of the community (e.g., gays), while those with less politicized governing institutions are more insulated from such political demands? The evidence from the remaining unconventional cities shows precisely this. As we will see, Valley City, with its hybrid manager-mayor form of governance, has provided a somewhat less receptive venue for gay rights activists than Metro City has; Hill City, with its pure city manager form of government, exhibits even less responsiveness to gay interests. By contrast, the two cities (Port and Western) whose governing institutions are at least as politicized as Metro City's are, like Metro City, very responsive to gays.

Port City

Consider the case of Port City, which has a dramatic history of adopting policies beneficial to the gay, lesbian, bisexual, and transsexual community.[1] Starting in the early 1980s, as Port City's gay and lesbian community began to achieve a higher level of political representation and incorporation in the city's power structures, gay activists and officials pressed for a domestic partner registry and equal benefits for spouses and domestic partners of city employees. Although they failed several times, they formed electoral alliances with other groups to elect a gay rights champion as mayor in 1987 and new, more sympathetic, council members in 1986 and 1988. In 1989, the council passed and the mayor signed a domestic partner ordinance to provide the desired registry and benefits coverage. Before it could go into effect, however, the ordinance was challenged by a coalition led by religious conservatives and was subjected to a referendum later that year. In a close vote, citizens rejected the proposed ordinance. In 1990, however, the voters approved a watered-down version of the proposal placed on the ballot by council initiative. In 1991, the conservative opposition made one last attempt to undo the policy at the ballot box, but that effort failed by a wide margin, and domestic partner benefits for city employees were finally secured.

By the mid-1990s, alliance building, political mobilization, and electoral strategizing had yielded a stunning level of political representation and incorporation in the city's power structures. This was dramatically illustrated by the city council's unanimous passage of an ordinance in 1996 that would be supremely controversial in most cities. It allows the city clerk or a deputized volunteer to perform same-sex wedding ceremonies at city hall or elsewhere for couples who register as domestic partners. The city's chief administrative officer expressed the hope that Port City would become a destination spot for gay and lesbian tourists seeking to have a civil ceremony. Two months later, a mass public "wedding" ceremony involving 163 gay and lesbian couples was held, with the mayor and nine of the eleven council members in attendance, despite the objections of the city's Roman Catholic archbishop. With the national media covering the event, Mayor John Green was quoted in a local paper as claiming, "We're leading the way here . . . for the rest of the state, and the rest of this nation, to fully embrace the diversity and the legitimacy of people in love, regardless of their gender or sexual orientation."

In 1998 and again in 1999, in a public gesture of the city's response to the emergence of a movement to ban same-sex marriage in the United States, the mayor and a host of other city officials presided over two more mass ceremonies recognizing the domestic partnerships of gay and lesbian couples. In 2000, two weeks after the passage of a statewide initiative banning gay marriage, Mayor Green, virtually the entire city council, and other city officials showed their continuing resolve on the gay marriage issue when they presided at the fourth such mass ceremony.

The political power of gays and lesbians in Port City, as well as the city's determination to serve as a model for the nation with respect to gay rights, was even more dramatically illustrated by the city's adoption of an ordinance that goes well beyond conventional domestic partner benefits ordinances. In May 1996, three leaders of one of Port City's most powerful gay-lesbian Democratic clubs drafted a policy that would require all contractors doing business with the city to certify that they did not discriminate between registered domestic partners and legal spouses in providing health and other benefits to all their employees, no matter where they resided. The equal benefits ordinance targeted thousands of city contractors and vendors, including many national and multinational corporations. A total of about $1 billion in city business was at stake.

The three club leaders persuaded seven of the eleven city council members to place the policy initiative on the council's agenda as a proposed ordinance. The timing of this initiative was strategic: council elections were scheduled to take place only a few months later on November 5, and none of the incumbents seeking reelection would want to risk alienating the formidable gay vote by opposing the measure. The final vote on the proposal occurred one day before the November 5 election. According to a member of the human rights commission, who was a close observer of events at this stage of the process, all parties involved were well aware of the bold and unprecedented nature of their undertaking and of the likely challenges if the measure became law. And all shared a common vision of this new legislation as a model for the nation in advancing gay rights. To demonstrate that such a seemingly radical policy innovation was practical and feasible, however, it was important to take great care in crafting legislation that would not only survive legal scrutiny but also allow "flawless" implementation. Gay and lesbian activists worked closely with the city attorney's office to come up with a final draft of the ordinance that was as legally bulletproof as possible.

Mayor Green made a public commitment to sign the new ordinance, and support on the city council was building toward unanimity. At the council's public hearings, virtually all of the city's gay and lesbian organizations, clubs, and groups endorsed the proposed legislation. The main opposition came from conservative religious organizations, particularly the Roman Catholic archdiocese, and from some business leaders who were concerned about the possible financial impacts of the ordinance and by the inclusion of opposite-sex domestic partners in the coverage.

On November 4, 1996, the council approved the equal benefits ordinance by a ten-to-zero vote, with one councilman absent. Three days after the general election, Mayor Green signed the ordinance into law amid much celebration and national news coverage. The task of developing standards and guidelines for implementing the ordinance was assigned to the lesbian, gay, bisexual, transgender, and HIV division of the city's human rights commission. Division staff collaborated with gay council members and with the mayor in educating city contractors about the new law and working out clear, reasonable, and enforceable guidelines for implementing it. For example, when the Roman Catholic archbishop objected on religious grounds to the term "domestic partner" in the certification language required of a nonprofit Catholic service organization, a compromise was arrived at to substitute the phrase "spousal equivalent," thus allowing certification to proceed without overt rhetorical violence to religious doctrine.

On June 1, 1997, with the guidelines in place, the equal benefits ordinance became effective. Under the new law, a "domestic partner" is defined as "any person whose domestic partnership is currently registered with a governmental domestic partnership registry." Contractors unable to end discrimination despite demonstrable good-faith efforts can still comply with the law by offering a cash-equivalent benefit to employees with domestic partners. Subcontractors are not required to comply, nor are contractors that do less than $5,000 of business with the city per year.

As of June 30, 1999, 8,005 contractors had submitted compliance paperwork to the human rights commission, and 92.7 percent were found to be in compliance with the law. Complying companies have headquarters in 41 states and more than 700 cities across the country, although 88 percent are located in the state and 43 percent in Port City. A number of multinational corporations, including some that do only a modest amount of business with the city, have adopted nondiscriminatory benefits policies for all their employees as a direct result of Port City's new law. Many other large corporations that have no contracts with the city adopted equal benefits for domestic partners anyway, in most cases to stay competitive with rival firms. The human rights commission estimates that at least 30,000 domestic partners now receive equal benefits as a direct consequence of the new law. In late 1999, one of the nation's leading gay rights organizations reported that Port City's equal benefits ordinance was responsible for 76 percent of all employers nationwide that offered domestic partner benefits.

Three lawsuits have been filed against the city challenging the legality of the ordinance, mainly on the grounds that local governments lack the authority and jurisdiction under the U.S. Constitution to make policies of this sort. The city attorney's office, with the full support of the mayor and the city council, has vigorously defended the new ordinance against those challenges. In the most important of these cases to be decided to date, a federal district court judge issued a partial decision in April 1998 that upheld the ordinance but limited its application to a firm's local employees and to those elsewhere who were actually working on city contract projects. Nevertheless, only twenty-seven companies have opted to use this provision to restrict coverage, and several of the companies involved in the lawsuit have since voluntarily adopted full and equal benefits for their employees.

Port City thus epitomizes a city that has embraced a number of far-reaching gay rights policies and stood by them despite some opposition from the community and some legal challenges. It also illustrates the significance of highly politicized institutions in the development and implementation of that policy stance. In this city, where the mayor is directly elected, council elections are highly politicized, and numerous clubs and other political party–like organizations are active, gay rights activists aggressively use electoral strategies to gain a platform, and elected officials are key players in gay rights policy development. In contrast with other cities that would avoid even considering such a controversial matter with an election looming, in Port City, significant gay rights legislation has been enacted in the lead-up to local elections.

Although it is not as dramatic as the Port City case, politicized Western City also exhibits a high level of responsiveness to gays (see table 6.1 and the appendix). The more interesting comparisons emerge when we consider unconventional cities with less politicized governing arrangements, such as Valley City, where the gay rights agenda has advanced far less.

Valley City

In the late 1990s, gay rights activism and the local government response in Valley City were shaped by a history of successful efforts against gay rights in the area, led by local evangelical churches. In the late 1970s, gay activists requesting gay pride resolutions were repeatedly turned down by the city council, a gay human rights week resolution was voted down, and a proposal that would have outlawed job discrimination countywide based on sexual orientation was defeated in a 1980 referendum.

The defeat of that referendum increased local politicians' reluctance to show any sympathy toward gay rights issues. According to the leaders of some gay and lesbian organizations, officials are more supportive of gays than they once were, but twenty years later, people still remember what happened, and some politicians are absolutely opposed to pro-gay ordinances for fear of the religious right. That defeat, however, created the spark for more sophisticated political organizing by local gays and lesbians. In 1984, Sonya Williamson and Chad Clifton founded a political action committee that, over the years, has given tens of thousands of dollars to the campaigns of politicians who support gay issues. By the late 1980s, the city council easily passed the sort of proclamations in support of gay pride week that had once been so controversial, and in 1991, Valley City gays held their first gay pride parade, even though the event lasted only about ten minutes.

Perhaps more important than such political organizing was the development of a private-sector strategy for advancing gay rights and benefits. In 1990, a private university in Valley City became the first in the state to pass a domestic partner policy for students. Two years later, its faculty voted to extend same- and opposite-sex domestic partner benefits to faculty and staff. In 1991, a local corporation announced the implementation of domestic partner benefits for its employees, and in 1992, the city was the site of a key conference bringing together more than thirty companies nationwide that had adopted or had plans to adopt domestic partner benefits. In the spring of 1993, in a meeting with more than sixty gay and lesbian employees, an area CEO received a standing ovation when he announced that domestic partner benefits would be instituted. Gay activists lauded corporate support for their issues, recognizing that interest from certain CEOs and other high-tech leaders was critical to their movement. Quickly, the area became the most fertile ground in the nation for organized gay and lesbian employee groups. Within a year, it was reported that more than half of the nation's thirty or so companies that offer domestic partner benefits were high-technology firms, and that most were based in the Valley City area.

In this changed climate, Valley City officials pursued gay rights policies, but in a low-key fashion. Valley City required all contracts to contain nondiscrimination clauses that included sexual orientation as a protected category. In 1997, the city council, led by Mayor Mary Simpson, approved domestic partner medical benefits for city employees under union contracts. The police union, however, was excluded, because police union leaders had objected on the grounds of cost. Mayor Simpson's initiative was handled in the city council's executive session and evoked little fuss. The only opposition came from two council members. Both Marcia Miller, a likely mayoral candidate, and Matthew Major voted against the two-year contract with the Municipal Employees Federation because they believed the decision to grant such benefits had been made behind closed doors, allowing the public no chance to comment on the new policy. Both alleged that the city manager had failed to inform council members of the plan to offer the benefit in negotiations with the union—an allegation denied by both the city manager and other council members. Whether the council knew what was going on or not, it is clear that the public was not notified until the last minute. A memorandum on the general terms of the agreement was not made available until the day of the council meeting, even though the specifics had been ironed out with the union a month earlier. The following spring, Miller lost the mayoral race to a candidate who was a firm supporter of health benefits for domestic partners of city employees.

The city's domestic partner policy was the result of the combined efforts of the leaders of the gay community and the personal convictions of Mayor Simpson, whose daughter is gay. But the manner in which the policy was adopted suggests that it was politically delicate. The mayor acted on the issue six months before she was slated to leave office, and she used quiet, behind-the-scenes methods so as not to crystallize opposition. Gay activists believe that Simpson failed to introduce the issue during her first term for fear that she would not be re-elected, even though activists urged her to pursue the issue, reminding her that the county had instituted these benefits for its employees in 1995.

The tentative and "below-the-radar" character of gay rights policy adoption in Valley City may stem from the fact that the gay community is not particularly active at the grassroots level. Gays in this community are often described as relatively apolitical and quiescent. Their quiescence is commonly attributed to their affluence and the widespread availability of domestic partner benefits in the area's high-tech firms. In fact, the political action committee mentioned earlier is the only organized gay group in Valley City, and although it continues to make campaign contributions and hand out endorsements, it does not have much grassroots activism.

Thus, although Valley City's hybrid of reformed and nonreformed political institutions has allowed some electoral organizing by gays, gay rights policy making is often handled in depoliticized ways or eschewed altogether in favor of private-sector benefits. In Hill City, the governing institutions are even more reformed and depoliticized than those in Valley City, and as a result, the responsiveness to gay demands is even more limited, despite a strongly mobilized gay community.

Hill City

According to a local newspaper article, Hill City is "sometimes described as the San Francisco of [this region]" because of its visible and highly mobilized gay and lesbian population and because the community is viewed as a progressive and welcoming place for gays to live. The city has a rich array of gay and lesbian social and political organizations and activities, some of which have a predominantly local focus, and some of which are statewide lobbying organizations.

In line with the liberal-progressive and tolerant character of the community, Hill City has long-standing ordinances (dating to at least the early 1980s) banning discrimination in employment, housing, and public accommodations, each of which includes sexual orientation as a protected category. Throughout the 1990s, the gay and lesbian community's version of a gay pride celebration was a festival held at Fiesta Gardens, a community park. The event appears to be well established and noncontroversial.

When the city council decided in 1993 to provide health insurance coverage to city employees' unmarried partners, regardless of gender, it sparked a controversy. Although the policy applied to both heterosexual and homosexual couples, the decision was clearly a response to pressure from gay activists. In particular, the Hill City Lesbian-Gay Political Caucus had been pushing for the measure. Before making its decision, the city had its human resources department investigate similar programs in other cities and generate an estimate of the cost, which it determined would be a little over $700,000 in the first year for an estimated 472 domestic partners or dependent children.

Hill City's adoption of the domestic partner ordinance was far from unopposed. For example, a Christian fundamentalist who writes a newspaper column and has a local talk show mobilized forces to oppose the measure on the grounds that it would use taxpayer funds to support immoral relationships. Within six months, local opponents of the domestic partner benefits policy — headed by Concerned Citizens, a group whose leader is the pastor of a local Baptist church — had gathered the necessary signatures for a referendum on the issue. Forces in support of the ordinance also mobilized into a coalition that included the Hill City Women's Political Caucus, a Latino health organization, and a number of other political, religious, and business groups.

A recent event in a nearby suburban jurisdiction provided important ammunition for supporters of the domestic partner policy. A major computer company had been negotiating with nearby Crafton County for a tax break that would enable it to build a customer service center that would employ 1,700 people, but county commissioners had raised objections to the company's health benefits policy, which covered domestic partners. When this nearly caused the deal to collapse, the commissioners withdrew their objections. A member of the Hill City coalition in support of the domestic partner ordinance was quoted in the local paper as claiming that its purpose was "to protect Hill City's jobs by keeping our national reputation from being damaged by the same radical right organizers who almost stopped [computer company] from bringing 1,700 jobs to [Crafton] County."

The initiative appeared on the ballot at a complicated time, however. It was slated for the regular election, at which four council members' seats would also be contested. These members had won office as part of a sweep that established the dominance of a liberal, environmentally oriented faction on the city council. As the election approached, it became clear that some neighborhood organizations were disaffected with the direction the city council had taken. The president of a council of neighborhood organizations claimed in a local newspaper interview that city residents "are wearying of City Councils that delve into far-flung national and international issues such as apartheid, grape boycotts and Colorado's initiative on gay rights." Citing the city's domestic partner ordinance, she argued that "the city is passing a lot of rules and regulations it cannot afford to enforce." Meanwhile, gay activists in the community saw the fight to keep the policy as part of their larger fight against homophobia and their ongoing struggle against the religious right.

The ballot proposition that would void the city's domestic partner policy passed handily, with 62 percent in favor and 38 percent opposed. As a result, members of the winning coalition announced that a new conservative era for Hill City had arrived. But there was not necessarily clear-cut evidence that the election signaled a swing to the right. Progressive candidates got the vast majority of the votes, even though there were conservative candidates on the ballot.

City officials were confronted with the fallout from the successful ballot initiative in June 1994, when three gay couples sued the city for cutting off their insurance benefits and the ACLU considered representing a police officer who had lost his benefits when the proposition was passed. The couples' lawsuit was based on claims of breach of contract and unfair insurance practices. The ballot initiative appears to have had longer-term consequences as well, in terms of tempering officials' propensity to respond to gay activists' demands in this area. While noting that many private companies in town have domestic partner coverage, the city manager does not foresee the city government attempting to provide such coverage again anytime soon. He says, "That one is going to be tougher. For whatever reason, that one got people's ire up."

These case histories, coupled with the summary evidence in table 6.1, indicate that the degree of responsiveness to gay interests differs even among unconventional cities. An institutional explanation would posit that those differences are linked to differences in political institutions, and indeed, the pattern of the cases suggests that they are. Port City, Western City, and Metro City, with their directly elected mayors and generally more politicized environments, exhibit the highest levels of responsiveness to gay and lesbian interests and demands. Valley City, with its hybrid government, exhibits a more limited responsiveness to gays, and even that responsiveness took a low-visibility approach to the issue. Hill City, with its completely professionalized, city manager form of government, was overridden by the citizenry in its attempt to provide domestic partner benefits.

One might argue, of course, that these differences stem from differences in the strength, sophistication, and mobilization of the cities' respective gay communities. The match between the extraordinarily high level of gay political strength and mobilization in Port City and that city's exceptional pro-gay policy leadership certainly invites such an interpretation. However, the Hill City and Valley City cases contradict such an interpretation. Despite the apolitical and quiescent character of the gay and lesbian community in Valley City, that government did more for gays and lesbians than did Hill City, where gays are highly mobilized.

But what role do political institutions play with respect to gay politics and policy making in conventional cities? The institutional explanation in its most general form posits that cities having governing institutions that are more politicized will be more responsive to community pressures than will cities with reformed institutions that buffer public officials from community pressures. But the question is, what community pressures? So far, that has not been problematic, because in unconventional cities, there is presumably a rough alignment, or at least a sympathetic resonance, between the interests of the gay and lesbian community and community preferences more generally. But in cities with conventional subcultures, the opposite is true. Unless gays constitute an extraordinarily substantial and well-organized special interest—something that is not, by definition, very likely in a conventional city—politically motivated officials in such cities would be expected to be more hostile to gays (and more responsive to prevailing, traditional values); under the same logic, cities with professionalized city manager governments would be expected to have the necessary insulation from politics that allows for responsiveness to gay rights demands, despite an inhospitable subculture.

The results from the relevant study cities are too mixed to provide substantial support for this institutional interpretation. Although examination of one pair of conventional cities with contrasting political institutions yields results consistent with the interpretation, the other pair yields results precisely the opposite of that interpretation.

Coastal City versus Lake City

Consider the case of Coastal City, whose city manager form of government might be expected to allow for responsiveness to gays despite its conventional subculture. In many ways, its subculture is hardly a promising venue for gay rights initiatives. Not only is the community in a relatively conservative state, it is also the home of numerous organizations on the Christian right, some of them very high profile; still other such religious organizations lie just across the border in a neighboring city. As a consequence, the community and its environs are frequently the source of antihomosexual rhetoric, such as when a coalition of Christian right organizations began a national campaign against homosexuality. The community does have some gay-related organizations and institutions, but not surprisingly, their number and level of activism are well below what one might find in any number of major U.S. cities. The gay community does not hold an annual gay pride parade, as many cities do; instead, for eleven years it has held an annual gay pride picnic in a prominent city park. One member of the regional gay and lesbian pride coalition that organizes the event indicates in a local newspaper interview that the picnic is not only less expensive but "also less threatening to local sensibilities than a political rally or parade." Even so, the gay pride picnic has caused controversy among police officers, who were shocked at the idea, and in a newspaper article from 1996, a Coastal City resident is quoted as saying that she "had every intention of writing to [the] City Council" because she was "furious that something like this is allowed. How can they take over our park like this?"

In this context, it is not surprising that there is no local antidiscrimination ordinance that includes sexual orientation, let alone domestic partner benefits. What is surprising is that the city government has recently been involved in policy developments that reveal a pro-gay use of local government authority. Specifically, the city manager made a decision to change the city's personnel policies to explicitly state that there will be no discrimination on the basis of sexual orientation. The proposal came from the city's equal employment opportunity advisory committee, then chaired by Jack Fellows. Although committee members were ready to accept a nondiscrimination policy, a domestic partner benefits policy, which Fellows also suggested, was more controversial and was omitted from the committee's recommendation to the city manager's office. The city manager was very open to the idea of adding "sexual orientation" to the list of categories protected against employment discrimination and signed off on the change in April 1995, after review by the human resources department.

When the city council learned of the executive order, "All hell broke loose," says the city manager. The Christian Communications Board began calling and pressuring council members, who in turn put pressure on the city manager. However, the city manager saw the matter as "strictly an administrative change in our own personnel policies, rules, and regulations" and refused to undo the policy; the city council eventually backed down.

Although not a particularly expansive gay rights policy by the standards of unconventional cities, Coastal City's antidiscrimination policy is a pro-gay stance in a setting that is generally very hostile to a gay rights agenda. In this case, a professionalized city government was clearly the key to the adoption of this controversial policy.

This contrasts nicely with the situation in Lake City, where a high-profile, directly elected mayor and elected council members have been avoiding gay rights action out of a clear sense of the adverse electoral consequences in that conventional city. Surprisingly, Lake City was among the first cities in the nation to prohibit discrimination on the basis of sexual orientation. That provision was part of the city charter adopted in the early 1970s, and the political dynamics surrounding that decision were not altogether clear from our fieldwork in the 1990s. However, given the predominantly African American population of the city, there is little support for discrimination against any group of people.

Yet Lake City has failed, despite repeated attempts by gay rights activists, to extend its tolerance for diversity to the realm of domestic partner benefits. In 1996, the city council refused to bring a domestic partner benefits ordinance to a vote because it was linked with a same-sex-marriage ordinance. There is limited support for the latter, and both measures would have been defeated, according to one council member who is highly supportive of gay rights. Furthermore, gay rights activists were reportedly pushing the city council to vote on the two issues shortly before the November election. The council responded by evading both issues, and no action was taken for two years.

In 1998, the city council tried to respond discreetly to requests for domestic partner benefits by authorizing the mayor to issue an executive order providing the benefits, but he dodged this "opportunity." Subsequently, a council member reported that he introduced a domestic partner benefits ordinance by linking it to the case of a grandmother left to care for the two children of a deceased city employee. The issue was tabled, however, and the council member who introduced it is no longer in office. But the effort to expand the definition of domestic partners to include groups of cohabiting people other than homosexuals or unmarried couples seems to reflect the political realities of council members who must run for reelection in a city with a relatively conventional subculture.

Indeed, interviews with Lake City council members suggest that if the domestic partner ordinance were brought to a vote, it just might pass. Still, many leaders in the city's large Christian and Muslim religious communities vehemently oppose homosexuality. These religious leaders are also active in politics and often provide valued endorsements for candidates running in the nonpartisan elections for city council and for mayor, so their opposition could make it difficult for these officeholders to win reelection. Therefore, the vote would need to be timed to avoid affecting their reelection prospects, according to current members of the city council.

Border City versus River City

Whereas Coastal City and Lake City yield precisely the contrast that an institutional interpretation would call for, the contrast between Border City and River City is quite the reverse. Despite its full package of reformed institutions (city manager; nonpartisan, at-large city council elections), Border City officials (unlike the city manager in Coastal City) could not stand firm behind controversial gay rights policies. In 1992, the city council passed, by a seven-to-two vote, a human rights ordinance that prohibited discrimination in employment, housing, and public accommodation and included a controversial clause extending the protection to sexual orientation. Spokespersons for both Stonewall Border City, which represents the gay community, and Citizens against Special Rights, a coalition of community groups opposed to the ordinance, emphasize that its passage was the result of the gay community's electing politicians who were sensitive to gay rights issues.

In 1993, Citizens against Special Rights gathered enough signatures to put a referendum on the ballot that would ban what it termed "special rights" for homosexuals. The referendum passed by an overwhelming majority (62 to 38 percent) and amended the city charter to prohibit municipal protection based on sexual orientation, status, conduct, or relationships. The passage of the referendum had immediate economic repercussions when the city lost an estimated $35 million in convention business.

Six days after the referendum was approved by voters, gay rights groups sued the city, claiming that the charter amendment violated their rights. In August 1994 a district court judge ruled that the amendment was unconstitutional and ordered the city to pay nearly $400,000 in attorneys' fees and court costs to the gay rights attorneys.

Then, in a complete reversal of its original commitment to a gay rights ordinance, the city council voted five to three to appeal the district court ruling. Those in favor of the appeal explained that their decision was based primarily on the notion that because nearly two-thirds of the voters had indicated their opposition to a gay rights ordinance, elected leaders had a duty to file the appeal. Indeed, pressure to toe the line of majority sentiment in the community was strong. Anti–gay rights organizations were waging political battles that focused on defeating city council candidates who supported gay rights. The groups targeted all five of the city council members that Stonewall Border City had endorsed in 1993, publicly vowing to campaign against them if they ran for reelection.

The city council voted in March 1995 to repeal the sexual orientation part of Border City's human rights law, by a slim five-to-four majority. Councilman Doug Tupol cast the deciding vote. This came as a surprise to many in the gay community, because as ceremonial mayor of Border City when the ordinance passed, he had gone on record in the local newspaper, stating, "The passage of the Human Rights Ordinance is the city's pledge that all people will be treated with respect and dignity." Yet, compelled by the immense support for the antigay initiative, Tupol informed the public that he would reverse his earlier position and vote to remove sexual orientation protection from the city's human rights ordinance. Many supporters of the gay rights ordinance protested boisterously, displaying anti-Tupol signs in council chambers that read, "Dykes against Tupol," "Closets are for bigots," "Waffle House," and "Tupol kiss the dyke vote goodbye."

Ultimately, a U.S. Court of Appeals declared that gays were not entitled to municipal protection and that the amendment violated no one's constitutional rights. As a result, the referendum outcome prevailed, and gays and lesbians could not be accorded any specified rights under Border City's municipal code. In 1996, the U.S. Supreme Court struck down a voter-approved amendment to the constitution in another state that would have overridden local gay rights ordinances. Using that case as a reference, the Supreme Court ordered a review of Border City's anti–gay rights referendum by the district court. However, in 1997, the referendum was upheld as constitutional by a unanimous decision of the district court panel.

For the director of Stonewall Border City, the referendum and its aftermath highlighted the difficulties gay activists have with the Border City community. As she explains, "You have a lot of people who are allies when they are with you, and you know them to be progressive minded. But, you live in a conservative city. . . . If you have aspirations of higher political office, you may not be willing to stand with the gay community. . . . There are some political officials who have stood with us and they get torn apart in the media. So, I imagine that support for gay rights is a hard line to walk."

Even more damaging to an institutional interpretation is River City's experience with gay rights. River City might not be expected to be fertile ground for gay rights issues and causes. It is not a particularly cosmopolitan city; in fact, the ACLU director describes it as "parochial" and "insular" and "conservative, both politically and socially, . . . in the working-class, conservative sort of way." He notes that virtually none of the private companies in River City have progressive policies with respect to gays, such as domestic partner benefits. And until quite recently, the city's gay community was not well organized, either politically or socially. There were no gay pride parades or related events in the late 1980s; these have appeared only in the past five years or so. Most important from an institutional point of view, this city's highly politicized governing institutions should make it virtually impossible for local officials to ignore the pressure of the city's traditional, parochial, conventional subculture and embrace gay rights policies. But River City officials have done just that, pursuing gay rights very aggressively.

Initially, it did not seem that River City's gay rights history would be very remarkable. The city amended its antidiscrimination ordinance in 1991 to include sexual orientation, but it took two tries. On the first try in 1988, the proposal was highly controversial and created "all sorts of ruckus, such as ministers claiming that God would withhold all the city's water if it was passed," according to a gay activist. He notes, "There was a lot of community backlash," and council support "just wasn't there" on the first attempt. When the makeup of the council subsequently changed, the gay community thought the time was right to try again. The human relations director explains that gay rights activists "went to [the] council and found a backer," and then they were successful. In addition, a gay activist explains that between the first and second attempts, gay activists became "better organized, documented things better," and mounted a dramatic and successful challenge when gay rights opponents tried to challenge the proposed ordinance via a petition drive that called for a change in the city charter.

Passage of the ordinance was facilitated by other factors, according to a gay activist. The city council typically reflects a fair amount of "social conscience," and some members have been active in the black community. Another council member has a "huge union history," and even though unions are not as important in the city as they once were, that union heritage is still "worked in" when matters of social justice are at stake. The ACLU director explains that although the city as a whole is not progressive on gay rights, the city council was able to move "ahead of the curve" of public opinion on this issue. The gay rights ordinance "comes out of [two named neighborhoods]," where there is a large university population and where the health care industry has brought in a lot of professionals and progressive thinkers. The two council members representing these two districts served as key sponsors of the ordinance and would repeatedly emerge as key spokespeople in follow-up policy developments.

In the years immediately following passage of the nondiscrimination provision for gays, there was little contention. In fact, the ordinance was extended in 1997 to include transsexuals. In the spring of 1999, however, the relative quiet surrounding the gay rights policy ended with a jolt when River City became embroiled in a battle that the local ACLU director describes as "really the first civil rights struggle for gay men and lesbians in River City, aside from passing the ordinance." When the University of Hull—a major public research university—refused to extend medical benefits to the same-sex partner of faculty member Mary Roth, she filed a formal complaint in 1996, citing the city's ordinance as the basis of her claim that the university was discriminating on the basis of sexual orientation. The city's human relations commission, which handles such complaints, apparently moved slowly through the processes of fact-finding and deliberation, finding probable cause in the spring of 1997 that Hull had discriminated in this case and that a full-blown hearing was warranted. The matter received little public attention during this period, but in November 1998, when the university filed a motion to dismiss the by-then nearly three-year-old complaint on the grounds that the ordinance exceeded the scope of the state's Human Relations Act, which does not include sexual orientation as a protected category, the case emerged as a very public issue indeed. By then, the ACLU had signed on to represent Roth and two other university employees who had joined the case. And, in its efforts to show that Hull's decision to deny domestic partner benefits constituted discrimination based on sexual orientation, the ACLU planned to depose a number of current and former Hull trustees and administrators on various matters, including their personal beliefs about homosexuality.

The director of the city's human relations commission opted for a low-profile public stance at this stage, befitting the commission's quasi-judicial role as arbiter of the formal hearing on the matter. Other city officials aggressively and publicly lined up in opposition to the university's challenge to the gay rights ordinance. In February 1999, for example, a council member who had been a key supporter of the ordinance joined in a protest outside the building where Hull trustees were meeting. The city attorney was quoted in the media as stating that the university's challenge to the city's gay rights law was "offensive," and she urged River City's human relations commission to reject it. Addressing Hull's argument that the city ordinance was unenforceable because state law does not include such a provision, she noted that the city's 1958 fair housing law, a point of pride for many in the community, was "meant to prevent race discrimination at a time when no similar state law existed."

However, the city had one embarrassing problem—it did not offer domestic partner benefits to its own employees. That would quickly change. In early April 1999, the city announced an agreement with its white-collar unions to provide health benefits to same-sex partners and common-law spouses and plans to extend these benefits to the other unions representing city employees. Little more than a month later, the city extended the same benefits to its nonunionized employees. Two council members who had sponsored the city's gay rights ordinance nine years earlier introduced the bill to extend the benefits, and the measure passed by a vote of five to two (with two absent), with little debate or protest.

For their part, Hull leaders held fast in their battle to vindicate the university's position, despite a faculty resolution against them, a student hunger strike, and student protests at graduation ceremonies. In June 1999, the city's human relations commission denied the university's motion that Roth's discrimination complaint be dismissed on the grounds that it had been improperly brought before the commission. The commission did not, however, rule on the university's direct challenge to the ordinance's validity and therefore to the commission's authority to hear the case, arguing that the issue of jurisdiction should wait until there was a finding of discrimination.

In November 1999, the state legislature hurriedly passed legislation to protect state universities, including Hull, from local requirements demanding same-sex-partner health benefits. Hull officials promptly asked the human relations commission to dismiss the lawsuit, but it refused. Hull then asked a county court for a restraining order to prevent the commission from proceeding with the case. Ruling that, because of the recently enacted state legislation, River City's human relations commission did not have jurisdiction in the case, the county judge issued a temporary restraining order and later a permanent one, ordering the commission to cease further investigation of the discrimination complaint involving Hull.

According to a simplistic version of the institutional explanation, city government should have been less inclined to favor gay and lesbian interests in River City, South City, and Lake City than in the other two conventional cities because of the significance of electoral imperatives to their political institutions. Those electoral imperatives would be expected to deter public officials from risking their political futures by pursuing pro-gay policies in the face of a community context where such a stance is controversial at best. Lake City perfectly fits this interpretation, but River City should evidence the same fear of electoral backlash and the resulting avoidance of pro-gay policy making. Instead, River City officials took an openly and aggressively pro-gay stance in an extended showdown with a major university and with the state government. Furthermore, Border City and Coastal City should, in contrast to Lake City, show less resistance to gay rights based on officials' desire to avoid political risk. The Coastal City case fits this expectation perfectly, with the politically insulated city manager able to proceed with civil rights protections for gays despite a hostile community context. However, Border City's experience is the mirror image of Lake City's, with plentiful evidence of officials backing away from a pro-gay policy in the face of antigay community opinion and antigay political organizing.

Clearly, city council members as well as chief executives must deal with gay-related issues in these cities. So an institutional interpretation that hinges primarily on the distinction between cities with mayors and those with city managers may be part of the reason for the mixed findings. Yet a focus on the city council as an institution does not really account for the pattern observed here either. Two council members elected from unusually progressive, gay-friendly districts clearly played an instrumental role in the surprisingly pro-gay history of River City. Thus, one might be tempted to conclude that the presence of district elections in River City, but not in Border or Lake City, provided a better basis for a "minority" interest (i.e., gays) to achieve policy responsiveness in a subcultural environment that would not otherwise be conducive to it. However, Coastal City, with its at-large elections, accomplished the same thing, albeit via administrative action and despite council resistance. Hence, although political institutions clearly shaped the pattern of responses to gays in unconventional cities, the responses of conventional cities do not appear to be patterned according to institutional imperatives.

ECONOMIC EXPLANATION

There is very little evidence that economic considerations function to deter cities from gay-friendly policies and actions. Admittedly, some officials voiced financial concerns about domestic partner benefit proposals. For example, this concern was cited as a reason for the mayor's initial veto of domestic partner benefits in Metro City. Furthermore, the cities whose recent actions are least favorable to gays—Border City, South City, and Lake City—are all declining cities. However, as noted elsewhere in this volume, the economically challenged cities are also by and large cities with conventional subcultures. Although Lake City's failure to adopt domestic partner benefits may stem in part from its acute financial distress, the case evidence points more to political sensitivities involving a controversial, morality-related topic in a conventional setting; similarly, Border City's experience reveals that morality rather than money was at stake.

Instead, the case evidence suggests that, to the extent economic considerations are important, they act in several ways to *encourage* a gay-friendly stance on the part of local officials. For one thing, cities with strong economies have resources, allowing them some latitude in taking the lead on gay issues (DeLeon 1999)—an explanation that perfectly fits the Port City case. More indirectly, the composition of the local economy may make a difference. Cities with strong positions in the "new economy" are also expected to be more responsive to gays. Some studies (Black, Gates, Sanders, and Taylor 1999; Bishop 2000) report a high correlation between the concentration of unmarried partners and the concentration of high-tech businesses, or between the concentration of gay and lesbian couples and the concentration of high-tech industry (Florida 2002). As one observer puts it, "gay men and lesbians are the canaries in the new-economy coal mine" (Bishop 2000); new-economy firms also seek the amenities, diversity, and inclusive cultures that attract gays and lesbians to a community. Or, as Florida (2000) argues, the prevalence of gays is a "leading indicator of a place that is open and tolerant," and those characteristics are highly important both to high-tech workers and to the "creative class" more generally.

This interpretation is well supported by both the Western City and Valley City cases. There is also justification for extending the interpretation to those cities that are new-economy wannabes. That is, cities that have begun a transformation to high-tech postindustrial development may be especially eager to maintain an image of progressiveness on gay issues. River City's aggressive fight against Hull's challenge to an expansive view of gay rights should be viewed in light of the city's efforts to move from a declining industrial past to a sophisticated and prosperous postindustrial future. As one gay activist there noted, "High-tech industry generally frowns on attacks against gays and lesbians from the legislative point of view." In this context, a progressive policy stance makes good economic sense.

INTERGOVERNMENTAL EXPLANATION

Finally, we turn to the intergovernmental explanation. Table 6.2 shows the state policy context for gay rights in the study cities at two points in time: 1996, near the beginning of the study period (equivalent information for 1994 was not available), and 1999, near the end of the study period. As the table shows, some states embraced policies favorable to gays, such as the inclusion of sexual orientation in state civil rights and hate crime laws, and some states adopted policies adverse to gays, such as bans on same-sex marriage and state laws criminalizing sodomy. Indeed, some states had a mixture of both. The summary scores (in parentheses in the first column) were calculated by adding +1 for each pro-gay policy adopted or antigay policy not adopted by the city's home state, and −1 for each pro-gay policy not adopted or antigay policy adopted, resulting in a possible total of 4 in each year. The state governments of two of the unconventional cities had the highest possible pro-gay scores in both 1996 and 1999 (Valley and Port). One state with a neutral score in 1996 had become more pro-gay by 1999 (Western), one with a modestly pro-gay score in 1996 had become equally antigay by 1999 (Hill), and one with the highest antigay score possible in 1996 had become only slightly less antigay by 1999 (Metro). There is less diversity in the state contexts of the conventional cities. That set is dominated by states that were quite hostile to gays; only two of the cities (Border and South) are in states that had neutral scores, and none of the conventional cities are in states where governmental policy was pro-gay in either 1996 or 1999.

Table 6.2 State Policy Context for Gay Rights

Study Cities and Summary Scores	Civil Rights Law Includes Sexual Orientation		Same-Gender-Marriage Ban		Hate Crime Law Includes Sexual Orientation		State Law against Sodomy	
	1996	1999	1996	1999	1996	1999	1996	1999
Unconventional								
Valley City (4, 4)	X	X			X	X		
Hill City (2, –2)					X			X
Metro City (–4, –3)			X	X			X	
Port City (4, 4)	X	X			X	X		
Western City (0, 2)				X				
Conventional								
Border City (0, 0)								
River City (–2, –3)			X	X				
South City (0, 0)								
Lake City (–4,– 4)			X	X			X	X
Coastal City (–2, –4)				X			X	X

See text for an explanation of summary scores.
Sources: National Gay and Lesbian Task Force 1996; Hawes 1999.

For all the conventional cities, then, both the state policy context and the local subcultural context are unfavorable for gay rights—a situation that would lead us to expect a pattern of "legitimated inaction" in each of the conventional cities (see table 6.3). This is consistent with Coastal City's avoidance of any gay rights action beyond a narrow nondiscrimination policy for city employees. But River City's epic battle to uphold a gay rights policy in the face of a hostile state legislature is evidence of "compensatory action" rather than "legitimated inaction." And although the lack of pro-gay action in Lake City is superficially consistent with "legitimated inaction," the gay community's lack of political sophistication and mobilization and elected officials' concerns about majority sentiment are the dominant themes in that case; there is no need for officials in Lake City to use state constraints as an excuse for inaction, and no evidence that they did so. Hence, the intergovernmental explanation does not add much to our understanding of the handling of gay issues in conventional cities.

Among unconventional cities, the more variable state policy context summarized in table 6.2 provides an interesting set of possibilities. Valley and Port Cities' state policy context is highly favorable to gays, and Hill City's was

Table 6.3 Typology of Local Action vis-à-vis State Government: Gay Rights

	For Cities "Culturally" Predisposed to:	
Status of State Policy	Pro-Gay Action	Inaction or Antigay Action
Constrains gay rights policy making	*Compensatory action* Metro City	*Legitimated inaction* Coastal City Lake City **River City**
Empowers gay rights policy making	*Legitimated action* Valley City Port City Western City Hill City (early years)	*Underutilization*

Cities in bold exhibit policy histories inconsistent with expectations shown in the framework.

Because their state policy context is, on balance, neutral with respect to gays, Border City and South City cannot be placed in the matrix.

moderately favorable to gays in the early part of the study period; this, in combination with these localities' subcultural context, would be expected to yield "legitimated action," and the evidence from all three cities is consistent with this. By contrast, the state context is unfavorable to gays in Metro City, leading to the expectation of a conflictual relationship between the city and state government as the city engages in "compensatory action." Metro City's sustained court battle with the state insurance commissioner and attorney general over domestic partner benefits is precisely what the intergovernmental explanation would predict. Though not as gay-friendly as Port and Valley Cities' state governments, Western City's state context has become increasingly more favorable to gays in recent years, and its contemporary experience is reasonably consistent with the "legitimated action" expected. Thus, Western City's effort to offer domestic partner benefits was sustained by a state court of appeals, and although there was no same-sex-marriage ban in place to complicate the city's effort to institute a domestic partner registry, the provisions of that registry had to be carefully crafted to avoid raising opposition in a state where a same-sex-marriage bill had been introduced, only to die in committee. Beyond this, the Western City experience yields a bonus insight about the potential importance of intergovernmental relations. Its earlier experience with a state-level antigay ballot initiative effectively sealed a working partnership between gay activists and city officials.

GAY RIGHTS AND THE POLITICS OF RACE

Racial and ethnic factors were not included in the explanatory approach that framed the design of the research on which this book is based. However, other scholarship on gay rights at the local level has uncovered evidence that race is an important consideration in the politics of gay rights at the local level, with black Baptist leadership sometimes opposing gays, and other religious conservative opponents mobilizing blacks against an expansion of gay rights (Wald, Button, and Rienzo 1996; Button, Rienzo, and Wald 1997). In a related vein, in their study of the election of openly gay local public officials, Button, Wald, and Rienzo (1999a, 204) found that there is some "antagonism from African-Americans" to the electoral advancement of gays and some unwillingness to view gays as an oppressed minority. Instead, there is evidence that "some blacks perceive gays as more affluent and less disadvantaged than many in the African-American community and therefore . . . less deserving of minority status."

Given these findings, it is worth considering whether there is parallel evidence of a racial dimension to gay rights politics in these study cities. The last column in table 6.1 shows the percentage of each city's population that is African American. There is considerable variation in the racial composition of the study cities, with three predominantly black cities (South, Metro, and Lake), one (Border) that is within a few percentage points of being majority-minority, and another where blacks are a substantial component of the population (River); in the remaining five communities, the African American population is not numerically prominent. If the politics of race is important for gay rights, we would expect South, Metro, and especially Lake City to be less receptive to gay rights than the other cities in their respective subcultural categories. The overall pattern is disappointing with respect to this expectation. In fact, the city with the largest black population and a long history of black mayors (Lake) is one of only two conventional cities to have a nondiscrimination ordinance that is applicable to gays. Furthermore, even though it is the only unconventional city that is predominantly black, Metro City has both a nondiscrimination ordinance and domestic partner benefits, which are typical of unconventional cities. Only South City fits what a "politics of race" explanation would suggest.

If we go beyond the pattern of outcomes presented in table 6.1 to reconsider some details about the political processes behind these outcomes, there is a bit more evidence for a racial interpretation. In Lake City, it is particularly apparent that both the black mayor and the predominantly black city council have avoided pursuing domestic partner legislation for fear of electoral retribution by the politically active leaders of the religious community, who vehemently oppose homosexuality. Although gays in South City are not mobilized enough to exert significant pressure for domestic partner benefits, it is also apparent that the strongly religious character of the community (black Baptist churches are paramount in this regard) creates a hostile context for gay rights organizing.

This leaves the curious case of Metro City, where a majority black population and the powerful presence of black churches have *not* yielded the racial politics of hostility to gay rights found in the other two majority black communities. Opposition to gay rights came from other quarters, but the black community and black churches were apparently neither a source of opposition nor a target for mobilization by other opponents of gay rights. Instead, racial politics there worked in favor of gay rights. A city council member explains that Metro City's long tradition as the center of the nation's civil rights movement engenders a very special context that tempers any opposition to gay rights.

CONCLUSION

For gay rights issues, local culture matters. The subcultural distinction of unconventional and conventional cities improves our ability to anticipate and understand the types of stances city officials take on gay issues. Admittedly, the overlap between cultural type and economic status means that we cannot ignore the potential importance of economic considerations. To the extent that economics play a role in gay politics and policy making at the local level, it occurs through enhanced pressure for gay-friendly policies in places that have, or aspire to have, successful high-tech development and similar features of the new economy. The importance of institutional arrangements is less clear. Whereas unconventional cities exhibit precisely the pattern that an institutional explanation would lead us to expect, the evidence from conventional cities does not fit the pattern. Similarly, an intergovernmental interpretation fits the evidence from the unconventional cities but not the conventional ones. In short, although unconventional cities overall are more favorably inclined toward gays than conventional cities are, institutional features and the state context help explain which of the unconventional cities are the most pro-gay. Among conventional cities, the only thing that matters above and beyond subculture is the presence of a high-technology economic development initiative.

7
Drugs, Health, and Local Politics

Few issues in American politics have been as politically potent as the drug issue. The political potency of this issue stems from the ease with which the abuse of narcotics and other illicit drugs for recreational purposes can be defined as a morality problem. Under this definition of the problem, drug use is "an evil, a bad habit, a weakness in virtuous character, a vice which leads to further debauchery and immorality" (Nolan 2001, 15). Those who profit by trafficking in drugs are, of course, viewed as an even greater evil. The definition of drug users and drug traffickers alike as immoral has provided the impetus for a long history of U.S. policy that features use of the criminal law to resolve the drug problem. Thus, from the Harrison Narcotics Act of 1914 to the Comprehensive Drug Abuse and Control Act of 1970 to the numerous anti-drug laws enacted in the 1980s and 1990s, federal policy has involved not only legal restrictions on the sale of drugs but also increasingly harsh legal penalties against individuals for possessing and using drugs. During the Reagan administration, "zero tolerance" became the policy, meaning that even small-time, casual drug users would be targeted by the authorities because, in the words of Nancy Reagan: "The casual user cannot morally escape responsibility for the action of drug traffickers and dealings. I'm saying that if you're a casual drug user you're an accomplice to murder" (as quoted in Sharp 1994, 56).

But this is not the only definition of the problem of drug abuse. Scholars of the history of drug policy note that, in addition to the criminal model of the problem, a medical model, or what Nolan (2001, 15) calls the "therapeutic paradigm," has competed for attention. From this perspective, drug abusers and addicts have a "disease or disorder that needs some form of treatment" (Nolan 2001, 16). Dwelling on whether their behavior is moral is irrelevant from this point of view, given the need for a therapeutic response.

There have been one or two brief moments in U.S. history when the medical model rose to prominence, such as President Richard Nixon's 1971 initiative to provide federal support for the then-experimental use of the synthetic drug methadone to keep addicts off heroin (Sharp 1994, 27) and President Jimmy Carter's short-lived efforts to have his drug policy adviser, Dr. Peter

Bourne, redirect antidrug efforts toward more creative drug treatment approaches (Sharp 1994, 37). However, the criminal model of the drug problem has consistently been favored over the medical model. Politicians have found it more politically useful to rally the public behind law enforcement–directed wars on drugs than to mobilize the public for large-scale therapeutic efforts. Since the 1960s, the federal antidrug budget has included funding for both types of activities, but the bulk of the funds—typically about two-thirds—has gone toward law enforcement to pinch off the supply of drugs; much smaller amounts have been devoted to programs to stanch the demand for drugs. Drug treatment funding is only a portion of the latter category, which also includes educational programs aimed at prevention.

Because the dominant perspective on drug use is a morality-based one that views drug abuse as a character flaw at best and criminal behavior at worst, public policy innovations that emphasize other aspects of the drug abuse problem have a difficult row to hoe. By the early 1990s, however, the nation's seemingly endless war on drugs had created some serious negative consequences at the local level that made room for just such innovations. For one thing, the flood of arrests that stemmed from law enforcement policies targeted at both drug traffickers and lower-level drug possessors put tremendous pressure on the already overburdened urban courts, leading to a slowdown in case processing time (Terry 1999, 3). Beyond this, the emphasis on a criminal rather than a medical approach to the drug problem meant that many individuals whose drug abuse had led them to crime did not receive any substance abuse rehabilitation. There is evidence that substantial numbers of individuals in jail or on probation have substance abuse problems. For example, in the late 1990s, a Columbia University Center on Addiction and Substance Abuse study showed that 80 percent of offenders in the criminal justice system are substance abusers (Tauber and Huddleston 1999, 7). To the extent that the treatment and rehabilitation side of the drug problem is ignored, a root cause of these individuals' dysfunction is not dealt with head-on. Not surprisingly, many law enforcement and judicial actors became frustrated with the endless merry-go-round of processing the same individuals over and over again.

Finally, the emphasis on a criminal definition of the drug problem has exacerbated public health problems involving sexually transmitted diseases. In particular, an important vehicle for the spread of HIV, the virus that causes AIDS, is the use of contaminated needles by injection drug users. Contrary to mythological interpretations of needle sharing as a ritualistic behavior among addicts, intensive fieldwork has shown that needle sharing results when the addict's inelastic demand for such injection equipment meets the scarcity and high price of needles that must be bought on the black market because of state criminalization of drug paraphernalia possession (Fernando 1993). Any proposed change in these laws, even for the purpose of preventing the transmission of HIV, runs afoul of the definition of drug addicts as morally depraved and their drug use as criminal behavior.

Despite such resistance, two policy innovations relevant to these problems have emerged: drug courts and needle-exchange programs.

DRUG COURTS

Drug courts are designed not only to focus on drug cases but also to take a new approach to the disposition of those cases—specifically, to put the full weight of the court behind the diversion of suitable defendants to drug treatment programs. As the case histories in this chapter show, drug courts differ in their eligibility requirements for defendants to receive this treatment-focused approach, but most drug courts focus on individuals who are drug users (rather than drug traffickers) and whose drug use has led them into a cycle of non-violent crime to support their habits. Although a variety of treatment programs are used, the key is the continued involvement of the drug court judge as the defendant proceeds through treatment. As Terry (1999, 7) notes, the drug court concept has "turned traditional judges into substance abuse problem solvers." Drug court judges do not simply refer defendants to drug treatment programs; instead, defendants must appear before the judge on a regular basis to report their progress. The judge decides what to do when urine tests show that a defendant has faltered, offers encouragement, and congratulates those who successfully complete the program. This radically changes the character of the relationship between the judge and the defendants, who now become "clients." "The judge engages the clients directly, asks personal questions, and encourages them in the treatment process. Judges interact with clients in a manner more like proactive therapists than dispassionate judicial officers" (Nolan 2001, 40).

By placing the authority and involvement of the court and the activism of the judge behind the activity of treatment professionals, drug courts are expected to enhance treatment programs' effectiveness in rehabilitating drug abusers. Most important, this approach is intended to break the cycle of drug abuse and minor crimes committed to support the drug habit; it is intended to stop individuals from being arrested again and again for similar infractions because the root cause of their dysfunctional behavior was not addressed. Although some preliminary research evaluating drug courts has begun, by 2000, that body of research evidence was still quite weak (Nolan 2001, 130; Terry 1999, 15), especially with respect to demonstrating improvement in recidivism rates. Nevertheless, this innovation diffused quite rapidly. Since the implementation of the first drug court in Dade County, Florida, in 1989, more than 800 similar courts have emerged (Nolan 2001, 39).

Traditional courts that handle only drug cases, called "specialized drug courts," also exist. Their purpose is simply to expedite the process by taking advantage of the expertise of court personnel who deal only with drug cases. These cases are handled along conventional, criminal law–based lines. To distinguish drug courts in the sense used in this chapter from these efficiency-oriented specialized drug courts, some scholars have suggested the term "dedicated" drug courts (Terry 1999, 1).

NEEDLE-EXCHANGE PROGRAMS

Needle-exchange programs (NEPs) are designed to fight the spread of HIV infection among intravenous drug users, who traditionally engage in the practice of sharing "dirty" needles. NEPs provide free, clean needles to drug addicts in exchange for their used needles. At the same time, many NEPs incorporate a broader purpose, using the occasion of contact with drug users to encourage them to get drug treatment and other health services (Bertram, Blachman, Sharpe, and Andreas 1996, 170). There is a compelling body of evidence that NEPs do reduce the sharing of dirty needles and the spread of HIV (Hurley, Jolley, and Kaldor 1997; Broadhead, Van Hulst, and Heckathorn 1999, 48). Still other studies provide reassuring evidence that NEPs do not encourage the use of intravenous drugs (Heimer and Lopes 1994).

However well-intentioned, NEPs are problematic, because most states have drug paraphernalia laws that criminalize the sale or possession of needles and syringes without a prescription or for the purpose of using illegal drugs. In the mid-1990s, all but five states had such laws (Normand, Vlahov, and Moses 1995, 75). Nevertheless, NEPs have been operating in many places where they are technically illegal. In fact, the Centers for Disease Control and Prevention reports that there were 131 needle exchange programs functioning in eighty-one cities in thirty-one states as of 1998 ("Update: Syringe Exchange Programs" 2001, 2709). NEPs are often created by community activists whose dedication to AIDS issues leads them to defy local laws (Kirp and Bayer 1999, 179–80). As illustrated in several of the cases in this chapter, needle-exchange operations are sometimes publicly endorsed by city or county officials and sometimes indirectly supported by local authorities, such as when public health officials discreetly disseminate information about NEPs to their clients or police officials agree not to arrest NEP workers and clients.

Meanwhile, the federal government's stance ranges from outright hostility to NEPs to a hands-off approach that passes this politically charged issue on to the states. On eight occasions, Congress has passed bills with "provisions that barred or inhibited federal funding for needle-exchange programs," taking a firm position that any harm reduction potential that such programs might have is "subordinate to the need to sustain a consistently punitive, anti-drug message" (Bertram et al. 1996, 171). In 1998, the Clinton administration chose to extend the ban on funding while simultaneously endorsing the value of needle exchange. The ban has been sustained ever since.

Drug courts and needle-exchange programs have been implemented in a number of cities and counties, even in the face of the potential political flak if opponents mobilized the public to decry the immorality of drug abuse. Although these innovations were "fueled by undercurrents felt on the local level that were different from the themes and solutions emphasized in national [drug] policy" (Goldkamp 1999, 167), they have not been uniformly attractive in all localities. Indeed, as the case histories in this chapter illustrate, the localities' experience with these innovations has ranged from ready acceptance and smooth implementation to politically inspired conflict to outright hostility and rejection based on moral grounds. The first task is to assess the similarities and differences in these communities' experiences with drug courts in light of subcultural differences and then to consider what role institutional arrangements, economic context, and intergovernmental relations played in the development of these courts.

SUBCULTURAL EXPLANATION: DRUG COURTS

A key hypothesis guiding all the analyses in this volume is that the character of the community subculture has a bearing on local officials' handling of morality policies. In the case of drug courts specifically, we would expect localities with unconventional subcultures to be more accepting of the idea than would localities with conventional subcultures, on two grounds. First, unconventional communities might be more supportive of policy innovations in general because of their relative sophistication and cosmopolitanism compared with the traditionalism and provincialism of conventional settings. Second, unconventional cities might be more receptive to drug courts because they are viewed as less harshly punitive, which would appeal to unconventional subcultures' antiauthoritarian strands and tolerance of alternative lifestyles.

The results in table 7.1 are consistent with this hypothesis. Even though the pervasiveness of drug courts suggests that there are few differences between conventional and unconventional communities' acceptance of them, it is quite clear that conventional communities were, as a set, slower to adopt this innovation. One conventional community has not yet established such a court.

In addition, it is possible that there are real differences among communities with respect to the motivations for establishing a drug court, the specific character of the drug court, the nature of the obstacles that had to be overcome to create a drug court, and the extent of political conflict surrounding the court's adoption and implementation. Drug courts may have been more politically controversial in some settings than in others. In particular, we would expect there to be more conflict over their establishment in more politicized settings. Likewise, some communities may have limited the drug court's scope and functioning, while others may have institutionalized a comprehensive and ambitious version of a drug court. Brief descriptions of the history of drug court development in the study cities provide the raw material for exploring these possibilities.

With respect to subculture, the case details reinforce the conclusion from table 7.1 that drug courts fare better in unconventional settings, in the sense that more full-blown, ambitious versions are implemented. Consider, for example, the contrast between conventional South City and unconventional Metro City.

South City

A drug court has been established in South City's home county, South County. However, the establishment of a true, treatment-oriented, "dedicated" drug court (Terry 1999, 7) came relatively late to South County, delayed by both community politics and conflict with the state government, which controls the creation of local courts. As early as 1991, the state legislature had created a temporary specialized drug court in South County, with federal funding support, in response to a crush of drug-related cases that was clogging court dockets. However, this court had none of the essential features of a dedicated drug court. Most notably, there was no commitment to court-supervised drug treatment rather than conventional prosecution and sentencing.

As expiration of the federal grant loomed in 1994, South County officials were having difficulty convincing the state legislature to make the drug court a permanent one. There were concerns about the cost of creating a new, permanent court division and questions about whether the heavy caseloads of county judges were overstated. The local district attorney, judges, and defense attorneys supported the idea of a specialized drug court, but their argument was grounded exclusively in terms of promoting the efficient handling of drug cases rather than transforming the character of their disposition.

Table 7.1 Status of Drug Court Innovation, by Community Subculture Type

Study Cities	Drug Court Established	Year Established	Restrictiveness of Eligibility
Unconventional			
Metro City/County	Yes	1997	Moderate
Western City/County	Yes	1994	Low
Port City/County	Yes	1994	Moderate
Hill City/County	Yes	1993	Moderate
Valley City/County	Yes	1995	Low
Conventional			
Lake City/County	No	—	—
River City/County	Yes	1998	High
Border City/County	Yes	1996	Low
South City/County	Yes	1997/1999	Moderate
Coastal City/County	Yes	1998	Very High

In late 1995, in the midst of this discussion, County Commissioner Glen Jervis (a white Republican) took the lead and suggested a discussion about creating a drug court that would actually focus on drug treatment and the types of defendants who could benefit from such an approach. He was quoted in a local newspaper as saying that he would favor such a drug court if there were funding for it and "if we did the drug court concept right." Jervis got several local judges, the public defender, and other officials to participate in preliminary discussions of the idea, but control of resources constituted an obstacle. In early 1996, Jervis and other county commissioners were engaged in a tug-of-war with the county's elected sheriff over the control of asset forfeiture monies derived from drug arrests. Those monies had been controlled exclusively by the sheriff, and Jervis argued that they should be controlled by the county commission, which would allow the funds to be used for drug prevention programs and other purposes as well.

Ultimately, local officials agreed in 1997 to create a dedicated drug court, to be financed initially with federal grant monies received from the state government and matching local funds. Perhaps most important, the county had a new district attorney, who took the lead in articulating the treatment orientation of the new drug court, acknowledging his awareness of how such courts worked in other cities. According to District Attorney Doug Grout, the new drug court would be for misdemeanor rather than felony drug users who owned up to their drug addiction and volunteered to undergo intensive treatment with the court's supervision. Signaling his commitment to the program, the county sheriff provided over $40,000 in asset forfeiture monies to be used as matching funds for the federal grant. Initially, the new program was expected to handle about 500 drug defendants, but it could be expanded quickly if additional federal funding was obtained. Later that year, the member of Congress representing South County—a high-profile black politician from South City—announced the award of a substantial, additional federal grant for South County's drug court.

Federal funding allowed South County to establish a temporary, part-time drug court, which operated with little controversy for two years. But because of resource constraints, the demands of a huge felony caseload in the jurisdiction, and the perception that no judge should shirk his or her share of that larger caseload to specialize in minor drug cases, the new drug court also took on cases from the regular court docket. These cases did not fit the narrow specialization for which the court was allegedly created, and this limited its ability to provide intensive drug treatment follow-up, as a pure drug court would. More important, full institutionalization would eventually require state legislation to authorize the drug court as a permanent court division, as well as the county commission's allocation of funds for the court. That price tag was not trivial. In addition to construction costs of over $250,000 for a new courtroom and chambers, proponents indicated that the yearly operating costs would be over $750,000. When the state legislative session convened in early 1999, South County's district attorney took a lead role in lobbying for support for the drug court, joined by South County's elected chief executive. Grout argued that the drug court was not soft on crime; rather, defendants processed through the drug court were subjected to more intensive supervision and given harsher penalties for failure than were other drug offenders. The tough talk was apparently effective; the state legislature provided the required authorization in the spring of 1999. Getting local funding, however, was not an easy matter, especially since the county commission was in the midst of a budget-cutting exercise in the summer of 1999. Grout did have the carrot of federal funding to dangle before the commission, because that funding was assured at least for the costs of the actual drug treatment. The costs of court personnel would have to be borne by the county, however, which would require a tax increase. Ultimately, the necessary local funding to fully institutionalize the drug court was pieced together in the fall of 2000 with the help of South City's mayor, who committed $250,000 in asset forfeiture funds from the police department's drug-related law enforcement.

Conventional South City's drug court experience illustrates how both cost constraints and a lack of conviction about the need for such a court can make it difficult to institutionalize a true drug court, although the community finally got to that point. By contrast, the case of unconventional Metro City shows how widely shared beliefs about the desirability of an expansive treatment orientation and a high degree of cooperation can smooth the way past resource constraints.

Metro City

In Metro City's core county, the impetus for the development of a drug court came from a group of governmental and nongovernmental actors who had already come together in 1993 to collaborate on solving problems related to drug and alcohol abuse. The organization they formed, Newfound Beginnings, was chaired by a retired CEO from a major corporation in the community and included a number of leaders from other businesses, nonprofit organizations, and local governments. The organization was supported with grant funding from both a foundation and Metro City.

By early 1995, Newfound Beginnings was already committed to developing a drug court. They sought the support of long-term county judge John Everett, who was skeptical at first and asked many tough questions about the concept. Once the leadership of Newfound Beginnings was able to convince Everett that the drug court was a good idea, he took a leading role in pushing for the court and ultimately agreed to serve as its presiding judge.

According to a member of Newfound Beginnings, the concept of a drug court was not controversial, but getting the resources to establish the court was a challenge. The organization requested federal grant funds for the program and got the state legislature to commit matching funds. A substantial federal grant to support the drug court was awarded in the spring of 1996, and a U.S. attorney active in Newfound Beginnings acknowledged that Metro City's mayor and the Metro County commissioner were instrumental in garnering the grant.

The new drug court began operations in the spring of the following year with the full support of the district attorney, who noted that nearly half his caseload involved drugs. The district attorney assigned an assistant from his office to the drug court. At least one of the county commissioners also expressed public support for the drug court, noting in a local newspaper interview that it involved a combination of "stern administration and true compassion." The program targets drug-abusing defendants with no violent criminal record. Prior to adjudication, they must agree to participate in the treatment program. Consistent with the public-private partnership approach that characterized the development of the drug court concept, counseling was initially provided by a variety of public, private, and nonprofit drug treatment institutions; in addition, there is weekly drug testing and regular sessions before the drug court judge. Upon successful completion of the program, the original charges are dismissed.

One year later, the program had grown to include well over 200 participants, and officials were celebrating the opening of a new drug court treatment center built with the program's grant funds. Although the program's failure rate was not trivial—sixty-five had been dropped from the program for not abiding by the rules—there was no evidence of controversy about or political challenge to the drug court.

By the second anniversary of the drug court, some problems were beginning to surface, however. A total of about 400 individuals had been admitted to the drug court, but only 35 had successfully completed the program; about half had either quit the program or been dropped. Commenting publicly on this disappointing performance, the district attorney noted that the drug court was not being adequately used, in the sense that only 35 graduates in two years simply did not put enough of a dent in the problem. He argued that the drug court needed to develop a residential (i.e., inpatient) treatment center, which he believed would be more effective than outpatient drug counseling. Like the district attorney, the director of a drug counseling program in the community argued that the drug court needed a more elaborate array of after-care services for drug abusers, which could reduce the recidivism rate. These arguments all took the tone of supporting the drug court concept in principle while pushing for a more expansive or elaborate drug court effort. Consistent with this, the county commission signaled its continuing support for the drug court by budgeting $1 million for its operations so that staffing could be expanded. Judge Everett initiated a collaborative effort with the county's pretrial services office to find a way to supervise drug court clients to prevent recidivism, but without unduly burdening the probation department. The judge acknowledged that the drug court needed a better way to track graduates to replace the passive approach of waiting to find out whether such individuals had been rearrested.

The South City and Metro City cases suggest that although both conventional and unconventional communities have drug courts, those in conventional cities may not be as fully developed or as true to the treatment orientation. At one time or another, South City's drug court was either a specialized, but not a true treatment-oriented, drug court or a part-time treatment-oriented drug court that was expected to handle nondrug cases as well. This contrasts with the full-blown drug court developed in Metro City, with more and more services being added with the blessing and financial support of local officials. Except for Border City, the other communities in the conventional category have similarly limited versions of functioning drug courts (see the appendix for additional case histories). For example, the drug court in River City's core county has highly restrictive eligibility criteria; these criteria limited the number of drug court cases to such an extent that a substantial chunk of grant funding had to be returned. Coastal City's very small and highly specialized drug court deals only with drug and alcohol abusers who are arrested for driving under the influence.

INSTITUTIONAL EXPLANATION: DRUG COURTS

The key similarity across the study sites is that the development of drug courts was largely a matter of entrepreneurial action on the part of public officials rather than a direct response to public pressure for such an innovation. Metro City and River City come closest to being exceptions to this generalization; in the former, a collaborative group of public- and private-sector leaders pushed for the drug court, and in the latter, the addiction services specialists at a major hospital used a pilot project to leverage the interest of public officials. More generally, however, drug court development in these communities exemplifies Nolan's (2001, 42) claim that the creation of drug courts is a social movement of political actors: "Typically, social movements are conceived as collective social behavior seeking to effect change from outside the political processes. In the case of the drug court movement, contrastingly, the major agents of change are the political (or, more specifically, the judicial) actors themselves."

One interpretation of drug courts suggests that this controversial innovation has been able to take root so broadly because politically insulated officials took the lead role. To the extent that judges are appointed and have to face the voters only rarely and on relatively low-key, noncontested retention ballots, they can afford to push for an innovation such as a drug court without fear that a political opponent will mobilize voters on morality grounds and use the issue against them.

However, in contrast with Nolan's observation, the major agents of change in these communities were not necessarily judicial actors. In only two sites (Western and Coastal) was the movement judge-led. In another (Border), a judge and a county commissioner played a coequal role in fostering the drug court, whereas in Port City, a local legislator and an assistant district attorney were the entrepreneurs. In Valley City's home county, the district attorney took the lead role; likewise, South County's district attorney was ultimately the successful policy entrepreneur, after a county commissioner had failed in the attempt. The team of public-private actors featured in the Metro City case included a wide array of public officials, and development of the drug court in Hill City's core county also featured the collaboration of a team of officials. In short, the change agents for drug courts at the local level include a variety of elected officials who could very well face political fallout from drug court leadership.

A connection would be expected, however, between institutional arrangements and subcultural influences. Thus, in conventional settings, where there is more hostility to an innovation that overrides traditional moral sentiments about drug use, the presence of politicized institutions that maximize governmental responsiveness to the public would spell trouble for drug courts. By contrast, drug courts can be successfully developed and implemented in conventional settings if there are professionalized, depoliticized institutional arrangements that insulate officials from public accountability. The reverse logic would be expected to hold in communities with unconventional subcultures. In such settings, the community would be much more receptive to, perhaps even demanding of, innovations that challenged the drug war status quo. Political institutions that heighten public officials' accountability provide a transmission belt for translating these popular preferences into policy innovation; by contrast, political institutions that depoliticize governance and neutralize popular accountability remove a key incentive for public officials to pursue the development of drug courts.

Assessing this hypothesis with respect to drug courts is complicated by the fact that county rather than city officials are typically the key actors. Hence, the characterization of the study sites' political institutions used for other topics must be replaced with an alternative, county-level characterization that features the most relevant public officials here—judges, district attorneys, and, to a lesser extent, county commissioners. Unfortunately, there is relatively little variation in county-level political institutions, at least among the sites used for this study. District attorneys and county-level legislators are elected in each of the counties on partisan ballots, and in most of them, judges are elected as well. Nevertheless, there are some institutional differences, particularly with respect to judicial selection, that point to a greater level of politicization in some counties than in others. In Western County, for example, judges are initially appointed for a two-year term by the mayor, whose choices are restricted to candidates approved by a bipartisan commission; judges are then subject to a retention ballot every four years. By contrast, judges in Port County are elected on a partisan ballot in hard-fought, high-profile contests, befitting this community's approach to local politics as a blood sport. Some of the other study sites approximate Western County's model, in that judges are elected, but on a nonpartisan ballot (Valley, Lake, and Border Counties); others, with partisan elections (or ostensibly nonpartisan elections that feature heavy-duty party endorsements), approximate the more politicized model of Port County (River, Metro, Hill, and South Counties). Coastal County judges are not elected locally at all; they are chosen by a vote of legislators in the statehouse.

But do these differences in relevant political institutions really have an impact on the development and implementation of drug courts? The case evidence suggests that they do not. The South County case outlined earlier shows that some difficulties were encountered in establishing a drug court there, and one might be tempted to attribute these problems to the elected district attorney and partisan judiciary. However, despite the fact that it too is a conventional community with a politicized district attorney and judges, River County developed and implemented drug courts with no apparent controversy or political conflict. Even more damaging to the institutional explanation is the fact that the only conventional city that has been unable to develop a drug court is Lake City, which has nonpartisan judicial elections. Further, the conventional community that has most significantly restricted its drug court, to keep it from offending local moral sensibilities, is Coastal City, whose local judiciary is selected at the state level. In short, drug courts have *not* had a tougher row to hoe in the conventional counties whose relevant political institutions are more open to traditional local values; if anything, the case studies suggest the reverse.

The institutional interpretation fares no better when we consider the unconventional communities. For one thing, the two that have experienced the most controversy and political conflict over drug courts are Western City and Port City.

Western City and Port City

Western City's drug court, which began operating in the summer of 1994, was the brainchild of district court judge B. J. Janeway. The judge had heard about the drug court established in Dade County, Florida, and began pushing the idea of creating one in Western City, out of frustration with the ineffectiveness of the regular prosecution and sentencing of drug offenders. Law enforcement agencies and prosecutors in Western City, in tune with national "no-tolerance" policy trends, were arresting and prosecuting greater numbers of individuals for both drug possession and drug trafficking. As a result, the courts were becoming bogged down with drug cases, and drug users were just cycling through the system again and again. Janeway hoped to institute a special court for minor drug offenders that would emphasize treatment and the opportunity to have felony convictions removed from their records upon successful completion of the program.

Judge Janeway's vision was realized when Lou Randall became the district attorney. Randall supported a drug court even though, as he acknowledged in a local newspaper article, "people are going to say that we're mollycoddling drug users under this program." With relatively few resources, the fledgling drug court was launched in 1994, with Janeway serving as the presiding judge. Randall assigned four deputies and an investigator full-time to the court. There was only a tiny amount of grant money to tide the operation over while Janeway sought additional funding for more courtroom personnel, as well as staff for counseling and supervision programs. The fledgling operation was assisted to some extent by the fact that, three years previously, the state government had mandated a research effort to identify which treatment programs were effective for various categories of drug abusers.

One year later, the drug court celebrated its first anniversary amid numerous success stories and the receipt of a $200,000 federal grant to support its operations. The additional resources were clearly needed. In its first year, the drug court had handled about 2,000 cases, compared with the 1,000 Janeway had planned for and the 3,800 cases handled by all the other divisions of the local court system put together. Indeed, by its second anniversary, it was clear that the drug court was being deluged with cases, handling more than 3,000 in its second year of operation. The escalating caseload was attributed to the increase in drugs flowing into the state in general and the metro area in particular, as well as to the Western City police department's policy of targeting minor drug users for arrest.

In 1996, the drug court faced an equally important challenge when it became an issue in the election campaign for district attorney. Randall was being challenged by former assistant district attorney Hank Feldman, who critiqued the drug court in a local newspaper for giving out unduly light sentences and thereby turning the city into "the Big Easy for drug dealers." Feldman vowed that, if elected, he would put an end to the drug court.

In response to this challenge, Randall began to back away from the treatment-oriented approach that is the core of the drug court concept. Instead, he argued that the drug court was actually tougher than the system it had replaced, on several grounds. For one thing, in the past, minor drug cases had been given low priority in a court system swamped with cases, leading to frequent plea bargains down to trivial sentences. Explicitly acknowledging the community's political subculture, Randall also argued in a local newspaper article that the jury pool in Western City was "nine miles to the left of Mao Zedong" and hence unwilling to convict minor drug offenders under the traditional criminal approach.

Feldman continued to center his campaign around a critique of the drug court, but ultimately, Randall won reelection, with nearly 62 percent of the vote. Despite the fact that he had prevailed, Randall acknowledged to the press that the campaign had caused him to reexamine the drug court and to ask whether it was working as well as it should be. By the same token, he had "a growing sense of bipartisan support" of the "need for treatment as well as law enforcement."

Like Western County, Port County has experienced conflict and controversy over its drug court. In the Port County case, that conflict stemmed from a dispute between the district attorney and the public defender over the scope of the program; the former wanted to limit the program to first-time nonviolent defendants arrested for possession or use of small amounts of drugs, and the latter wanted to include defendants whose nonviolent crimes stemmed from the need to support their drug addiction. The drug court was initiated along the lines of the restrictive vision favored by the district attorney, but it took in a disappointing number of cases. Nevertheless, the district attorney opposed any attempt to broaden the program; he was facing reelection and feared that opponents would criticize his involvement in a more expansive drug court. Controversy also surfaced over statistics suggesting that the court had an unduly high failure rate (see the appendix for further details).

Western and Port Counties thus have many similarities with respect to conflict and controversy over the drug court experience. But their institutional similarity is limited to the fact that the district attorney is elected on a partisan ballot, which is true of virtually all the study cities. The two communities could not be more different with respect to their relevant judicial institutions. Western County has the least politicized judiciary, while Port County has a highly politicized judiciary. Instead of leading to contrasting outcomes, however, these institutional differences led to similar outcomes. The highly politicized judicial and prosecutorial arrangements in Port County should have propelled officials to act with confidence on drug courts, knowing that the innovation fit the local subculture. Instead, electoral accountability seems to have gotten in the way of drug court development. Again, an institutional interpretation falters.

Hill City and Valley City

Similarly, Hill City's home county has a more politicized judiciary and governing institutions than Valley County does. Hence, of these two unconventional communities, we would expect more aggressive and confident development of drug courts in Hill County. Instead, the reverse is true. Valley County's drug court was adopted largely in response to a growing court caseload stemming from its state's "three-strikes" law. In late 1994, the entire county court system was reorganized for greater efficiency, and creation of a specialized drug court was part of this arrangement. Within a year, this specialized drug court was transformed into a true, treatment-oriented, "dedicated" drug court. The district attorney, who was first elected in 1990, was key to this transformation. Under his leadership, a program was developed that focused on drug treatment as an alternative to jail time for drug offenders. County court judges approved the drug court in the fall of 1995, and the county council approved funding that same year for additional staff in the district attorney's office to monitor the program and ensure its compliance with county standards. Although it was initially targeted toward hard-core drug users, the district attorney immediately pressed for expansion of the program to deal with minor cases as well.

In Hill County, a drug court was initially developed as a pilot project in the fall of 1993. With information about the highly acclaimed Dade County, Florida, drug court fresh in their minds, the local judiciary collaborated with the district attorney's office, the county's department of mental health and mental retardation, the probation and pretrial services offices, defense attorneys, law enforcement officials, and Hill City to develop a program modeled on the Dade County experience. Funding for the pilot project was provided by Hill County and three state government offices—the governor's office, the department of criminal justice, and the state agency dealing with alcohol and drug abuse.

The program was intended to deal with very minor drug offenders—those arrested for possession of drugs, provided they had no record of serious drug dealing, violent felony crime convictions, or other felony crimes still to be adjudicated. Designers of the program allowed for other types of offenders to enter the program as well through an appeal to a committee that includes individuals from the judiciary, the pretrial services department, the district attorney's and public defender's offices, and the community. Defendants must sign on for a yearlong program, during which time adjudication of their charges is deferred; charges are dismissed if they successfully complete the program. Participants undergo daily urine tests for the first two weeks, as well as detoxification with acupuncture treatment and drug counseling; then they move on to other counseling, such as Narcotics Anonymous. In addition, they face the usual round of regular appearances before the drug court judge to report on their progress.

One year after the drug court began operations, funding difficulties loomed on the horizon. The state grant monies that had provided the bulk of its funding were due to dry up at the end of the summer of 1995, and Hill County had not yet received any federal funds, although those operating the drug court intended to apply for such funds. In the meantime, Hill County commissioners were asked to provide funding for the program, but because of budget problems besieging the county, they cut back the scale of drug court operations to a cohort of about fifty to sixty offenders per year. County officials exhibited support for the drug court in principle but continuously attempted to piece together financial support from external sources while avoiding a commitment of local funds. By the end of its fourth year of operation, only 200 individuals had completed the program, and by the end of the fifth year, slightly more than 250 had graduated. Eventually, the county's efforts to get external resources began to pay off. In late 1997, the drug court received a small federal grant to pay for computer equipment, and the following summer, it was awarded a more substantial grant of federal funds.

As this narrative shows, Hill County's drug court suffered from resource limitations that reflect an overreliance on external sources of funding and cautiousness about committing local funds. This is a far cry from what we would have expected from a community with an unconventional subculture and institutional arrangements that should motivate judges, district attorneys, and other relevant officials to forcefully pursue this innovation. By contrast, officials in the less politicized setting of Valley City's home county readily came up with the necessary commitment of local funds and launched their drug court with little ado. In short, as with all the other focused comparisons, the institutional explanation is not well supported by the evidence.

ECONOMIC AND INTERGOVERNMENTAL EXPLANATIONS: DRUG COURTS

Assessing the impact of the local economic development context on drug court development is complicated by the overall confounding of economic status and community subculture in these case study communities. As a result, the greater receptivity to drug courts in unconventional communities may actually reflect a greater receptivity in settings that are economically secure. And greater receptivity to drug courts in economically secure settings is precisely what one would hypothesize, based on the fact that policy innovation is generally linked to the availability of resources.

However plausible such an interpretation may be, there are grounds for minimizing the significance of economic development with respect to drug courts. First, the experiences of Metro County and Coastal County provide evidence that undercuts an economic development explanation. Although Metro County is the only unconventional community in the declining category, it joined the other unconventional communities in forging ahead with a drug court. Coastal County, which is the only conventional community that is economically secure, generated only a minimalist version of a drug court, while counterparts in the much more economically precarious Border County developed a substantial drug court. Second, although drug courts, like other innovations, often require what appear to be new budgetary resources, they also are touted as saving tax dollars; that is, the per-client cost of supervised treatment is less expensive than jail, and a reduction in the recidivism rate will mean fewer law enforcement and court costs in the future. From this point of view, drug courts, unlike other policy innovations, can also be appealing in settings where a declining economy puts a strain on local government budgets.

Perhaps the most important reason that economic status is not a big factor in these communities' experiences with drug courts is the significance of the intergovernmental context. The federal government has been highly supportive of drug court development. That support has come not only in the form

Table 7.2 Status of Needle-Exchange Programs, by Community Subculture Type, Chief Executive Type, and Economic Status

Study Cities	Type of Existing Needle-Exchange Program	Local Officials' Policy Stance toward Program
Unconventional		
Growing		
Port City/County	Officially endorsed	Policy endorsement and subsidy
Valley City/County	Officially endorsed	Policy endorsement and subsidy
Western City/County	Underground	Official but symbolic support
Hill City/County	Underground	Indirectly supported by public health officials
Declining		
Metro City/County	Underground	No official support
Conventional		
Declining		
Lake City/County	Officially endorsed	Supportive, except for some police harassment
River City/County	Underground	Briefly tolerated by street-level officials; then crackdown
Border City/County	None	Nonresponsiveness
South City/County	None	Nonresponsiveness
Growing		
Coastal City/County	None	Nonissue

Cities in bold have a professional, city manager government.

of symbolic affirmation through the endorsement of high-level officials but also in the form of more detailed information sharing and, even more important, resources. A program office for drug courts was established in the Justice Department in 1995, dedicated to helping localities plan, establish, and expand such courts. Federal funding specifically for drug courts grew from $12 million in 1995 to $40 million in 1999; previously, other federal funds directed to the states in block grant form were used to assist drug courts (Nolan 2001, 42). The importance of these federal resources is evident in many of the case study narratives presented here.

SUBCULTURAL EXPLANATION: NEEDLE-EXCHANGE PROGRAMS

The first part of this chapter showed that a community's handling of drug courts is shaped to some extent by community subculture, with unconventional communities providing a more favorable setting. For needle exchange, the impact of community subculture is even more dramatic. As table 7.2 shows, unconventional communities are markedly more receptive to needle-exchange programs than are conventional communities. NEPs exist in all five unconventional cities, and in two of them, official endorsement allows them to operate openly and receive public resources. In another city, the local government provides symbolic endorsement but is holding back from officially operating a program or providing direct assistance to the existing underground NEP until a change in state law makes that legal. By contrast, needle exchanges exist in only two of the five conventional cities. In one of those, the NEP is a small, underground operation; although it was originally tolerated by the police, higher-level public officials have since cracked down on its operations.

If anything, this skeletal overview understates the greater receptivity of unconventional communities to NEPs. Consider the dramatic case history of needle exchange in unconventional Valley County.

Valley County

It is a misdemeanor to possess a hypodermic needle without a prescription in this state, and it is illegal to provide hypodermic needles to others without a prescription. However, as early as 1991, Valley County officials were at odds with a conservative Republican state administration on this issue. That year, Valley County's assistant district attorney, Corey King, chose to drop charges against Gavin Lowe, who had been arrested for needle possession and distribution. Lowe, who had founded a national organization to prevent the spread of AIDS among intravenous drug users, publicly interpreted King's decision as approval of needle-exchange programs. The following year, King again dropped charges against a needle-exchange activist—this time, a public health worker who was also a participant in the voluntary NEP operating in the community. The public health worker's arrest had been a staged protest event— he had demanded that the police arrest him. But because of a similar case prosecuted in a nearby county, King was very much aware that jurors are sympathetic to defendants' claims that they break the law by necessity; in fact, jurors had even been known to join NEPs after hearing such arguments.

Despite the growing climate of sympathy for needle-exchange activists, the state's attorney general and the Republican governor opposed needle exchange on the grounds that it would condone drug use. In the fall of 1993, the governor vetoed legislation that would have legalized needle exchange, saying that NEPs undercut the message that people should not abuse drugs. The sponsor of the vetoed bill claimed that this was a case of political posturing in an election year.

Despite state officials' refusal to empower needle exchange through a

change in state law, several county officials signaled their support for the practice. In January 1994, the AIDS health services director asked the county health
department to endorse an NEP, arguing that the county should go beyond just
giving the green light to an underground, voluntary operation. In fact, he argued, the county ought to operate an exchange itself; by doing so, it could ensure that other elements of drug control were included, such as counseling.
Criminal justice officials were also supportive. Both police and prosecutors
avoided taking action against known needle-exchange operations.

In September 1994, the Valley County commission unanimously declared
the spread of HIV among injection drug users to be a local emergency—a declaration intended to provide legal cover for county health workers to operate
an NEP. The emergency declaration would have to be reissued every fourteen
days in order to sustain the legal authority to conduct a needle exchange. The
AIDS program at the county hospital was set to oversee the exchange, which
was expected to cost over $20,000 a year out of the hospital's AIDS budget.
However, the county program would initially serve only about 50 of the estimated 15,000 people injecting themselves with street drugs. The new program
absorbed an existing underground NEP run by volunteers, who were invited to
continue working with the county, without pay. The two-year-old volunteer
group already served about 40 drug users a week in Valley City's downtown,
each week swapping 500 to 600 potentially contaminated needles with clean
ones to limit the spread of HIV.

As with the privately run program, the county-run NEP was not likely to
be hassled by law enforcement. District Attorney King was quoted in a local
newspaper as stating that the law "is somewhat in flux right now," and the "police have taken the view that they have more important things to do than go
after health officials." At the county hearing on the matter, there was no opposition. A local newspaper quoted a county legislator, who explained, "There's
a lot of information out there about how well these programs work," and
"people in this community are just well-informed."

In December 1994, Valley County's NEP began operation, giving out clean
needles twice a week to drug addicts who brought in dirty ones. By the spring
of the following year, the county had incorporated the needle exchange into its
street operations against AIDS, using a van that appeared twice a week at
places far from residential neighborhoods. Information about these locations
was somewhat guarded; health workers worried about vigilantes, and addicts
were skittish or paranoid. The police seemed unlikely to go after the program,
however, especially since prosecutors considered such cases to be unwinnable.
The exchange drew 30 to 40 people each time, and they turned in 500 to 700
syringes an evening.

The Valley County exchange stayed in close touch with the city's police department. According to a police spokesman, the NEP caused no problems, and police viewed needle exchange as a public health rather than a law enforcement issue.

In the summer of 1995, however, Valley County's exchange was threatened by the action of the state attorney general, who issued an opinion that needle exchanges were illegal, despite local governments' use of "state of emergency" declarations. The attorney general ruled that state law allowed for no such gray areas but indicated that he did not intend to push the issue by cracking down on needle exchanges. The ruling was viewed as a form of political posturing being used by the attorney general to gain favor with conservative groups in the state.

A year later, the attorney general took a much harsher tone. In May 1996, he threatened to sue county legislators, or even jail them, if they persisted in operating needle exchanges. In light of this threat, Valley City legislators, by a vote of four to one, abruptly canceled public money for the NEP. They did, however, vow to change the state law that made operating such programs a felony. One county legislator was quoted in the local newspaper as saying, "I find it very exasperating to have another public office litigate us to try and prevent us from doing what is right for the health of the community." The chair of the county legislature explained that, given the prospect of felony charges, they had no choice. County legislators still held out hope that a private group would volunteer to continue the biweekly exchange.

In fact, the volunteer group that had previously run the NEP quietly started to do so again. A nationally recognized nonprofit group that helped fund NEPs nationwide gave the group a "start-up kit" of 10,000 syringes and needles to keep it running. It also gave the group a $5,000 grant, enough to purchase about 67,000 more needles. Although the volunteer group received no public funding, the county sent one person out to the needle-exchange site to pass out health literature, condoms, alcohol wipes, and bleach and to dispose of the used syringes. The county notified the attorney general's office that it planned to continue its involvement in public health efforts related to the needle exchange but would not be involved with the needles directly, which placated the attorney general.

In the years that followed, Valley County's voluntary NEP operated largely without controversy, with the indirect involvement of the county. Because public health officials worked in close proximity to the needle exchange and often had needles in their possession in order to conduct educational programs about the bleaching of used needles, the legality of their actions was questionable. Potential difficulties were averted when, in May 1999, the Valley City chief of police issued an order not to take enforcement action against AIDS program staff possessing hypodermic needles en route to or from the needle-exchange sites.

However, it was clear that the constraints on county involvement were limiting the operation. By September 1999, the NEP was reaching only about a third of the county's estimated 15,000 drug addicts, according to one health official, who also pointed out that 285 county residents had died from AIDS contracted through contaminated needles.

Nevertheless, as late as 1997, the governor's office was still resisting a change in the state law regarding needle exchange. That year, he refused to sign a bill that would have allowed city councils in four locations—including Valley City—to establish pilot NEPs for two years, to be evaluated by a state university. The governor was backed by the state's associations of police chiefs and law enforcement officers.

Finally, in 1999, the governor and the legislature reached a compromise that would legalize the underground NEPs being operated in Valley County and elsewhere. Under the agreement, cities and counties that authorized NEPs using emergency public health ordinances would be immune from prosecution. Valley County's health officer, one of many local advocates of needle exchange, said that he would recommend that the county legislature take an active role in funding and establishing an exchange program to take the place of the underground one that had been operating since the withdrawal of county funding in 1996.

Valley City's case dramatically illustrates the level of official commitment to needle exchange in that unconventional community. (Port City's similar, but less dramatic, case history is detailed in the appendix.) By contrast, consider Lake City, the only conventional city to institutionalize a needle-exchange program.

Lake City

In the early 1980s, the Lake City health department tried to create a needle-exchange program. The mayor at that time opposed needle exchange, and a dispute over changes in the city's ordinance involving the possession of syringes led to a stalemate. By the late 1980s, an underground NEP, run by a community activist named Cal Vann, was operating in an area containing a number of homeless shelters. Ultimately, Vann did not participate in policy-making activities that culminated in the city's adoption of an official NEP in the 1990s, although local newspapers credit his work with helping people recognize the need for such a program Instead, the key lobbying group for needle exchange was New Transitions, a nonprofit organization.

In 1996, the city council unanimously approved an NEP, which began operation on December 1. This program replaced one run by the parent agency of New Transitions, which had simply taught intravenous drug users how to disinfect used needles with bleach. New Transitions and another nonprofit organization, Latino Community Resources, now contract with the city to provide needle-exchange services, with funding from the state's AIDS foundation. Laminated cards issued by these two organizations exempt needle-exchange participants from the law against the possession of drug paraphernalia. The NEP run by New Transitions operates out of a thirty-five-foot van that parks at seven sites two times a week for two hours at a time. In addition to needle exchange, the mobile unit provides HIV services, hepatitis testing, and wound care. New Transitions has 1,300 registered participants. About 15 percent of its clients are tested for HIV, and about 15 percent are referred for drug treatment.

According to a city council member, key to the decision to officially support needle exchange were the efforts of the health department's deputy director. He and New Transitions staff succeeded in convincing at least one councilwoman to support the program. At a public hearing held on March 28, 1996, all the people who testified (nearly twenty) asked the council to amend the drug paraphernalia ordinance to permit needle-exchange participants to distribute syringes without a prescription. According to a councilman who is also a pastor, there was very little correspondence from the "faith community" on needle exchange, although another council member had heard Baptist pastors argue that it would only encourage people to use drugs. Overall, needle exchange was not a well-publicized issue, and there was no substantial protest against it, although neighborhood groups expressed concern about the location of the service because of the possibility of drug users spilling out into the neighborhoods.

In the years since, the NEP has operated with minimal city involvement and minimal controversy, although implementation involved some problems with the police, and funding has been an issue. With respect to the former, police officers acknowledge that, from their point of view, NEP participation should not be used as an excuse to violate the drug paraphernalia law. It is their opinion that exchange participants might simply sell the needles, and they report getting complaints about needles being found on school grounds. These comments, along with those of New Transitions staff, suggest that there has been some low-level police harassment, although New Transitions reports that none of its staff has actually been arrested in connection with the NEP. To alleviate tensions with the police, New Transitions works with the community relations departments of the local police precincts, providing them with copies of the protocol and the license that participants carry.

With respect to the funding issue, Lake City's NEP was in financial jeopardy in 1997. That year, its mayor joined with the mayors of four other cities to make a high-profile pitch to the Clinton administration to allow the use of federal funds for needle exchange, but that effort failed. Because the state's health bureaucracy was so reliant on federal funds, it could no longer provide funding for an NEP. Fortunately, Lake City's needle-exchange operators managed to solicit private donations, obviating an immediate need to turn to the city for funding. In the years since, however, New Transitions staff have continued low-level, long-term lobbying efforts to lay the groundwork for city funding. By 2000, the city had hired a new public health director, from a city that provides funding for a needle exchange. New Transitions staff was optimistic about his ability to get the city to spend money on needle exchange, but it seems that the issue is no longer on the city council's agenda. A recently elected council member was not even aware that the city had an NEP.

Comparison of Lake City's experience with that of Valley City/County and Port County illustrates how the subcultural differences outlined in table 7.2 are actually understated. Lake City, the only conventional city to officially sanction an NEP, is not nearly as supportive as either of the unconventional cities that not only officially sanction their NEPs but also provide funding and have fought for their programs in the face of hostility at the state level.

Similarly, although Western City and River City each have "underground" NEPs, the case narratives (see the appendix) reinforce the greater receptivity of unconventional Western City to needle exchange. Although the bottom-line status of needle exchange is the same in the two communities, Western City council members have twice voted to endorse a legalized NEP (contingent on a change in state law), and the mayor has gone on record in support of an NEP; by contrast, in conventional River City, public officials have either avoided the issue altogether or delegated the matter to lower-level officials such as the deputy mayor, whose personal enthusiasm is countered by the hostility of the public health director.

INSTITUTIONAL EXPLANATION: NEEDLE-EXCHANGE PROGRAMS

Given the strong pattern of greater support for NEPs in unconventional than conventional cities, what role can be expected for the institutional explanation? Consistent with the theoretical framework guiding this volume, we would expect NEPs to receive more support in politicized unconventional settings than in professionalized unconventional settings; conversely, NEPs should encounter stronger opposition in politicized conventional settings than in professionalized conventional settings. Table 7.2 offers no pattern to support such an expectation. Among unconventional communities, the pair with a professional chief executive has the same range of NEP outcomes as the three with politicized, mayoral arrangements. Among the conventional communities, the two with professional, city manager governments have policy stances that are at least as inhospitable to NEPs as the other conventional communities.

Thus, the most straightforward version of the institutional explanation is of no help here. There are obvious reasons for the limitation of such an explanation. One is that, in some localities, county government rather than or in addition to city government is involved in the needle-exchange issue. Where county and city government are merged, as they are in Port City, Western City, and Coastal City (i.e., there is no county chief executive or legislature separate from the city government), this is not a complication. But in other places, it can be, especially if the character of county institutions on the politicized-professionalized dimension is not the same as the character of city government. Another problem for the institutional explanation is that governing institutions other than the city council and the chief executive can be important sources of leadership or policy shaping on this issue, either dictating or counteracting the policy stance taken by the chief executive and city council. The latter is well illustrated by Hill City's experience.

Hill City

By 1994, Hill City was already several years into a low-level dispute over needle exchange. In 1991, the joint Hill City-County HIV commission had put its weight behind the concept of a needle-exchange program, suggesting that Hill City and Hill County establish one. But city and county officials apparently did not take up that call to action. In 1994, police officials continued to maintain that they could not legitimize such a program because it violated federal law. According to the local newspaper, the assistant police chief at the time acknowledged that AIDS activists had explicitly asked the police to empower an NEP by simply agreeing to ignore it. But, the police official said, "It's narcotics paraphernalia. It's illegal in this state, and before you could do something like this, it would require a change in state law. If they do it, they're subject to arrest, and they know that . . . we certainly don't want to be in a position of promoting narcotics usage, so we're against it for that reason."

In addition to the citizens on the HIV advisory board, there were other local officials who supported an NEP. For example, Pam Caraley, the director of an AIDS program at the joint city-county mental health and mental retardation unit, was also a volunteer with a community organization dedicated to AIDS education, and that organization was thinking about starting an NEP. The local newspaper cites Caraley as arguing, "We always keep saying that we're hoping to get one started, that we want to do something like that. The research shows it doesn't lead to increased [drug] use."

Although its origins are somewhat cloaked in secrecy, a semi-underground NEP has been started and continues to function in Hill City; it is not officially endorsed by the city government but receives unofficial support from several quarters. For example, a recently arrived official with the city-county health department indicated his awareness of the informal NEP operating in the city and mentioned that some of the staff members in the HIV unit had approached him about providing support for it. His comments suggest that he thinks an NEP is a good idea, and, within the constraints set by the illegality of drug paraphernalia distribution, his office is trying to be cooperative. He believes that they "should do everything that's legal to do." Currently, whatever relationship exists between his agency and the NEP is unofficial and informal. Some of the clients at the health department's clinic ask about the NEP, and staff members give out literature on it. But, he stresses, "we ourselves do not, by law, participate" in the actual NEP. It is his understanding that the needle exchange operates out of a van that goes to various locations to distribute clean needles. When he first arrived, he asked if the police allowed this and was told that if the activity did not create a nuisance or draw a lot of attention, the police would not bother it.

According to the city manager, however, Hill City is unlikely to endorse an official NEP. In part, this is because of existing state law. It is also because the police chief, who is very conservative and is currently dedicated to getting small-time crack dealers off the street, would not want to encourage it.

In Hill City, the subcultural context means that the community might be relatively receptive to an NEP, but with a city manager form of government, the community does not have a chief executive with the political incentive and high profile necessary to champion such an innovation, as the Western City mayor did. The story would end there were it not for the existence of a well-established public health bureaucracy whose leadership is dedicated to this innovation. Hence, the existence in Hill City of an underground NEP that gets at least indirect, informal support from public officials is attributable to a different form of leadership.

South City and Metro City

Although it functions in the opposite direction, the significance of the local public health establishment is also illustrated in South City. In 1994, needle exchange was the subject of protest activity in South City, where public health functions are handled by a joint city-county health department. That health department was the target of a protest organized by the local chapter of ACT-UP, a gay rights organization that wanted to call attention to what it viewed as the city's and county's inferior efforts with respect to HIV/AIDS education and prevention generally and the need for the health department to institute an NEP. At the time, however, a spokesperson for the health department was quoted in the local newspaper as indicating that the department had "no plans to launch a needle-exchange program."

In a discussion of the reasons for this refusal to pursue an NEP, the current public health director argues that there is no need for such an approach because statistics show that a relatively small proportion of the population is engaged in intravenous drug use. The 1994 decision not to respond to pressures for an NEP has been sustained ever since. According to the public health director, no individuals or groups in the community have advocated for it since 1994, nor is it something that the health department has advocated.

It is not at all clear that there are more intravenous drug users in Hill City than in South City. However, the opinion of both the former and the current South City public health directors is that other HIV risk factors are more important and that needle exchange is not really needed. It appears to be this rather than (or in addition to) any subculturally based pressure on the city's politicized chief executive that accounts for this community's failure to develop an NEP.

In a similar vein, the Metro City experience suggests that core city mayors who might otherwise support NEPs will pull back in the absence of strong support from public health authorities and elected officials at the county level. In 1995, a group of Metro City residents announced that they intended to start an underground NEP using private donations, primarily their own funds. These activists were acutely aware that needle exchange was against state law, but they believed that it would be futile to try to get the state legislature to change that law. A spokesperson for the activists was quoted by the local newspaper as stating that although they would prefer to have a legal program, they were not going to "wait around while people are dying." Interviews with various Metro City leaders and discussions with public health students at a Metro City University confirmed that such a program is under way.

On several occasions, representatives of the group running the NEP have approached top-level staff members in Mayor Lipton's office to discuss how the city could play a more open and supportive role in the program. The mayor has said that if the county commission approached him about an NEP, he would support it; however, the fact that the city does not have a health department (that is a county function here) limits what the city could do. There is no evidence that the Metro County health department is involved, although, like most health departments nationwide, it has a unit for the prevention of AIDS and sexually transmitted diseases. An assistant to the mayor indicates that if either of two local universities launched a pilot NEP, the police department would tolerate it.

ECONOMIC EXPLANATION: NEEDLE-EXCHANGE PROGRAMS

Economic considerations appear to be largely irrelevant to city decision making with respect to NEPs. On theoretical grounds, one might expect the more economically secure, growing communities to be more receptive to needle exchange than the declining cities for two reasons. First, declining cities have fewer resources, which are crucial for innovation. Second, and perhaps more important, are the city image issues. Public endorsement of an NEP is, after all, a public acknowledgment that there is an intravenous drug problem in the community—hardly an attractive characteristic. Hence, whereas the ample development assets of growing communities might enable them to ignore the risks of this dent in city image, declining cities' desperation for investment would presumably make them much less willing to do so.

However, table 7.2 shows that there is no evidence to support these expectations. As a set, the declining cities include one with an officially endorsed NEP, two with underground NEPs, and two with none; the growing communities include two with officially endorsed NEPs, two with underground NEPs, and one with none. This is hardly a strikingly different pattern. Furthermore, Coastal County, the only conventional community that is economically secure, has shown no interest in needle exchange, whereas the most economically distressed of all the conventional cities, Lake City, has endorsed an NEP. Its history shows that Lake City has encountered challenges in funding the NEP, but the program has been sustained nonetheless.

INTERGOVERNMENTAL EXPLANATION:
NEEDLE-EXCHANGE PROGRAMS

The intergovernmental context, in the form of state policy on needle exchange, is, in one sense, very important. Indeed, public officials in some of the study cities attributed their lack of an NEP primarily to state law prohibiting such a program. This is certainly the case in Border City. The idea for an NEP was proposed in the early 1990s, but city prosecutor Tony Cantwell explains that the proposal never even made it in front of a committee because law enforcement officials were so vocal in citing the laws restricting the possession of hypodermic needles and drug paraphernalia. The police officials argued that making an exception for needles given to drug addicts to prevent HIV infection would yield an unworkable law. As a result of this opposition, the idea was immediately dropped. Cantwell notes that "it was proposed on Monday and shot down on Tuesday and [has] never been heard of since. It died a very quick death." Similarly, a city council member explains that the city's official position is that NEPs can work and have proved to be effective, but there are legal barriers in the state to their use.

However, legal constraints at the state level cannot explain why some cities support needle exchange and others do not, because state-level legal constraints are present for all the study cities. Yet localities such as Valley County and Port City have defied these constraints and engaged in political battles that eventually led to changes in state policy. Other localities have taken a formal stance in favor of needle exchange and are currently working for change at the state level, and still others have found subtle ways to informally subvert state policy to allow the operation of underground NEPS. Finally, some localities have simply accepted that state laws prevent needle exchange.

CONCLUSION

There are a number of important parallels in these stories of local governments' adoption of two drug-related innovations, but the contrasts are instructive as well. Subcultural influences, for example, are important in both cases, but much more so for needle exchange than for drug courts. Drug courts have been established in conventional as well as unconventional places, and although their development lagged in conventional cities, the delay was of limited duration. An important difference involving the intergovernmental context may help explain the lesser significance of subcultural factors for localities' response to drug courts. The key here is the important role of the federal government in fostering drug courts, compared to the resistance of the federal government and the outright hostility of state governments to needle exchange. The availability of federal resources has leveled the playing field, empowering officials in communities that otherwise would not be favorably oriented to such an innovation to welcome drug courts; in contrast, state laws prohibiting the distribution of drug paraphernalia provide both an obstacle and a ready excuse for local officials in communities that would not welcome such an innovation in any case.

The second consideration that helps explain the capacity of conventional cities to approximate unconventional cities' response to drug courts is the character of the innovation itself. In contrast with NEPs, drug courts have both a tough, authoritative side and a caring, rehabilitative side. Indeed, this "unique combination of a therapeutic perspective with the continued exercising of state control contributes to the drug court's broad appeal. . . . Judges are cognizant of which aspects of the drug courts play well to which audiences and do their best to emphasize particular features accordingly" (Nolan 2001, 53). NEPS, in contrast, put all the emphasis on a therapeutic approach and thus constitute a much more blatant challenge to the moral values of those who see drug use as sinful. Hence, politicians in conventional cities are seriously constrained from pursuing needle exchange by the traditional values and moral stances that are an essential part of that subculture. But with drug courts, political actors in conventional settings can more easily finesse the issue so that the affront to traditional values is minimized.

8
A Contingent Approach to Understanding Morality Politics

The preceding chapters explored the role of subcultural, economic, institutional, and intergovernmental explanations for local government's stance on five different morality issues. That exploration has generated an interesting pattern of conclusions. Those conclusions, and their implications, are the focus of this chapter.

Perhaps the most obvious conclusion is that the various explanations are not equally relevant for each morality issue topic. Table 8.1, which summarizes the results, shows this clearly. City subculture, for example, is crucial for understanding differences in these cities' handling of drug issues, gay rights, and abortion; it is not particularly useful for understanding differences in their handling of the sex industry or gambling. Meanwhile, an explanation keyed to economic considerations is critical for understanding the sex industry and gambling and, to a lesser extent, gay rights; economic considerations do not appear to play a role in cities' handling of abortion-related conflict or the pair of drug issues considered in this volume.

Before delving further into a discussion of the other differences and the strengths and weaknesses of the various explanations, it is important to acknowledge that the unequal role these explanations play, based on the topic, has important implications for conceptualization and theory building with respect to morality politics. Clearly, morality issues are not all the same. They are not driven by the same dynamics nor shaped by the same factors.

Some scholars of morality politics would find this unsurprising. At least one distinction among morality issues has already received widespread recognition—a distinction between contentious and consensus morality issues. Contentious morality issues feature closely divided public opinion, whereas consensus-type morality issues are ones in which a clear majority is on one side of the issue (Mooney and Lee 2000). In a related vein, Meier (1999) draws a distinction between morality issues that fit a "sin" politics scenario and those that involve "redistributive" politics. In the former, the issue is defined in such

Table 8.1 Evidence Supporting the Major Explanations of Morality Policy
Stance, by Morality Issue

	Drug Courts/ Needle Exchange	Gay Rights	Sexually Explicit Business	Abortion Clinics	Casino Gambling
Subcultural	Yes	Yes	No	Yes	No
Institutional	No	Yes[a]	No	No	Some
Economic	No	Some	Yes	No	Yes
Intergovernmental	No	Yes[a]	No	Yes	Yes

[a]For unconventional cities only.

a way that there is only one legitimate side to the issue; "no one is willing to stand up for sin" (683), and "opposition is the equivalent of joining the other side at Armageddon" (685). For morality issues of the redistributive type, alternative frames allow the existence of competing sides, each with the legitimacy to generate substantial support (685).

The distinction between consensus, or sin, morality policy and contentious, or redistributive, morality policy is potentially very important. Meier (1999), for example, notes that the politics of sin leads to poorly designed policy. The one-sided character of a sin issue means that policy making ignores compromise, bypasses expertise and analysis, and does not take misperceived preferences into account (686). In contrast, when a morality issue is redistributive in character, "opposition may prevent the rapid escalation of policy in a direction with little prospect of success" (686). Meanwhile, Mooney and Lee (2000, 233) find that different factors shape morality policy making for contentious and consensus issues. On a morality issue of the contentious sort, policy outcomes reflect majority public opinion (even though the majority may be a slim one); on a morality issue of the consensus sort, policy outcomes are driven by the ideological stance of party activists rather than by public opinion.

But does the distinction between contentious (or redistributive) policy and consensus (or sin) policy provide a useful basis for understanding the results generated in this volume? Initially, this might seem like a promising path to pursue. The topics considered include ones that have been used to exemplify contentious morality issues (abortion, gay rights), ones that have been used to exemplify consensus morality issues (drug issues), and issues that have yet to be categorized. This seems to invite consideration of whether the pattern of performance of the subcultural, institutional, economic, and intergovernmental explanations hinges on whether the policy at issue is a contentious or a consensus one.

On closer inspection, however, the distinction between contentious and consensus morality policy is problematic. For one thing, whereas the distinction seems clear at the conceptual level, when one attempts to distinguish real-world issues on these grounds, the results can be murky. How one-sided does opinion have to be for an issue to be considered a consensus one? Based on the World Values Survey items that Smith and Tatalovich (2003) use in their exploration of redistributive morality policy, the 54 percent to 46 percent split in the United States (in 1995) between those who say that homosexuality is never justified and those who say it is sometimes or always justified seems to place the gay rights topic squarely in the contentious policy issue category; meanwhile, the 74 percent who say that using illicit drugs is "never justified" seems to place this topic in the consensus category. However, it is unclear whether the 61 percent who say that prostitution is "never justified" is enough of a dominant majority to make this a consensus issue; yet the nearly two-thirds majority on one side of the issue seems too much for this to be characterized as contentious. Hence, as Mooney and Lee (2000, 226) acknowledge, "there is a continuum . . . rather than a categorical shift from consensus to contentious."

Dividing issues into contentious and consensus ones is further complicated by the fact that, for any given topic, a variety of issue definitions is possible. For example, gay rights at the local level encompasses issues ranging from whether an antidiscrimination ordinance should be adopted to how local officials deal with gay pride events to whether local governments should adopt legislation that provides the same benefits (such as health care coverage) for gay and lesbian couples as is provided for spouses. Although there appears to be something like a consensus at the national level on civil rights for homosexuals, public opinion is much more divided on whether homosexuality is morally acceptable, and it is even less favorable when people are asked their general opinion of gays and lesbians as a group (Smith and Tatalovich 2003, 224–45).

If we attempt to define a policy topic more narrowly and precisely, however, we might miss the evolving character of the topic as activists and issue entrepreneurs attempt to frame the issue in a way that is to their advantage. Meier (1999, 685), for example, notes that most issues "have the potential to be transformed from the politics of sin to the politics of redistribution simply because most policy issues are multidimensional. . . . The key issue is framing and whether or not one group is successful in framing the issue as one of sin."

Not surprisingly, then, national public opinion on a number of morality topics has changed over time as different dimensions of the issue have been emphasized by issue entrepreneurs and as activists have transformed the issue by linking it to other issues. For this reason, Mooney and Lee (2000) are able to contrast the politics surrounding a contentious policy issue with the politics surrounding a consensus policy issue while focusing on a single topic—the death penalty—but at different times. In short, even if a policy topic is defined more specifically, its categorization as a contentious or consensus issue is up for grabs because of the potential for change over time.

Because the analyses in this volume focus on a fairly narrow time frame (the latter half of the 1990s), major changes in issue definition are less likely than they would be for a longer-term study. For analyses of morality issues at the local level, however, there is a practical problem that dwarfs the substantial complexities of contentious and consensus issues. That problem is the lack of consistent and comparable poll data (in many cases, the lack of any poll data) to assess the contours of public opinion on these topics at the local level. Presumably, aggregate public opinion at the national level masks substantial differences in public opinion in different places. But without city-specific opinion poll data, it is not possible to classify issues into the consensus and contentious categories on a city-by-city basis.

Given these complexities and impracticalities, the discussion here must forgo any reliance on the conceptual distinction between consensus (sin) and contentious (redistributive) issues. In some ways, this is just as well. If morality issues are so multidimensional and open to framing effects that any one of them can be a consensus issue at one time or place and a contentious issue at some other time or place, then complexity truly begins to overwhelm our capacity to draw general conclusions about any morality topic, let alone to compare the politics of different morality topics. It is this latter task—comparing the politics of different morality topics (defined on somewhat broad, substantive grounds)—that is invited by the results in table 8.1.

PURE MORALITY VERSUS MATERIAL MORALITY POLICIES

Is there a categorization of these morality policy topics that can provide a theoretically satisfying account of the results in table 8.1? A combination of induction and deduction suggests that there is such a categorization, one that distinguishes pure morality issues from material morality issues. Pure morality issues are ones in which the competing sides and the competing issue frames they offer are all grounded in morals rather than material benefits or economic stakes. Material morality issues, in contrast, are ones in which there is a clash between morals and money. That is, the competing sides and their issue frames include both morals-based interests and at least one side with economic stakes in the issue, typically industry groups.

For the topics considered in this volume, two (gambling and sexually explicit businesses) fit squarely into the material morality category. Only the opponents of gambling frame the issue as a moral one, focusing on the sinfulness of an activity that stems from character weakness and destroys family values. On the other side are gambling industry forces with economic stakes in the issue, especially casino executives and investors, who argue for the benefits of an activity that will bring tax revenue and economic development to communities. Similarly, the issue of sexually explicit businesses evokes moral outrage from those who see it as sleaze, smut, and indecency. On the other side are two kinds of proponents—those who frame the issue in terms of free speech values and, more important here, industry forces (owners of nude dancing clubs, X-rated theaters, and the like) who have economic stakes in the issue and who frame it not only in terms of freedom of expression but also in terms of economic contributions to the community through licensing and tax revenues and attractiveness to convention and tourism efforts.

The topics considered in this volume also include some that exemplify pure morality issues—drug courts and needle exchange, and access to abortion and the associated issue of protest at abortion clinics. In principle, one might imagine some industry forces or other entities that have economic stakes in these issues; most notable are abortion providers and perhaps drug treatment providers, who might gain city contracts and client referrals if government policy turned away from the criminal model of drug use and toward a more medical-therapeutic one. However, economic stakeholders are not essential to these issues in the way that they are for casinos or nude dancing clubs. And, as the case histories in this volume illustrate, the unfolding of controversies over these issues has involved a host of morality frames about the rightness or wrongness of abortion, the free speech rights of protesters, whether clean needles and drug treatment alternatives to imprisonment unduly weaken the message of the evil of drug use, and so forth. In short, these issues have little or nothing to do about economic self-interests.

The topic of gay rights is somewhat more difficult to define as either a pure morality or a material morality issue. In part, the problem arises because the cluster of issues involving gay rights at the local level includes some (e.g., anti-discrimination ordinances) that do not appear to entail industry forces as economic stakeholders and others (e.g., domestic partner benefits) that verge into economic territory, especially if the framing of the issue involves matters such as the cost of health care benefits. Even more important, economic stakes can be a subtle (or not so subtle) frame for any of these gay rights issues because gay-friendly city policies have been linked to success in attracting business investment, especially high-tech business. In their case study of conflict in conservative Williamson County, Texas, over the granting of tax breaks to a high-

Table 8.2 Evidence Supporting the Major Explanations of Morality Policy Stance, by Morality Issue and Type

	Pure Morality Issues		Material Morality Issues		Hybrid
	Drug Courts/ Needle Exchange	Abortion Clinics	Sexually Explicit Business	Casino Gambling	Gay Rights
Subcultural	Yes	Yes	No	No	Yes
Economic	No	No	Yes	Yes	Some

tech company (Apple Computer) that provided domestic partner benefits to its employees, Chong and Marshall (1999, 91) explicitly note the ways in which both morality and economic stakes can be involved. Because the economic stakeholders on gay rights issues are not industry forces per se, but rather taxpayers and their government representatives, whose interests are community growth and solvency, gay rights is a bit of a hybrid.

Table 8.2 extracts some of the evidence presented in table 8.1, reorganized in light of the distinction between pure morality and material morality issues. The table highlights a key finding of this study involving a trade-off between the subcultural explanation and the economic explanation. For pure morality issues, subcultural differences are of substantial importance in accounting for different city responses, but the economic explanation is of no utility; by contrast, for material morality issues, the economic explanation "works," and the expected pattern of variation in city responses by subculture does not emerge.

Stated another way, subcultural differences are very important for our understanding of morality issues, *unless they are eclipsed by economic considerations.* This does not occur on a random basis. Rather, it appears that economic considerations supplant the subcultural explanation only when industry forces have clear-cut material stakes in the issue or when an issue has strong implications for the community's economic development. Chong and Marshall (1999, 116) criticized scholars' tendency to view morality conflicts as "involving essentially symbolic issues and to separate them analytically from economic conflicts over material outcomes." These results suggest that Chong and Marshall are partly correct. Morality issues can involve a conflict between economics and morality, and on issues such as gay rights, gambling, and sexually explicit businesses, economic considerations can be as important as or more important than the moral considerations that are reflected in subcultural differences. However, not all morality issues evoke material stakeholders. For some of these issues, competing frames focus solely on social norms, religious values, and the other "symbolic" matters to which Chong and Marshall refer.

This contingent view of the importance of subcultural and economic considerations has an important bearing on the responsiveness of local morality policy. On the basis of their study of morality policies in several postindustrial countries (including the United States), Smith and Tatalovich (2003, 11) concluded that "the content of morality policy is non-representative of public opinion," and "morality policy is rule by elites—not the people." This claim is quite startling. Scholars of the responsiveness of national-level public policy to mass public opinion in the United States have long noted that responsiveness is highly likely on the types of morality issues considered here, in large part because of the presumed salience of such issues to the general public (Page and Shapiro 1983, 181; Geer 1996). Likewise, scholarship on specific morality issues at the state level has been dominated by findings of consistency between public policy and majority public opinion. Norrander and Wilcox (1999), for example, found that states' abortion policies are closely aligned with public opinion. This clash of conclusions about the responsiveness or nonresponsiveness of morality policy to public opinion at the national and state levels sets the stage for a similar question at the local level.

This study does not examine variation in mass public opinion per se. Instead, it focuses on differences in cities' subcultures, measured in terms of the different clusters of demographic variables that divide communities into those where particular population groups and the nontraditional lifestyles and values they represent are relatively prominent, versus those dominated by population groups associated with traditional lifestyles and conventional values. For pure morality issues, there is clear consistency between community subculture and the policy stances taken by local officials. But should this be interpreted as being the equivalent of responsiveness to the general public?

The answer, I believe, is yes. To some extent, however, this answer clashes with prevailing interpretations of morality politics. Although the variables used here to conceptualize conventional versus unconventional culture are sometimes used in studies of morality policy making at the state level (and occasionally at the local level), they are typically not used as proxies for mass public opinion. More frequently, they are introduced as indicators of interest-group strength or potential mobilization. In his study of variation in the stringency of pornography regulation at the state level, for example, Smith (2001, 193) treats the percentage of a state's population that is Catholic and the percentage belonging to a Protestant fundamentalist denomination as reflecting the degree to which each of these groups can "use the political process to redistribute its values." Similarly, Haider-Markel and Meier (1996, 336) explicitly view the prevalence of gays and lesbians in the population as a "potential political resource" for gay and lesbian interest groups; lacking state-level information on that factor for the year of their study, they used another indicator of interest-group potential that, in the context of this study, might have served as an indicator of unconventional culture—the number of gay bars, businesses, and newspapers per 1 million population.

I believe, however, that the prevalence of gays in a community, or of churches or church adherents in general or Protestant fundamentalists in particular, may or may not translate into mobilization by organizations advocating on their behalf. In communities where one or the other of these population groups is prevalent, however, they will be notable components of local officials' constituencies, as well as important elements in shaping the local subculture as either unconventional or conventional. To the extent that the policy stances taken by local officials are consistent with the principles and constraints of that local subculture, I believe that it makes more sense to interpret the match as responsiveness to the public (in the sense of responsiveness to prevailing, subculturally defined values) rather than responsiveness to elite special interests. Like Mooney and Lee (2001, 182), we can thus conclude that "the values held by citizens are well reflected in pure morality policy, whether through religious affiliation or political ideology."

But this is true only for pure morality issues. For material morality issues, the picture is quite different and more consistent with Smith and Tatalovich's (2003) claims. Local policy on these material morality issues appears to be elite-dominated, in the sense that the policy stance is shaped by industry interests with economic stakes rather than by responsiveness to the local subculture.

THE TROUBLE WITH INSTITUTIONS

In addition to the economic and cultural explanations, a straightforward version of institutional theory, with a long heritage in urban scholarship, guided this inquiry. The institutional explanation is based on the distinction between cities with governing arrangements that are "reformed" (city managers as chief executives and at-large elections) and those with "nonreformed" governing arrangements (directly elected mayors and district elections). Because of the greater accessibility and more politicized character of the latter, compared with the more insulated and professional character of the former, there were strong grounds for expecting that these differences would influence cities' handling of morality issues, just as they have long been theorized to affect overall expenditures, economic development activities, and many other urban policy outcomes.

But as table 8.1 shows, the institutional explanation does not fare very well. For only two of the policy topics is there any evidence that institutional differences had the theorized impact. And even in those cases, institutional differences were of limited importance. With respect to gay rights, for example, there is evidence of politicized chief executives (mayors) being more likely than professionalized city managers to drive the city's policy stance in a direction consistent with the city's subculture, but this pattern is evident only in unconventional cities, not conventional ones. And in the gambling case, we saw that the lack of a strong mayor to spearhead efforts to transform casinos from moral anathema to economic salvation can deter a conventional city from pursuing casino development, but this institutional issue of a leadership vacuum was not relevant among the unconventional cities.

There are a number of ways to interpret the weakness of the institutional explanation. Most simply, we can acknowledge that other empirical studies on the impact of differences in local governing structure have yielded conflicting findings (Benton 2002b). Thus, the results here might be viewed as simply one more addition to the set of studies concluding that differences in institutional arrangements do not matter, which is countered by an equally substantial set of studies finding the opposite.

Another possibility is that, for morality issues (much more so than for other issues), public officials may take positions on the basis of personal, moral convictions rather than the usual political imperatives and constraints associated with their roles. There are indeed hints of this sort of thing in the case histories examined in this volume. At least one informant in River City interpreted the mayor's accommodating stance on abortion clinic protest as a reflection of his strong Catholic beliefs and Catholic seminary experience. And Western City's black mayor changed from opposition to support of a needle-exchange program after being personally moved by evidence of children contracting HIV from their drug-abusing mothers. Political institutions are typically said to matter because they carry incentives for certain behaviors and disincentives for others; they reduce uncertainty in the decision-making process, and they "provide stability in collective choices that otherwise would be chaotic (Clingermayer and Feiock 2001, 3). But if individual moral convictions based on personal characteristics and experience are the driving force behind officials' positions on morality issues, idiosyncratic factors would undercut the patterns expected on the basis of institutional incentives and disincentives.

Yet another possibility is that we should interpret the weak performance of the institutional explanation in the same light as the growing chorus of analysts who have begun to challenge the meaningfulness of the distinction between reformed and nonreformed institutions of city government. This chorus includes a number of voices pointing out the growing hybridization of cities' governing institutions, such as the trend toward the introduction of at least some district council seats into otherwise reformed city governments and the addition of city manager–like chief administrative officers to city governments with directly elected mayors (Frederickson and Johnson 2001; Frederickson, Wood, and Logan 2001). This blurring of the distinction between reformed and nonreformed city government pushes institutional analysis based on that distinction toward irrelevance.

Still other critics have challenged the theoretical premises behind the approach that undergirds so much urban institutional analysis. As noted earlier, the core theoretical premise is that cities having more politicized institutions, such as directly elected mayors, will be more responsive to a variety of demands and pressures from the public than are cities with professional and insulated city manager–type governments. Hence, cities with more politicized institutions (i.e., nonreformed governments) are conventionally hypothesized to tax and spend more, undertake a broader array of economic development efforts, and the like. Consistent with that premise, the analysis in this volume has been guided by the expectation that mayors (and, to a lesser extent, council members elected by districts) are more likely to take policy stances on morality issues that are responsive to the community's prevailing subculture. Campbell and Turnbull (2003), however, shift the attention from the politicized-professional dimension to the fact that mayor-council government involves a separation of legislative and executive powers, while council-manager government does not. When this dimension of difference between nonreformed and reformed government is the basis for theorizing, the usual hypotheses (e.g., the expectation of greater spending by nonreformed governments) do not make sense. Instead, Campbell and Turnbull (2003, 24) argue that the separation of powers, by itself, may lead to either higher or lower spending. More specifically, they argue: "If the separation of powers successfully introduces checks and balances that increase the responsiveness of both the administration and council to voters' demands, then it is likely to curb expansionary tendencies of the public bureaucracy and lead to lower spending. On the other hand, the separation of powers typically gives the executive specific agenda control or veto powers in the budgetary process. Agenda control and veto power change the decision-making dynamics in ways that are difficult to predict" (24).

In effect, these writers are suggesting that if the key difference in the institutions of local governance is whether there is separation of powers, predictions about the impact on expenditures become nearly impossible. And if spending outcomes are highly contingent on the vagaries of how mayors choose to take advantage of their powers vis-à-vis the city council, there is even less hope that we can find clear-cut patterns of the impact of these institutional powers on morality policy decisions.

Perhaps the most important reason for the weakness of the institutional explanation in this study is that the distinction between reformed and non-reformed institutions of general-purpose city government simply does not begin to encompass the variety of other local governing institutions that are involved in decision making about the morality issues of interest here. In particular, it is clear from the case histories that a variety of county officials, such as county legislators, district attorneys, public health officials, and judges, may be involved.

Unfortunately, the state of theorizing and empirical research about these county-level institutions is too limited to offer a useful analytical hook. In fact, very little research of any kind has been done on county governing institutions. As Benton (2002a, 4) notes, "Scholars have viewed county government as an inconsequential part of local government and therefore have largely ignored them as subjects of study." The relatively small body of research that does focus on the institutional arrangements of county government tends to adopt the same reformed versus nonreformed distinction that dominates research on city government. The result is theoretically unsatisfying, because the meaning of "reform" for county governments is not the same as it is for city governments. For example, Schneider and Park's (1989) study of the expenditure patterns of county governments found that county governments with either appointed professional executives or elected chief executives spent more and performed more functions than did traditional county commission governments (which are characterized by a small number of legislators who also perform executive functions by committee). DeSantis and Renner (1994, 291) note that since "reform" of county government involves a move away from the commission type to one with a unified executive, Schneider and Park's results might be construed as being inconsistent with the long-held view that reformed governments spend less than nonreformed ones. Indeed, DeSantis and Renner (1994, 291) note that "the reformed county type that had the highest expenditures (county-executive) follows the same basic blueprint as the unreformed city type (mayor-council)," a result that leads them to conclude that "reformed county structures are correlated with policy outputs in the opposite direction of reformed municipal structures." But the apparent inconsistency is really a manifestation of the different meanings of "reform" for city and county governments.

Of course, this semantic confusion could be avoided by focusing more explicitly on the institutional features at issue for both city and county governments (i.e., appointed professional chief executive versus directly elected chief executive), ditching the rhetoric of reform altogether. Theorizing that distinguishes the institutional imperatives facing directly elected, politicized chief executives from appointed, professionalized executives could then be applied in the same fashion to officials from either level of government. But this does not fully solve the problem either. As noted earlier, some analysts are beginning to argue that other dimensions of difference in governing arrangements (e.g., separation of powers versus unitary systems) are more important than the difference between professional and political management (Campbell and Turnbull 2003).

Finally, even if there were agreement on the primacy of an analytical focus on professionalized versus politicized chief executives, there is still the challenge posed by the fact that the institutional arrangements of city government are nested within the county institutional context. The institutional context for decision making about many of these morality issues is thus a set of potentially complex amalgams. One possible amalgam is a city government with a professional city manager functioning within a county that has a directly elected county executive, along with one or more other directly elected officials, such as the district attorney or judges. Another possible amalgam is a city government with a directly elected mayor situated within a county that has an appointed, professional county manager, but again with a number of directly elected county offices. There are numerous other possibilities as well, including the situation in which the core city and the county are consolidated into a single entity.

Unfortunately, neither logic nor existing theory provides much help in framing our expectations about the impact of these various combinations on policy making of any kind, let alone decision making about morality issues in particular. There is, of course, a substantial body of research and theory on interlocal relations among municipalities—a body of research organized around the competing frameworks of public choice theory's diagnosis of the benefits of competition among municipalities in a fragmented metropolis and metropolitan reform theory's claims about the problems of fragmentation and the benefits of consolidation. However, research on city-county relationships is in its infancy, focuses primarily on competitive versus cooperative spending patterns, and does not include the character of governing institutions as an explanatory variable (Park 1997).

In sum, the key reason for the weakness of the institutional explanation in this volume is that so many different institutions are potentially relevant in morality issue decision making. Because these institutions involve complex arrangements of municipal institutions nested within a county government context, we lack a theoretical framework to account for the impact of these highly variegated institutional arrangements.

INTERGOVERNMENTAL CONTEXT

Ironically, if a major problem of the institutional explanation is the sheer diversity of relevant institutions (and the lack of theory on the impact of different combinations of these institutions), an important consideration for evaluating the intergovernmental explanation is the lack of variation. That is, for a number of the issues considered in this volume, the character of the opportunities and constraints set by state and federal policy action is largely the same for all large cities. This fundamental uniformity cannot help explain the diversity in cities' policy stances on those issues.

This is not to deny that the actions of the federal government and the states are very important in setting the context for local government action on morality issues. For example, Supreme Court decisions on obscenity and protected access to abortion clinics set a legal framework that empowers and constrains all local governments in their choices about prosecuting vendors of sexually explicit material and their decisions about managing abortion clinic protest. The federal government has been highly supportive of drug court development, providing information and funding in an effort to jump-start the diffusion of this policy innovation. Meanwhile, throughout the country, state laws on the possession and distribution of intravenous drug paraphernalia constitute a significant constraint on local governments' adoption of needle-exchange programs. Although these and a number of other federal and state laws and policies are an important part of the context within which local officials act, the resources and constraints they represent are more or less the same everywhere. They cannot, therefore, help explain differences in how localities deal with morality issues.

But when there *is* substantial variation in the intergovernmental context for decision making, an explanation keyed to that variation *does* help account for differences in local officials' policy stances. This was clearly the case with respect to abortion and gambling. There are notable variations across state governments in the restrictiveness of abortion policy, and whereas some states have explicitly refused to authorize casino gambling, others have adopted local option arrangements that empower city officials to move ahead with casinos. For these policy topics, the pattern of variation in local governments' stances is generally what would be expected on the basis of either the clash or the consistency between local subculture and state policy.

TOWARD THE FUTURE

This exploration of local government and morality policy ends with largely contingent conclusions. Either subculture or economics (but usually not both) can make a difference in how local officials respond to these issues, depending on whether the issue is a pure morality one or a material morality one. Likewise, only when there is variation in the intergovernmental context, typically represented by differences in state policy with respect to an issue, does the intergovernmental explanation contribute to our understanding of differences in local governments' policy stances. But on a number of morality issues, there is more uniformity than variation in the state policy context. These contingent conclusions are, I believe, an important step forward in understanding the differences in U.S. localities' approach to these issues.

By the same token, it is important to acknowledge the theoretical and empirical challenges that remain. The complexities of governance issues that involve both city and county actors, for example, underscore the limitations of institutional analyses that rely solely on distinctions in the character of either city or county institutions. These complexities also underscore the need for theoretical development concerning the bases for either cooperation or competition between city and county government; this theorizing will need to go beyond the usual thinking about service delivery and growth issues that underlies the debate about interlocal relationships among municipalities.

Finally, the generalizability of the conclusions drawn here might be questioned because of the limitations of a ten-city study. As noted in chapter 2, there is an inevitable tension between the comparative case study approach used here and the quantitative, "large N" approach. Nevertheless, it is possible to learn a great deal from only ten study cities, as the work of Browning, Marshall, and Tabb (1984) and other classic works have shown. Whether the patterns observed for the cities in this volume are as robust as the findings from other comparative case study analyses remains to be seen.

Appendix
Additional Case Narratives

ABORTION

Metro City: Pointed Neutrality

In Metro City, the abortion issue has not been prominent at the local level in recent years, but two abortion-related incidents provide a glimpse of local officials' staunch efforts to remain neutral on this issue. In 1996, the bombing of an abortion clinic just outside the city limits drew a response from Metro City officials. Police and other safety officials met with the operators of abortion clinics as a precaution to inform them of increased security measures that should be taken in the aftermath of the bombing.

In 1999, however, local officials took action that was, though ostensibly neutral, a blow to pro-choice advocates and at least symbolically reassuring to antiabortion forces, until it was overturned by the federal court. The Metro City transit authority refused to sell ad space to an abortion rights group that wanted to place advertisements in its trains, buses, and stations. A spokesman for the transit agency said that it has a policy against running ads on either side of a controversial issue. A group of about twenty women from the National Abortion Federation protested outside the transit authority's largest downtown station, claiming that their First Amendment right to free speech was being violated by the agency's refusal to run the ad. The group subsequently filed suit in district court, and in 2000, a federal judge ruled in favor of the protesters. As part of the settlement, the transit authority agreed to pay $100,000 in attorneys' fees to the abortion rights group and to advertise the group's message in 500 spaces inside buses, trains, bus shelters, and rail stations. To avoid such controversies in the future, the transit authority has changed its advertising policy and no longer accepts public-service advertisements from any group.

South City: Caught in the Middle

In South City, there are three abortion clinics. One is operated by Planned Parenthood, which also serves as an advocacy organization on the pro-choice side.

Reflecting the strong role of religion in this area, the local chapter of Planned Parenthood does not limit itself to a distinctively secular approach; it has sponsored worship services at a local church to commemorate the anniversary of the passage of *Roe v. Wade*. The South City chapter of the National Organization for Women, which has long been involved in providing escorts for women going to abortion clinics, joined in a nationwide call for the investigation of antiabortion clinic attacks as a terrorist conspiracy.

On the pro-life side, the community has a high-profile organization, Families for Responsible Living (FRL), dedicated to family values generally. It has been active in opposing abortion as well as homosexuality and pornography. The organization began distributing "voter guides" in 1991, featuring information about which candidates support prayer in the public schools, believe in the right to life of fetuses, and similar Christian right positions. A member of FRL's board currently serves as a county commissioner. In addition to this multi-issue organization, the pro-life side is represented in South City by at least three organizations dedicated to the abortion issue specifically—the local affiliates of two statewide right-to-life organizations and the local Committee for an Abortion-Free South City. Typically, these organizations "spread their message through mail-outs, fair exhibits and at the annual Walk for Life observed locally" every year.

Not surprisingly, then, this community is the site of relatively frequent protest activity, involving either antiabortion activists outside of clinics or activists on both sides of the issue at more general demonstration events. There is disagreement about the character of the protest activity at abortion clinics. The police chief describes it as being relatively small-scale and tame, and a Christian right activist depicts recent abortion protest at the city's clinics as something that does not involve confrontation. She knows many of the people involved in the "sidewalk counseling" and knows "how committed they are to not breaking any law." To her knowledge, none of the pro-life sidewalk counselors has ever been arrested. "Now, there's a lot of verbiage exchanged by the clinic owner and sidewalk counselors," she acknowledges, but that is all. When police have been called to the clinic, they simply caution both sides. Similarly, in describing the regular Saturday protests at the Planned Parenthood clinic, a key organizer of that activity was quoted in the local newspaper as claiming, "As far as confronting them [clients and clinic escorts] that's not what we want to do. We just want them to do their thing, and we do our thing."

By contrast, the director of one of the city's abortion clinics describes protesters as being much more aggressive and involved in illegal activities. She describes them as "screaming at everybody and blocking the drives" and says that when patients come in the evening and park in the lot across the street, the protesters "run over there and open the patients' car doors, causing some to drive off in fear." "It's just so intimidating, when you've got three or four people running up at you and throwing things at you and calling you baby killer or murderer."

However, this clinic director does not ask for police involvement. She explains, "I've given up on calling the police." According to her, when the police come, they say, "It's your word against theirs." By the time the police get there, the protesters are behaving peacefully. Furthermore, the patients being hassled would have to file complaints, which they would prefer not to do because it would compromise their privacy.

In 1992, two of South City's abortion clinics were vandalized, apparently by abortion protesters who sprayed noxious-smelling butyric acid into the clinics. In 1993, four individuals were arrested for trespassing after they chained themselves to a fence outside one of the city's abortion clinics. In March 1995, the four were found guilty of criminal trespass by a local jury and sentenced to the maximum penalty of thirty days in jail plus a $50 fine after they refused the judge's initial determination that they would be placed on probation if they agreed to perform community service and pay restitution of $125 each to the clinic. Both of these protest events appear to be unusually high profile and aggressive by South City standards, as evidenced by the fact that they are mentioned as touchstones by so many different informants, including a Planned Parenthood official, the police chief, the director of another abortion clinic, and a county commissioner.

Tensions around South City abortion clinics heightened noticeably in the wake of the abortion clinic shootings in Pensacola, Florida, in July 1994. The director of one of South City's clinics received death threats that she took seriously. The director of another clinic, which had already installed a fence and hired its own security guards, admitted that she asked the police department to tap the clinic's telephones, to intercept any telephoned threats, and that the police had done so. A high-ranking South City police official indicated that, in the wake of developments in Pensacola, he put his officers on alert. The South City police and fire departments and local prosecutors also joined with FBI and ATF (Alcohol, Tobacco, and Firearms) officials in a task force formed in August to deal with a potential conspiracy to incite clinic violence.

At the end of December 1994, abortion clinic shootings in Brookline, Massachusetts, once again evoked security concerns at South City abortion clinics, and at least one clinic administrator, Jane Galway, intended to request that federal marshals be assigned. Even before that request was processed, however, local police heightened their alert posture. Galway acknowledges that police cars cruised by the clinics on a regular basis. The U.S. attorney for the district explained in a local newspaper interview that, "clearly, the police department provides the first line of support . . . and they have agreed to notify the FBI and our office if there appears to be a violation of federal law." Within about three weeks, Galway backed off from her initial decision to request federal marshals, explaining that the clinic would beef up its own security instead.

In the aftermath of the bombing of an abortion clinic in Birmingham, Alabama, abortion clinic administrators in South City were once again mobilized in January 1998. Abortion clinic administrators and police officials acknowledge that the police once again escalated patrols near the clinics. In short, local law enforcement's response to potential security concerns indicates at least some show of intolerance of violence by abortion protesters. But the city has not taken a high-profile stance in this regard.

The city's attempt to stay out of the fray was most evident in its response to a 1996 incident in which about forty members of the California antiabortion group Operation Rescue West came to town and staged a two-hour demonstration at the corner of one of the busiest intersections, near one of the city's abortion clinics. The choice of this intersection during morning rush hour was intended to maximize the impact of their signs of bloody fetuses. Meanwhile, South City Planned Parenthood staged a rival protest across the street. Although there was some yelling back and forth, events unfolded peacefully. Despite the fact that this event involved an aggressive, out-of-town antiabortion organization staging a protest in a busy part of the city, using potentially inflammatory tactics and prompting a counterprotest, the city took no special action to manage the situation. (In other cities, word of such a protest led to substantial police mobilization and city council action to constrain the volatile group.) In South City, officials' choice to stay on the sidelines is reflective of their broader effort to stay clear of the abortion issue as much as possible.

GAY RIGHTS

Western City

In the latter 1990s, gay rights activism in Western City centered on the extension of spousal benefits to homosexual city employees in domestic partnerships. Securing protection from discrimination was not a major issue, because antidiscrimination policies have been in effect since 1991, when the city amended its code to make discrimination on the basis of sexual orientation unlawful in employment, housing and commercial space, public accommodation, educational institutions, and health and welfare services. However, the city's implementation of its nondiscrimination ordinance with respect to gays has been controversial on occasion.

In 1994, city officials were resisting pressures for domestic partner benefits for city employees. The city appealed a lawsuit in which a woman won the right to paid leave from her municipal job to care for her domestic partner. In this case, the state court of appeals ruled in favor of the city, finding that Western City had not discriminated.

In March 1995, 150 city employees signed a petition to change the city's definition of immediate family to include domestic partners, whether homosexual or heterosexual, and to allow them to use paid sick leave to care for their partners. Newspaper accounts indicate that the mayor's liaison to the gay community was instrumental in this petition effort. That same month, Western City's career service authority board officially expanded the definition of immediate family to include unmarried couples. Effectively, this change grants leave time to city employees who need to care for spousal equivalents.

Importantly, this decision did not extend other benefits, such as health insurance, to domestic partners, as the board does not have the authority to decide policies that entail financial costs. However, immediately following the decision, the mayor lauded the effort and called for the extension of full benefits to the families of gay employees. Just over a year later, the career service authority board officially recommended implementing a benefits policy for homosexual families. In September 1996, the city council passed (by a vote of eleven to one) the domestic partnership ordinance as recommended by the board. This ordinance applies to homosexual families only; unmarried heterosexual couples are not eligible to receive benefits for spousal equivalents. A spousal equivalent is an unrelated adult of the same gender with whom the employee is in an exclusive and committed relationship, who shares in household expenses, and who expects the relationship to last indefinitely. Employees with spousal equivalents must file affidavits notifying the career service authority of the relationship; gay couples who terminate their relationship must file a statement to that effect, and the employee is not allowed to declare a new spousal equivalent for six months. After council approval, forty-eight gay employees signed their partners up for health benefits, at a cost to the city of $1,700 each. Based on the experience of other cities with similar provisions, officials estimate that a maximum of 200 workers out of the city's 9,000 employees will eventually sign up.

Ultimately, this action led to a backlash when two citizens filed suit in district court in December 1996 to halt implementation of the domestic partnership ordinance on the grounds that it is inconsistent with the state's allowances for dependents—that is, that it illegally redefines the marriage relationship. The plaintiffs, who had threatened to sue during city council hearings on the ordinance, framed their concerns in terms of the fiscal impact of the change in eligibility for health benefits. In July 1996, the court threw out the lawsuit, and in October 1998, the state court of appeals ruled against the plaintiffs and allowed Western City to continue its policy (effective January 1, 1997) of granting benefits to the unmarried, same-sex partners of employees.

Finally, a city ordinance established a domestic partnership registry in late 1999 to allow unmarried domestic partners to certify their relationship and become eligible for insurance benefits offered by the city as well as by corporate entities. The provisions carefully avoided identifying these relationships as marriage. The coalition supporting this registry teamed senior citizens and gay and lesbian groups together in arguing that committed personal relationships deserve nominal recognition, even if other laws prevent (for same-sex couples) or discourage (for senior citizens afraid of losing Social Security and other benefits) formal marriage. In responding to these arguments, the council vote was unanimous, although one opponent, who had publicly called it "a worthless piece of legislation," was absent.

Western City's movement forward on domestic partnership issues was shaped by previous struggles in the state legislature over gay rights issues. Several years earlier, there had been a volatile court fight over a successful state ballot initiative that was not favorable to gay rights. Court injunctions ultimately prevented implementation of the initiative, but the political conflict mobilized the gay and lesbian community; because the initiative also nullified local ordinances in this strongly local control state, it gave the gay community and Western City officials a common goal. Initially, this mobilization was for defensive purposes, but over time, the organizations that had been established turned to other issues, including benefits for domestic partners comparable to those provided for heterosexual couples. Since their alliance with gays to challenge the statewide initiative, city officials have been receptive to other demands from the gay community. These issues are often referred to as sequential fights to broaden the benefits available to gays and lesbians, all contingent on the critical city council decision in 1995 to redefine who is considered immediate family.

To activists, these are civil rights issues with significant symbolic, rather than economic, meaning. To their opponents, these victories are further evidence of a decline in moral values, since equal benefits connote equal status. However, gays and lesbians are well organized and influential voting blocs in Western City politics. They rightly claim responsibility for the electoral victory of the city's first minority mayor, who supported the city employees' petition to change the definition of family, on the grounds that it was an issue of fairness. In addition, there is an advisory gay and lesbian council with access to the city council. As a local activist noted, the gay community is "pretty well off" here.

The downside to the local strategy, from the local activist perspective, is that local ordinances get you only so far. They "lack teeth" and remain riddled with exemptions and loopholes. A good example of this emerged in 1998, when the city faced charges from a statewide advocacy group that it had failed to enforce the gay rights portion of the antidiscrimination ordinance. The organization claimed that the city's antidiscrimination office had prosecuted only one case in the last seven years. Western City officials responded by noting that the antidiscrimination office has only two staff persons and a very limited budget and therefore has to be selective about the cases it takes on. They defended their record of settling the majority of cases before the filing of motions, explaining that although plaintiffs often prefer to take their cases to district court, where higher settlements are possible, that strategy is risky. Because there is no state law barring discrimination against gays, the city ordinance is not grounds for such a lawsuit, and such cases are usually thrown out of district court. For the advocacy organization, these explanations simply illustrate the limitations of a local government strategy for achieving gay rights. The Western City ordinance does not include a private right of action and constrains the antidiscrimination office, which can do only an initial investigation of a complaint; if no probable cause is found, that is the end of it—there is no other municipal option available beyond issuing a "cease and desist" order. From a civil rights perspective, the chances of achieving a positive result from this local office are modest.

Similarly, some local activists note the limitations of the domestic partner ordinance. For example, many parts of the ordinance allow insurance companies to make discretionary decisions, which could result in de facto discrimination. By contrast, gay activists believe that the domestic partner registry could serve as a basis for challenging the exemptions in the domestic partner ordinance. And despite their criticisms of some of the limitations of these gay rights policies, activists acknowledge that these local accomplishments set an example for other cities and for other employers. Implementation of Western City's domestic partner ordinance establishes a credible record of the actual costs and unanticipated benefits of granting equivalent benefits to domestic partners. These policies are therefore potentially important for economic development. Says one activist, "ignoring 10 percent of the labor pool in a tight economy" is not good business practice.

GAMBLING

River City

This state has a lottery, and it is also legal to bet on horse races or in small games of chance, but casino gambling is not authorized. The incumbent governor in the early 1990s was strongly opposed to gambling and had threatened to veto any bill authorizing it. This, coupled with the fact that a stalwart opponent of gambling, Representative John Cale, chaired the relevant house committee, stood in the way of pro-gambling forces. The incumbent governor was replaced in 1995, and incoming Governor Adam Putnam indicated that he would support legislation authorizing casino gambling if it included a provision for a statewide referendum.

Meanwhile, in the fall of 1994, River City's mayor announced the commissioning of a two-month feasibility study to examine the potential revenue that riverboat gambling would generate as well as the costs involved. The purpose of the study was to determine how hard the city would lobby the state legislature for the authorization of casinos. The deputy mayor coyly noted that the study could very well show that the costs outweighed the benefits, in which case they would be opposed to gambling, but he also noted that most cities were trying to develop entertainment facilities to attract visitors. This feasibility study was launched shortly after a gambling partnership announced its purchase of a site for a potential casino just outside River City, indicating that if the legislature authorized it, the casino and its associated resort could bring in 1,500 jobs.

In February 1995, Ray Ranatoni, a state legislator whose district includes the River City area, introduced a bill that would authorize riverboat gambling in communities where it had been approved by local referendum—the very provision that Governor Putnam had insisted on. Ranatoni claimed that riverboat gambling would be a boon for the state's economy, but his bill was opposed by Mainstream Consortium, a statewide lobby group for family values. The bill was immediately bottled up in committee by Cale, a Baptist minister whose opposition to casino gambling was legendary. In fact, Cale scheduled hearings on gambling to be held in the summer of 1995 in River City and in Bankton, another major city in the state. A River City council member testified that redevelopment of the riverfront was compromised by the uncertainty over riverboat gambling. The same hearing featured individuals presenting horror stories of how gambling had ruined their lives. It was quite obvious that Cale was using the hearings primarily as a venue to air the downside of gambling.

By the early fall of 1995, pro-gambling legislators were laying plans to introduce a bill that would provide for a statewide referendum on gambling.

The governor, who wanted a full airing of the issue, wanted the referendum moved back to the spring of 1996—a suggestion that was publicly endorsed by the mayor of River City. However, the legislature never authorized that referendum.

Similarly, although hearings on the legalization of riverboat gambling were held in 1996 in the statehouse and six different gambling bills were introduced during the legislative session, none of the bills was passed. The president of the River City–based antigambling group Not a Chance argued that the defeat of the gambling bills reflected a growing awareness locally and nationwide that the gambling industry's efforts to portray the issue as a straightforward matter of economic development constituted a deceit. Further evidence of the potency of antigambling forces at the state level emerged in 1997, when the governor's threatened veto stalled legislation that would have allowed slot machines at the various racetracks in the state, including one near River City.

In 1999, gambling issues once again surfaced in the state legislature. One proposal would have authorized nearly twenty riverboat casino licenses and slot machines at the state's racetracks. Evidence of the lucrativeness of slot machines was putting considerable weight behind the proposals of pro-gambling forces. One neighboring state was said to have more than tripled the revenue at its horse tracks since slot machines were introduced. Although the gaming industry was still in the picture, with one casino enterprise lobbying for riverboat gambling and another holding rights for a potential casino location in River City, spokespersons for the industry were beginning to indicate that the repeated failure of the state to authorize gambling was causing them to lose interest.

In February 1999, the statehouse passed legislation to have a statewide referendum in which voters would decide whether to have riverboat casinos, slot machines at the racetracks, and video poker in bars. Gambling opponents such as Not a Chance geared up to oppose the referendum even before the state senate had its turn at the legislation. Referendums in this state are technically nonbinding, but given the governor's insistence on one, it was clear that pro-gambling forces would have to win the vote of the people in order to get the governor to authorize gambling.

As the move toward a referendum heated up in the legislature, the River City council approved a motion to send correspondence to state legislators urging them to include two things in any gambling legislation: tax relief for city residents, and funding for gambling addiction programs. The motion was proposed by a city council member who is in favor of gambling because he sees it as an economic development measure.

As the time approached for the state senate to vote on the house bill authorizing a statewide referendum on gambling, both pro- and antigambling interests organized their forces and mounted heavy lobbying efforts. Gambling opponents included Mainstream Consortium and Not a Chance, which used church bulletins to reach people through the religious community. Organized religion, however, was somewhat split on the issue of gambling. The state's Catholic conference was expected to take no position on the referendum, because the Catholic Church traditionally relies heavily on some forms of gambling, such as bingo, for fund-raising. Some elements of the Catholic Church, such as a liberal Catholic community group with a strong presence in River City and some of the individual congregations in the city, were strongly opposed to the referendum and eagerly made use of the information provided by Not a Chance. The state's Jewish coalition also remained silent on the issue. In contrast, the state's council of churches registered high-profile opposition to the referendum, holding a rally at the state capital and vocalizing moral as well as economic reasons for its opposition.

The cast of characters on the pro-gambling side was predictable. The gaming business that held rights to a potential casino in River City had a noted lobbying firm working on its behalf in the state capital; another casino company, whose CEO was based in River City, also hired a lobbyist, as did other casino companies. In addition, bar owners, who had a stake in the video poker issue, were involved in the lobbying. Racetrack owners also weighed in on the issue, and racetrack workers held a rally at the state capital in support of the referendum. To everyone's surprise, what was to have been a clash of titans turned into an abbreviated, low-key matter as the state senate turned down the gambling referendum on the grounds that it would be unconstitutional without a full-scale debate on the merits of gambling.

River City's mayor was not an active, visible proponent of gambling during this period. He was on record as supporting a referendum, but on the issue of gambling per se, he claimed to have no position. Later developments hint at the reasons for the mayor's seemingly cooled interest in riverboat casinos. In September 1999, it was revealed that Representative Ranatoni, a leading figure in the effort to get gambling authorized, was the target of a federal investigation related to riverboat gambling. Ranatoni had originally been a strong supporter of the mayor in his initial run for office, but they later had programmatic disagreements and became bitter enemies. The mayor was ultimately reelected in 1997, with Ranatoni throwing high-profile support behind his opponent. In the spring of 2000, Ranatoni pleaded guilty to four counts of extortion, one of mail fraud, and one of tax evasion; in exchange, twenty-one other charges involving fraud and influence peddling were dropped. At the time of this writing, Ranatoni had not yet been sentenced, and the extent to which gambling-related matters were part of his crimes is unclear.

The mayor's enthusiasm for gambling cooled even more dramatically in the spring of 2000 when Grant Properties proceeded with plans for a hotel and commercial complex at a potential riverfront casino site. The land in question, which is in a prime area for development, had initially been purchased in 1994 from the city's Historical and Landmarks Foundation by Grant Properties in partnership with a casino company. By 2000, Grant Properties had bought out the casino company, although the latter still holds an option to develop a casino at the site if the legislature ever authorizes casino gambling. The mayor, however, was at odds with Jim Zillman, the president of the Historical and Landmarks Foundation, who had criticized a major redevelopment plan that the mayor was pushing elsewhere and for which he presumably needed support. The mayor publicly lambasted Zillman for selling the riverfront site to Grant Properties and the casino operator in the first place and for the subsequent approval of a development plan for the site that would take down a historic building. The mayor was quoted in the local paper as accusing Zillman of "selling River City's future to gambling interests on an important piece of riverfront property."

Meanwhile, there were interesting developments involving video poker machines. Although it is legal in this state to bet in small games of chance, and video poker games are a popular form of this type of gambling, state law makes it illegal for the machines to be altered to allow cash payoffs. Both city and county police were active in 1995 and 1996 in enforcing the law through investigations and periodic raids on establishments.

In contrast, in the spring of 1996, the city's planning commission recommended to the city council that it increase the number of video poker machines that establishments could have from five to seven, provided the establishment was in a commercial area, and that businesses with the larger number of video poker machines be exempt from the normally required amusement arcade license. The change, which had originally been proposed by two city council members, also increased license fees for the machines to $350 annually, up from $185. In July, the city council voted six to three to approve the planning commission's recommendation. The mayor vetoed the ordinance on the grounds that it would cause an increase in illegal gambling. Although some viewed the veto as merely a gesture in a feud between the mayor and the proposal's key sponsor on the city council, the mayor had in fact opposed the legalization of video poker machines as a member of the state legislature. He had also been pressed to veto the ordinance by the local antigambling group Not a Chance. The local paper later printed a clarification of the mayor's position on the issue, with the mayor stating that he opposed "incremental and arbitrary" increases in video gambling machines until the state legislature set up a system for gambling and a referendum on the issue had been held. In any case, the mayor's veto was overridden by the city council on a six-to-three vote in late July.

DRUG COURTS

Port City

The idea of a drug court in Port City and County was initially promoted by county legislator Alice Fane and assistant district attorney Mary May, who by 1992 were already interested in the idea. The idea was slow to develop, but Fane and May worked with a variety of other actors and, by January 1994, had garnered enough support to introduce legislation for a rehabilitation-oriented court for drug abusers, to begin operations in 1995. The court would be presided over by one judge and have a staff of counseling and medical professionals as well. The head of the Port County police department strongly endorsed the plan, which targeted nonviolent drug offenders. A municipal court judge who had been appointed by a Republican governor was also a key supporter and ultimately agreed to serve as a policy adviser to the new court. Fane worked with the county's public health department to develop the proposal, which ultimately envisioned an elaborate treatment program that could involve either inpatient or outpatient services and included counseling, drug testing, and even acupuncture. Those who successfully completed the program could have the charges against them dropped at the request of the district attorney.

However, instituting the drug court hinged on the receipt of federal funds, and a proposal for such funds was submitted in mid-1994. It was also constrained by a dispute between the district attorney and the public defender over the scope of the program. District attorney Fred Gunther argued that the program should be limited to first-time nonviolent defendants who had been arrested for the possession or use of small amounts of drugs. Public defender David Danfors argued that the drug court should also include defendants whose nonviolent crimes, such as burglary and even drug dealing, stemmed from the need to support their drug addiction.

By late 1994, the obstacles in the way of the drug court had been cleared. The public health department was awarded a substantial federal grant for drug court programming, and the dispute between the district attorney and the public defender over the scope of the program had been settled through a compromise: the court would target first-time drug offenders, as the district attorney preferred, but it would also handle a limited number of repeat offenders, thus opening the door a notch for the more expansive program preferred by the public defender. In the spring of 1995, the drug court began operations, and presiding judge Carol Waring, who had a graduate degree in social work, told the press that the drug court would provide early intervention and a demanding program that would help clients break out of the spiral of drug use and arrest. She also noted that, based on figures from other cities with drug courts, Port County was looking at costs of no more than $2,000 per drug court defendant, compared with the more than $20,000 per year that incarceration costs.

But eight months after the court's opening, there was evidence that the compromise over the scope of the program, which largely favored the district attorney's more restrictive view, had made the court's eligibility standards too restrictive. In addition to barring those with a history of arrests for violent crimes and those convicted of drug dealing, the drug court's focus on first-time offenders collided with the reality that most of these people were diverted into a program run by the state that was much less demanding (six months of less intensive counseling, compared with the drug court's one year or more of full-blown drug abuse rehabilitation). As a result, of the approximately 1,500 drug possession cases that were reviewed by the drug court, only 90 were eligible for drug court handling, and more than half of those 90 defendants chose to have their cases handled in the regular criminal court system rather than drug court. A spokesperson for Danfors noted that they were pressing to get the drug court's eligibility rules changed so that drug users arrested for crimes such as prostitution and petty theft could be included. The spokesperson claimed that Gunther was hostile to such a change because of worries that, in the political campaign he was facing, opponents could use his endorsement of a more expansive drug court against him.

In addition to the controversy over the scope of the drug court, there were concerns about its failure rate. When initial statistics were compiled on those who had voluntarily quit the program because they could not handle its rigors and those who had simply disappeared and were wanted on bench warrants, the failure rate was about 30 percent. This was high, according to an out-of-town expert who had served as a consultant to the designers of the Port County program. An assistant with the public defender's office quickly responded that Port County's failure rate was in line with the 30 percent failure rate reported by the U.S. General Accounting Office study on the subject, especially since many of the drug courts in other cities included mostly easier-to-handle, first-time drug offenders. Despite these difficulties and controversies, the drug court continued operations and in the spring of 1996 graduated its first class of ten defendants who had successfully completed the program. The original drug charges against them were dropped.

By the following spring (1997), the inability of the public defender's office, now run by Max Cahill, to get a more expansive eligibility standard appeared to be placing strains on the interorganizational cooperation that is critical to the drug court concept. Cahill removed the full-time assistant that he had assigned to work in the drug court, arguing that the caseload was simply too small to warrant such a use of his staff and that much of the decision making in the drug court involved treatment rather than legal matters. Furthermore, Cahill indicated a lack of support for the whole concept of the drug court, arguing that although such a specialty court has some advantages, the issue is whether the costs involved outweigh the benefits. To deal with the loss of the public defender's staff member, the drug court rearranged its operations, moving to a part-time schedule, using a full-time social worker to pick up the slack, and relying on a promise that the public defender's office would provide lawyers for defendants when necessary.

The following year brought good news for the Port County drug court—a promise of legislation to provide state funding for drug courts. Proponents of drug courts noted that this legislation and the governor's support showed that drug courts no longer polarized politicians on ideological grounds. But two years later, an unexpected threat to drug courts throughout the state emerged in the form of a ballot initiative funded by out-of-state figures who favor drug legalization. That ballot initiative, which was approved by a wide margin, stipulates that nonviolent, first-time drug offenders should not spend any time in jail and limits the sentence of most drug abusers to thirty days in jail. Because the drug court concept hinges on the court's authority to sentence participants to jail if they fail to meet the requirements of the treatment program, drug court proponents were appalled by the passage of the proposition. However, it is possible that some of the very weaknesses of the Port County drug court program figured into the politics of the proposition. A lawyer from Port County who helped draft it argued that the narrow eligibility standards of drug courts and their limited capacity statewide meant that the need for rehabilitation rather than imprisonment simply was not being met. In the wake of the passage of this proposition, Port County's officials have been struggling to adapt so as to keep the drug court functional while implementing the requirements of the proposition.

Border County

In Border City's home county, a drug court was established in 1996 with start-up funding from county government and a plan to leverage federal funds to further support the court. Two individuals were instrumental in pushing for the drug court—municipal judge Donna Harvin, who had a longtime interest in the concept, and county commissioner Jack Dolan, who hoped that the drug court would save money and reduce the need for more jail cells. But there is evidence that the drug court idea did not engender universal enthusiasm. None of the county's regular court judges were willing to preside over the new drug court. Harvin was willing, but in order to meet the state's legal requirements, the governor would have to first appoint her as a district court of appeals judge and then have her "retire" from that position to take up the drug court role. This gambit provided fodder for the chairman of the Democratic Party in Border County, who openly criticized the arrangement.

Despite the lack of interest on the part of the county's judges and the critique of the governor's appointment of Judge Harvin, the county moved ahead with the drug court under Dolan's leadership, and the court began operations in 1996. Unlike some drug courts, which restrict eligibility to first-time offenders or otherwise limit the scope of their operations, the Border County drug court immediately took on offenders with significant criminal histories. Judge Harvin was quoted in the local newspaper as noting that those were precisely the individuals who should be of interest to the court, because they are the "revolving door people who keep coming back to court, and that's where the problem is." The court-supervised treatment that these individuals commit to is quite elaborate. The program, which lasts for at least one year (it is extended for individuals who have lapses), involves either outpatient treatment or inpatient treatment at the county's own facility, and clients undergo three to four urine screenings each week.

Two years later, the court appeared to be a definite success story. Nearly 400 felony defendants had completed the court-supervised treatment program, and the recidivism rate was very low. Commissioner Dolan was basking in the glow of positive media coverage about the program, stating that when the program's graduates tell him that the drug court saved their lives, it makes being an elected official worthwhile. Local officials' interest in the creation of a second drug court was reported in the media. State officials, such as the director of the state's department of alcohol and drug addiction services, were also very supportive of drug courts at the county level, although they noted that the most attractive aspect for county-level officials was the money-saving angle. State officials were convinced that drug courts saved tax dollars, and they were instrumental in garnering federal grants to divide among the several county-level drug courts operating in the state.

Coastal County

Coastal County's drug court is unusual in several respects. First, it is one of only a few in the nation that is designed for misdemeanor defendants only. Indeed, the target cases for this drug court are even more specific, in that the court is intended for those whose arrest is for driving under the influence of drugs, alcohol, or both. Second, although it is called a drug court, many of the cases it handles involve defendants who are alcoholics rather than drug addicts. Finally, unlike in many other drug courts, successful completion of the treatment program does not qualify the defendant to have the charges dropped. The drug court's presiding judge acknowledges that the drug court would never have been accepted in this politically conservative community if defendants had the opportunity to clear their records.

This unusual drug court was pioneered by Judge Sheila Gunther, who instituted the court as a pilot project in 1997 with very little funding. Two years later, two offenders graduated from the tiny pilot project. That same summer, Coastal County was awarded a planning grant from the U.S. Department of Justice to pursue the drug court further. By the following summer (2000), fifty-four offenders had been admitted to the program, and eighteen had completed it. The program incorporates intensive drug treatment counseling and court-supervised monitoring.

In the process of implementing the pilot program and obtaining and implementing the planning grant, Judge Gunther assembled a team of collaborators, including an assistant county attorney and Dave Evans, an attorney in the public defender's office. In mid-2000, these individuals were hoping to get a federal grant that would enable them to expand the program. By this time, however, the drug court movement had progressed rapidly, spawning a national association of drug court professionals and a drug court office in the Department of Justice that had substantial experience with grant administration. As a precondition for qualifying for federal funding, Evans, Gunther, and others involved in the planning grant had to attend a series of seminars for drug court professionals. In an observation that reveals the degree of support (or lack thereof) for the drug court in the community, Evans noted that it was very important for them to get federal funding, because they could then get more state and local funding.

River County

River County lagged several years behind the unconventional communities in its initial efforts to institute a drug court. The primary instigator of the drug court idea in River County was U.S. Senator Ben Sandiford, a conservative Republican, who sponsored a meeting in early 1997 on instituting a drug court in River County. The inspiration for Sandiford's interest was a small, federally funded pilot project and research study launched in River City in 1991 by the addiction services unit of one of the city's nonprofit hospitals. This pilot project, which involved a group of nonviolent drug offenders being remanded for treatment instead of jail time, showed a high success rate (93 percent completed the program) and a two-year recidivism rate of only 30 percent, compared with a recidivism rate of nearly 80 percent for a comparison group. Moreover, the costs of the outpatient drug treatment were only $17 per day, versus $120 per day for imprisonment in the county jail. Hence, those responsible for the pilot project were able to claim that they had saved the county $2.5 million just by doing the study, and that even larger savings could be realized if a full-scale program were instituted. Energized by the results of this study, and with full awareness that federal money for drug courts was available under the 1994 crime bill, Senator Sandiford sponsored a meeting of the county jail warden, the district attorney, representatives of the county commission, drug rehabilitation specialists, and three county judges.

One of these judges, Donald Cicorelli, along with the district attorney, took up the mantle of leadership in pushing for a drug court. By July 1997, the two announced plans to launch the drug court in early 1998, using funding already in the county court budget. Judge Cicorelli emphasized the cost savings that could be realized, noting that the cost of jailing a single inmate for a year was approximately $22,000, while the estimated yearly cost for each individual handled by the drug court was $8,000. Furthermore, Cicorelli argued, the community would realize additional benefits to the extent that the drug court succeeded in transforming crime-prone drug addicts into productive individuals. A spokesperson for the district attorney's office also argued that, under the existing system, drug-addicted individuals arrested for nonviolent crimes were often sentenced to probation, but not necessarily with any attention to their drug problems and their need for treatment. Such individuals inevitably wound up being arrested again and again.

The drug court envisioned by the judge and the district attorney began operations in early 1998, targeting offenders whose nonviolent crimes stemmed from their drug addiction. At the discretion of the district attorney's office, appropriate offenders are referred to the drug court, although they first have to plead guilty. They are then assessed by the county's probation office for a determination of the kind of treatment services needed. The drug court makes use of a variety of services, ranging from treatment at a residential facility run by a nongovernmental organization to outpatient treatment under house arrest with electronic monitoring. Participants in the program can serve as much as two years and are monitored by probation officers. Once a month, they appear before the drug court judge, who discusses their progress with a team including representatives from the district attorney's office, the probation department, and the county office on drug and alcohol abuse. Throughout its first year of operation, the drug court functioned with little overt controversy and in fact began compiling a record with a remarkably small failure rate; very few of the initial defendants quit or had to be dropped from the program. In January 1999, the drug court received a substantial grant of federal monies through the state's commission on crime and delinquency that enabled it to continue operations for another year.

Toward the end of the second year, it became evident that River County's drug court had a problem of sorts. The eligibility rules were so restrictive that the number of individuals being handled by the court was embarrassingly small. The district attorney's office was using criteria that called for participants to be both nonviolent and repeat offenders; that is, they had to have lengthy enough criminal records as to be considered habitual. As a result of this restrictive interpretation of the focus of the court's efforts, fewer than 140 individuals had entered the drug court in its first twenty-one months of operation; in September 1999, there were only about 100 enrolled, even though the program had been budgeted for a capacity of 150. As a result, the county was required to return about 30 percent of the grant funding it had been given. The drug court's presiding judge noted publicly that the district attorney's office was the source of the problem. Sometimes, the judge complained, he encountered defendants whose records included numerous shoplifting or prostitution violations, some of which might have been plea-bargained down to misdemeanors. The district attorney was unwilling to refer such individuals to the drug court on the grounds that they had not committed enough felonies. In frustration, the judge was quoted in the local newspaper as claiming that he had actually said, "Tell them to go out and commit some more." In contrast, the probation officers involved with the program liked its small size and the correspondingly small caseload of twelve offenders for each probation officer. The normal caseload for probation officers handling violent offenders is more than 200.

Despite the drug court judge's complaints and the giveback of some grant funding, the River County drug court appears to have continued in much the same fashion. After nearly four full years of operation, slightly more than 200 individuals had entered the program, and as of October 2001, 126 were enrolled—still below the capacity envisioned for the program. By the same token, the drug court was generating very favorable program completion and recidivisim statistics.

NEEDLE-EXCHANGE PROGRAMS

Port City/County

In 1994, Port City continued to support and partially subsidize (about $250,000 per year) the underground, voluntary needle-exchange program (NEP) that had been operating in the city since the late 1980s. Such NEPs were illegal under state and federal law, so to circumvent this legal prohibition, every two weeks, the city council and the mayor declared a state of health emergency allowing needle exchange to take place. In 1995, the mayor and district attorney declared publicly that they would protect the NEP from attacks by conservative state Republicans. In 1996, the newly elected mayor and newly elected district attorney reaffirmed the commitment of their predecessors to support the program, protect it from its political enemies, and push for state and federal legalization.

Indeed, from the late 1980s until the present, the city's district attorney, police department, health department, city council, and city representatives in the state legislature and in the U.S. Congress—indeed, the city's entire political establishment, high and low—backed the NEP and, in some cases, openly dared state and federal officials to try to enforce the law on the city's well-guarded turf. As growing numbers of prestigious scientific studies demonstrated that needle exchange works to prevent the transmission of HIV without increasing drug addiction, the political pressure on the state and federal government intensified, peaking in 1998, an election year. In these debates and skirmishes, the Centers for Disease Control and Prevention and other leading scientific research institutions routinely spotlighted Port City's NEP as the nation's most effective.

In September 1999, the state's new Democratic governor signed a bill that freed this city and other local jurisdictions from the threat of state legal action for running their own NEPs. Falling short of outright legalization, the new law merely proclaimed official tolerance of a program that the governor and most state Republicans perceived as morally suspect and potentially dangerous. The law provided no state funding and required the city to continue issuing a state of emergency declaration every two weeks. Meanwhile, the city government, having played a critical leadership role in changing state and national policy on this issue, continues to issue its biweekly declarations of emergency and to support and subsidize the HIV Prevention Project's NEP.

River City

State law prevents NEPs from being official, and River City's NEP is more underground and informal than ever. It was started about four years ago by a drug user who simply went to a neighborhood known to have a drug problem and set up a table on the corner. Initially, it was a one-person operation, with no phone number, operating in a predominantly black neighborhood. The individual who started it then got in touch with a professor at a university in River City who had experience with NEPs from her years in the Bay Area. At her suggestion, they applied for a grant from the North American Syringe Exchange Network (NASEN), were funded, and were able to get better established. Grants help fund their supplies.

According to an activist working with the NEP, "Street cops knew, of course," and the needle-exchange volunteers "had a good relationship with them." The street cops quickly became aware of them because the volunteers are white, and they stood out in the black neighborhood. The street cops went out of their way to be helpful, indicating that they were there to help ensure the volunteers' safety.

However, the police bureaucracy took a different stance; it had to be less supportive because the operation is technically illegal. When neighbors complained about the NEP, police officials were unwilling to tolerate the street operation, so the whole needle exchange has now "gone underground"— that is, it still operates via networking and probably distributes more syringes than ever, but it has no street presence.

The activist also notes that city officials "have done their best to stay as far from us as possible." City officials know about them, she says, but in general they are not yet ready to publicly endorse them. However, at least one official, a deputy mayor, was very receptive to the idea of a needle exchange and was surprised to learn that the city did not already have one institutionalized. The existing needle-exchange operation, now functioning underground, approached him for help in "trying to get back on the street." In response, the mayor asked the city attorney to research the matter and come up with a legal report. This activist thinks that such a report has been compiled, but she has not seen it. Meanwhile, the county health department "has been a bit of a problem." Its leader, an African American man, is not only *not* receptive to needle exchange but also denies that there is an AIDS problem in the area. She describes him as being "really very obstructive" of their efforts. He has made statements that an NEP would "bring in every junkie from the tristate area."

In contrast, the needle-exchange volunteers have been well received by officials at institutions such as the University of Hull, various institutions in the medical field, and elsewhere. As a result of this, perhaps, the activist thinks that the pressure is on the county health department director, and she detects some softening in his opposition. They have also received endorsements from the warden of the county jail and from drug recovery organizations.

Meanwhile, the needle-exchange volunteers have undertaken a low-profile educational effort to try to build support in the community. Because River City "is a very small town in some ways" and "rather conservative" and is "still coming to grips that there's AIDS in River City," the idea of needle exchange is "hard to sell." But they are making contacts with neighborhood groups, using an informational approach, and trying to make sense of something that, to many people, "seems counterintuitive." They are hoping to get an agreement with the city that would make prosecuting needle-exchange volunteers a low-priority matter.

Western City

Western City's council has voted to institute an officially sanctioned NEP—a move that pits it against the state legislature, which has opposed such programs. Initially, the push for an NEP came from members of the planning committee that was created in 1994 in this and other cities by the state legislature for the purpose of improving the delivery of human services. In 1996, this committee developed a preliminary report advocating both an NEP and the decriminalization of marijuana. For political reasons, these recommendations were left out of the final report, but organized groups in the community continued to push for an NEP.

This advocacy essentially died in the absence of mayoral support, but groups such as a local AIDS organization continued to advocate at the state level for a change in the state law that prevented legal needle exchange. Their allies within state government included the governing board of the state health department, which officially endorsed NEPs in early 1997. The executive director of the governing board acknowledged that it was a hot-button issue and that she was concerned about sending mixed messages; nevertheless, she indicated her firm belief that needle exchange actually decreases drug use, as well as stemming the spread of disease. By contrast, the state's association of police chiefs took an official position against needle exchange. The state legislature defeated the 1997 bill that would have allowed local-option NEPs.

In June 1997, the issue was resuscitated when Western City's black mayor announced his support of needle exchange. Admitting that he had originally opposed such programs, the mayor explained that he had changed his mind because of the research statistics he had seen on children contracting HIV from their mothers, who had become HIV-positive through their own drug use or that of their sexual partners. While acknowledging concerns about sending the wrong message regarding drug use, the mayor argued that the existing system was not working. His proposal would institutionalize three NEPs in the city, each to be registered with the city's health department and sited at least one mile apart and at least 500 feet from residential neighborhoods or schools. Most important, the mayor's proposal, though symbolically staking out a position at odds with the state government, would not be implemented until the necessary changes in state law had been made. In contrast, a nearby community had opted to implement its NEP in advance of a change in state law by having the district attorney refuse to enforce the state's total ban on drug paraphernalia. Western County's district attorney, however, had made it clear that he would prosecute anyone who violated state law barring intravenous needle distribution, thus tying the mayor's hands in this regard.

The Western City council initially attempted to avoid the issue by tabling the mayor's initiative on the grounds that there were a number of unanswered questions, ranging from the city's potential liability for bad outcomes connected to dispensed needles to zoning issues to questions about NEPs' efficacy in getting addicts into drug rehabilitation. The city attorney's office immediately responded with a report finding that city liability for needle-exchange mishaps would be negligible if the city only registered and monitored the exchanges. Still, the city council delayed another month.

In December, however, the mayor's proposal was once again on the reluctant city council's agenda. One council member criticized the police department for not taking a public position on the proposal. This reveals the council's unwillingness to make an authoritative decision on this potentially explosive issue without the political cover provided by law enforcement endorsement. Worse still, from this perspective, is that the main police union in the city had come out publicly against the needle-exchange proposal. A spokesperson for the union was quoted in the local newspaper as saying, "Let's not be handing out needles so that people can commit a felony." Nevertheless, by a vote of eight to three, the city council approved the creation of NEPs in Western City, subject to changes in the state paraphernalia law. In 1998, a statehouse panel killed a needle-exchange bill. The state's association of police chiefs had once again lobbied against needle exchange, and that viewpoint prevailed.

Notes

1. LOCAL GOVERNANCE AND MORALITY POLICY

1. The historical narratives are based on fieldwork conducted by the author in four cities and by six associates in six other cities as part of a National Science Foundation–supported research project with the author as principal investigator (grant 9904482). The six faculty associates are Yvette Alex-Assensoh, Susan Clarke, Richard DeLeon, Janet Flammang, Michael Rich, and Marjorie Sarbaugh-Thompson. Each of the associates developed narrative case histories on each morality policy topic for their cities, based on newspaper compilations and interviews with local officials and community leaders. The historical narratives presented in this book are adapted from those case histories and in some cases use language taken directly from the narratives written by the associates.

2. STUDYING MORALITY POLITICS

1. For purposes of study city selection, a core variable representing each category of explanation was defined, and corresponding data were collected for each of the fifty-two cities in the United States with a population of at least 300,000. With respect to the city's economic health, population change (1980 to 1990) served as a rough indicator of where the city falls on the continuum from declining to booming local economies. With respect to the city's institutional arrangements, data on whether city council members are elected at large or by districts and whether the city's executive functions are under the control of an elected mayor or a city manager served as key indicators of where the city falls on a continuum from politicized (mayor, district elections) to professionalized (city manager, at-large elections). With respect to the sociocultural character of the community, the percentage of the population in nonfamily households served as a rough indicator of where the community falls on Rosdil's (1998) conventional-unconventional sociocultural dimension.

The fifty-two cities were winnowed down to those that are both ± 0.75 standard deviation from the mean on percentage of the population in nonfamily households and ±0.75 standard deviation from the mean on population change. This yielded a set of fourteen cities falling into one of four scenarios: high on nonfamily households and high on population growth (unconventional and growing); high on nonfamily households and losing population (unconventional and declining); low on nonfamily households and high on population growth (conventional and growing); and low on nonfamily households and losing population (conventional and declining). Study cities were chosen from each scenario to maximize the variance of the values of two of the key explanatory variables and minimize the problem of collinearity between those two explanatory variables. To accomplish the same goals with respect to institutional arrangements, study cities were selected within each scenario with an eye toward maximizing variation in both aspects of governmental structure.

4. MORALITY POLITICS—CASINO STYLE

1. Coastal City's aversion to gambling appears to be confined to casino gambling, however. Local officials were more receptive to horse racing. In the early 1990s, the state legislature authorized a single racetrack and its associated betting to be developed in the state, and many cities immediately swung into action, hoping to be chosen as the site for the track, including Coastal City. The normally high level of moral indignation about gambling in the community was muted in this case. Acknowledging that even the powerful Christian broadcasting operation located in the city "agreed not to oppose it, even though they are very much opposed to gambling," the city's chief of operations explained that "somehow, it got wrapped up in the sophistication of horses . . . if it had been a gambling boat or casinos or other forms of gambling, it would have been turned down two to one or three to one. But the 'sport of kings,' as they say, made up for the fact that they were involved in gambling."

In any event, Coastal City was not chosen to be the site of the track; instead, it was slated to be located in a distant county. Having lost its bid to have the track itself, local officials immediately showed their aversion to gambling by spurning proposals to allow an off-track betting (OTB) site in the community. The state's enabling legislation for the track had provided for up to six such sites, and the track developers were interested in placing at least one OTB site in Coastal City. But, in contrast with city officials' eagerness to get the track facility, there was no such eagerness to have an OTB parlor in the city. The city council did not immediately put the issue on its formal agenda, and at least one council member publicly indicated his opposition to OTB parlors, which he called unsavory. Although the out-of-state corporation building the track periodically expressed interest in opening at least one betting parlor in Coastal City, it eventually gave up.

5. LOCAL GOVERNMENT AND THE SEX INDUSTRY

1. There is, however, at least the potential for a difference, in that obscenity law in River City's state is based on a statewide conception of community standards. The key 1973 Supreme Court case on the matter, *Miller v. California,* specified what is required for sexually explicit material to be deemed legally obscene and hence not protected by the First Amendment. The Court indicated that the definition of obscenity hinges on "whether the average person, *applying contemporary community standards,* would find the work, taken as a whole, appeals to the prurient interest." In many states, localities are considered the relevant entities for defining contemporary community standards. But in 1977, when the state legislature revised the state's obscenity law to bring it into compliance with *Miller,* it chose a statewide rather than a local definition

of "community" for the purpose of determining contemporary community standards. This is perceived as making it more difficult for local prosecutors to get obscenity convictions, but there is no clear evidence to support that perception.

6. GAYS, RIGHTS, AND LOCAL MORALITY POLITICS

1. Like the other case descriptions, the Port City case material uses language directly from the historical narrative written by the project associate who did the fieldwork for that city—in this case, Richard DeLeon.

References

Agranoff, Robert. 2001. "Managing within the Matrix: Do Collaborative Inter-Governmental Relations Exist?" *Publius* 31 (Spring): 31–58.
Associated Press. 2002. "Abortion Protest Leader Charged for Behavior at Halloween Parade." Associated Press State and Local Wire, November 27.
———. 2003. "News in Brief from Central Pennsylvania." Associated Press State and Local Wire, February 5.
Bailey, Robert W. 1999. "Economism and Identity." In *Gay Politics, Urban Politics*. New York: Columbia University Press.
Barstow, David. 1999. "Giuliani Ordered to Restore Funds for Art Museum." *New York Times*, November 2, sec. A, p. 1, col. 6.
Bell, Daniel. 1976. *The Cultural Contradictions of Capitalism*. New York: Basic Books.
Benton, J. Edwin. 2002a. *Counties as Service Delivery Agents: Changing Expectations and Roles*. Westport, Conn.: Praeger.
———. 2002b. "County Service Delivery: Does Government Structure Matter?" *Public Administration Review* 62 (July–August): 471–80.
Bertram, Eva, Morris Blachman, Kenneth Sharpe, and Peter Andreas. 1996. *Drug War Politics: The Price of Denial*. Berkeley: University of California Press.
Best, Joel. 1998. *Controlling Vice: Regulating Brothel Prostitution in St. Paul, 1865–1883*. Columbus: Ohio State University Press.
Bishop, Bill. 2000. "Technology and Tolerance: [Hill City] Hallmarks." *[Hill City] High-Tech News*, June 25.
Black, Dan, Gary Gates, Seth Sanders, and Lowell Taylor. 1999. "Demographics of the Gay and Lesbian Population in the United States: Evidence from Available Systematic Data Sources." Working Paper 12. Syracuse, N.Y.: Center for Policy Research, Maxwell School of Citizenship and Public Affairs, Syracuse University.
Boger, Carl A. Jr., Daniel Spears, Kara Wolfe, and Li-Chun Lin. 1999. "Economic Impacts of Native American Casino Gaming." In *Legalized Casino Gaming in the United States: The Economic and Social Impact*. Edited by Cathy H. C. Hsu. New York: Haworth Hospitality Press.
Bouchard, Kelly. 2002a. "Suit Brewing on Partner Benefits." *Portland Press Herald*, September 11, p. 1B.
———. 2002b. "Benefits Policy May Settle Impasse." *Portland Press Herald*, November 14, p. 1B.
Broadhead, Robert S., Yael Van Hulst, and Douglas D. Heckathorn. 1999. "Termination of an Established Needle-Exchange: A Study of Claims and Their Impact." *Social Problems* 46 (February): 48–66.
Browning, Rufus P., Dale Rogers Marshall, and David H. Tabb. 1984. *Protest Is Not Enough*. Berkeley: University of California Press.

233

Burstein, Paul. 1999. "Social Movements and Public Policy." In *How Social Movements Matter*. Edited by Marco Giugni, Doug McAdam, and Charles Tilly. Minneapolis: University of Minnesota Press.

Button, James W., Barbara A. Rienzo, and Kenneth D. Wald. 1997. *Private Lives, Public Conflicts*. Washington, D.C.: CQ Press.

Button, James W., Kenneth D. Wald, and Barbara A. Rienzo. 1999a. "The Election of Openly Gay Public Officials in American Communities." *Urban Affairs Review* 35, no. 2 (November): 188–209.

———. 1999b. "The Politics of Gay Rights Legislation." In *Culture Wars and Local Politics*. Edited by Elaine B. Sharp. Lawrence: University Press of Kansas.

Campbell, Rebecca J., and Geoffrey K. Turnbull. 2003. "On Government Structure and Spending: The Effects of Management Form and Separation of Powers." *Urban Studies* 40 (January): 23–35.

Caudill, Steven B., Jon M. Ford, Franklin G. Mixon Jr., and Ter Chao Peng. 1995. "A Discrete-Time Hazard Model of Lottery Adoption." *Applied Economics* (June): 555–62.

Chambers, David L. 2000. "Couples: Marriage, Civil Union, and Domestic Partnership." In *Creating Change: Sexuality, Public Policy, and Civil Rights*. Edited by John D'Emilio, William B. Turner, and Urvashi Vaid. New York: St. Martin's Press.

Chong, Dennis, and Anna-Maria Marshall. 1999. "When Morality and Economics Collide (or Not) in a Texas Community." *Political Behavior* 21(2): 91–121.

Clark, Terry Nichols. 1998. "Overview of the Book." In *The New Political Culture*. Edited by T. N. Clark and Vincent Hoffmann-Martinot. Boulder, Colo.: Westview Press.

Clark, Terry Nichols, and Ronald Inglehart. 1998. "The New Political Culture: Changing Dynamics of Support for the Welfare State and Other Policies in Postindustrial Societies." In *The New Political Culture*. Edited by T. N. Clark and Vincent Hoffmann-Martinot. Boulder, Colo.: Westview Press.

Clarke, Susan E. 1999. "Ideas, Interests, and Institutions Shaping Abortion Politics in Denver." In *Culture Wars and Local Politics*. Edited by Elaine B. Sharp. Lawrence: University Press of Kansas.

Clingermayer, James C., and Richard C. Feiock. 2001. *Institutional Constraints and Policy Choice: An Exploration of Local Governance*. Albany: State University of New York Press.

Cocca, Carolyn E. 2002. "The Politics of Statutory Rape Laws: Adoption and Reinvention of Morality Policy in the States, 1971–1999. *Polity* 35 (Fall): 51–73.

Cohen, Jeffrey E., and Charles Barrilleaux. 1993. "Abortion Opinion and Policy in the American States." In *Understanding the New Politics of Abortion*. Edited by Malcolm L. Goggin. Newbury Park, Calif.: Sage.

Crothers, Lane, and Charles Lockhart. 2000. "Part I: Concepts and Applications." In *Culture and Politics*. Edited by Lane Crothers and Charles Lockhart. New York: St. Martin's Press.

Davis, Nanette. 2000. "From Victims to Survivors: Working with Recovering Street Prostitutes." In *Sex for Sale*. Edited by Ronald Weitzer. New York: Routledge.

Daynes, Bryon W. 1998. "Pornography: Freedom of Expression or Sexual Degradation?" In *Moral Controversies in American Politics*. Edited by Raymond Tatalovich and Byron W. Daynes. Armonk, N.Y.: M. E. Sharpe.

Deitrick, Sabina, Robert A. Beauregard, and Cheryl Zarlenga Kerchis. 1999. "Riverboat Gambling, Tourism, and Economic Development." In *The Tourist City*. Edited by Dennis Judd and Susan S. Fainstein. New Haven, Conn.: Yale University Press.

DeLeon, Richard. 1999. "San Francisco and Domestic Partners: New Fields of Battle in the Culture War." In *Culture Wars and Local Politics*. Edited by Elaine B. Sharp. Lawrence: University Press of Kansas.

DeLeon, Richard E., and Katherine C. Naff. 2003. "Identity Politics and Local Political Culture: The Politics of Gender, Race, Class and Religion in Comparative Perspective." Paper presented at the annual meeting of the American Political Science Association, Philadelphia, August 28–31.

DeSantis, Victor S., and Tari Renner. 1994. "The Impact of Political Structures on Public Policies in American Counties." *Public Administration Review* 54 (May–June): 291–95.

Dorris, John B. 1999. "Antidiscrimination Laws in Local Government: A Public Policy Analysis of Municipal Lesbian and Gay Public Employment Protection." In *Gays and Lesbians in the Democratic Process*. Edited by Ellen D. B. Riggle and Barry L. Tadlock. New York: Columbia University Press.

Downs, Donald. 1989. *The New Politics of Pornography*. Chicago: University of Chicago Press.

Eckstein, H. 1988. "A Culturalist Theory of Political Change." *American Political Science Review* 82: 789–804.

Elazar, Daniel. 1970. *Cities of the Prairie*. New York: Basic Books.

———. 1984. *American Federalism*. 3d ed. New York: Harper and Row.

Elliott, Donald S., and John C. Navin. 2002. "Has Riverboat Gambling Reduced State Lottery Revenue?" *Public Finance Review* 30 (May): 235–48.

Feiden, Douglas. 1999. "Brooklyn Art Exhibit Stirs Shock and Outrage." *New York Daily News*, September 16, p. 8.

Feiock, Richard C., and Gregory Cable. 1992. "Need, Institutional Arrangements, and Economic Development Policy." *Journal of Public Administration Research and Theory* 2(4): 378–98.

Fernando, M. Daniel. 1993. *AIDS and Intravenous Drug Use: The Influence of Morality, Politics, Social Science and Race in the Making of a Tragedy*. Westport, Conn.: Praeger.

Feuer, Alan. 2000. "Giuliani Dropping His Bitter Battle with Art Museum." *New York Times*, March 28, sec A, p. 1, col. 6.

Florida, Richard. 2002. *The Rise of the Creative Class*. New York: Basic Books.

Frederickson, H. George, and Gary A. Johnson. 2001. "The Adapted American City: A Study of Institutional Dynamics." *Urban Affairs Review* 36 (July): 872–84.

Frederickson, H. George, Curtis Wood, and Brett Logan. 2001. "How American City Governments Have Changed: The Evolution of the Model City Charter." *National Civic Review* 90 (Spring): 3–18.

Furlong, Edward J. 1998. "A Logistic Regression Model Explaining Recent State Casino Gaming Adoptions." *Policy Studies Journal* 26, no. 3 (Autumn): 371–83.

Geer, John G. 1996. *From Tea Leaves to Opinion Polls: A Theory of Democratic Leadership*. New York: Columbia University Press.

Goggin, Malcolm L., and Christopher Wlezien. 1993. "Abortion Opinion and Policy in the American States." In *Understanding the New Politics of Abortion*. Edited by Malcolm L. Goggin. Newbury Park, Calif.: Sage.

Goldkamp, John S. 1999. "Challenges for Research and Innovation: When Is a Drug Court Not a Drug Court?" In *The Early Drug Courts*. Edited by W. Clinton Terry III. Thousand Oaks, Calif.: Sage Publications.

Goode, Stephen. 1995. "Christians Say No Dice." *Insight on the News* 11, no. 36 (September 18): 15.

Goodman, Robert. 1995. *The Luck Business*. New York: Free Press.

Haider-Markel, Donald P. 1999. "Morality Policy and Individual-Level Political Behavior: The Case of Legislative Voting on Lesbian and Gay Issues." *Policy Studies Journal* 27(4): 735–49.

Haider-Markel, Donald P., and Kenneth J. Meier. 1996. "The Politics of Gay and Lesbian Rights: Expanding the Scope of the Conflict." *Journal of Politics* 58 (May): 332–49.

Hansen, Susan B. 1993. "Differences in Public Policies toward Abortion: Electoral and Policy Context." In *Understanding the New Politics of Abortion*. Edited by Malcolm L. Goggin. Newbury Park, Calif.: Sage.

Hawes, Dan. 1999. *1999 Capital Gains and Losses: A State by State Review of Gay, Lesbian, Bisexual, Transgender and HIV/AIDS-Related Legislation in 1999*. Washington, D.C.: National Gay and Lesbian Task Force. www.thetaskforce.org /downloads/cgal99.pdf.

Hays, Tom. 1999. "N.Y. Mayor Violated Art Museum's Rights: Judge." *Chicago Sun-Times*, November 2, p. 29.

Heimer, R., and M. Lopes. 1994. "Needle Exchange in New Haven Reduces HIV Risks, Promotes Entry into Drug Treatment, and Does Not Create New Drug Injectors." *Journal of the American Medical Association* 271: 1825–26.

Higgins, Michael. 2002. "(USA) Des Plaines Council OKs Negotiating for a Casino." *Gambling News*, August 21. http://www.winner.com.

Hunter, James D. 1991. *Culture Wars: The Struggle to Define America*. New York: Basic Books.

———. 1996. "Reflections on the Culture War Hypothesis." In *The American Culture Wars*. Edited by James L. Nolan Jr. Charlotttesville: University Press of Virginia.

Hurley, Susan F., Damien J. Jolley, and John M. Kaldor. 1997. "Effectiveness of Needle-Exchange Programmes for Prevention of HIV Infection." *Lancet* 349, no. 9068 (June 21): 1797–1801.

Inglehart, Ronald. 1977. *The Silent Revolution: Changing Values an Political Styles among Western Publics*. Princeton, N.J.: Princeton University Press.

———. 1988. "The Renaissance of Political Culture." *American Political Science Review* 82 (December): 1203–30.

Jackman, Robert W., and Ross A. Miller. 1996. "A Renaissance of Political Culture." *American Journal of Political Science* 40 (August): 632–60.

Judd, Dennis R. 1999. "Constructing the Tourist Bubble." In *The Tourist City*. Edited by Dennis R. Judd and Susan S. Fainstein. New Haven, Conn.: Yale University Press.

King, Gary, Robert O. Keohane, and Sidney Verba. 1994. *Designing Social Inquiry: Scientific Inference in Qualitative Research*. Princeton, N.J.: Princeton University Press.

Kirp, David L., and Ronald Bayer. 1999. "The Politics of Needle Exchange." In *Culture Wars and Local Politics*. Edited by Elaine B. Sharp. Lawrence: University Press of Kansas.

Klawitter, Marieka, and Brian Hammer. 1999. "Spatial and Temporal Diffusion of Local Antidiscrimination Policies for Sexual Orientation." In *Gays and Lesbians in the Democratic Process*. Edited by Ellen D. B. Riggle and Barry L. Tadlock. New York: Columbia University Press.

Leonard, Arthur S. 2000. "From *Bowers v. Hardwick* to *Romer v. Evans:* Lesbian and Gay Rights in the U.S. Supreme Court." In *Creating Change: Sexuality, Public Policy, and Civil Rights*. Edited by John D'Emilio, William B. Turner, and Urvashi Vaid. New York: St. Martin's Press.

Lieske, Joel. 1993. "Regional Subcultures of the United States." *Journal of Politics* 55 (November): 888–913.

Lineberry, R. L., and E. P. Fowler. 1967. "Reformism and Public Policies in American Cities." *American Political Science Review* 61(3): 701–16.

Lynd, Robert S., and Helen Merrell Lynd. 1956. *Middletown: A Study in American Culture*. New York: Harcourt, Brace, Jovanovich.

Martin, R., and B. Yandle. 1990. "State Lotteries as Duopoly Transfer Mechanisms." *Public Choice* 64: 253–64.

Maynard-Moody, Steven, and Michael Musheno. 2003. *Cops, Teachers, Counselors*. Ann Arbor: University of Michigan Press.

McFadden, David. 2003. "Bill Seeks to Restrict Needle Exchange." *Providence Journal-Bulletin*, January 30, p. C-1.

McFeeley, Tim. 2000. "Getting It Straight: A Review of the 'Gays in the Military' Debate." In *Creating Change: Sexuality, Public Policy, and Civil Rights*. Edited by John D'Emilio, William B. Turner, and Urvashi Vaid. New York: St. Martin's Press.

McLaughlin, Amy. 2002a. "Casino Opponents Keep an Eye on Local Activity, Write to State Gaming Board." *Chicago Daily Herald*, September 12, p. C11.

———. 2002b. "Group Gears Up to Oppose Des Plaines Casino Idea." *Chicago Daily Herald*, July 23, p. C2.

———. 2002c. "We're in, Des Plaines Says City Votes to Launch Casino Bid." *Chicago Daily Herald*, August 21, p. F1.

Meier, Kenneth J. 1994. *The Politics of Sin: Drugs, Alcohol, and Public Policy*. Armonk, N.Y.: M. E. Sharpe.

———. 1999. "Drugs, Sex, and Rock and Roll: A Theory of Morality Politics." *Policy Studies Journal* 27(4): 681–95.

Meier, Kenneth J., and Deborah R. McFarlane. 1993. "Abortion Politics and Abortion Funding Policy." In *Understanding the New Politics of Abortion*. Edited by Malcolm L. Goggin. Newbury Park, Calif.: Sage.

Miller, Eleanor M., Kim Romenesko, and Lisa Wondolkowski. 1993. "The United States." In *Prostitution: An International Handbook on Trends, Problems, and Policies*. Edited by Nanette J. Davis. Westport, Conn.: Greenwood Press.

Mooney, Christopher Z. 2001. "The Public Clash of Private Values." In *The Public Clash of Private Values*. Edited by Christopher Z. Mooney. New York: Chatham House.

Mooney, Christopher Z., and Mei-Hsien Lee. 2000. "The Influence of Values on Consensus and Contentious Morality Policy: U.S. Death Penalty Reform, 1956–1982." *Journal of Politics* 62 (February): 223–40.

———. 2001. "The Temporal Diffusion of Morality Policy: The Case of Death Penalty Legislation in the American States." In *The Public Clash of Private Values*. Edited by Christopher Z. Mooney. New York: Chatham House.

Morgan, David R., and Michael W. Hirlinger. 1991. "Intergovernmental Service Contracts: A Multivariate Explanation." *Urban Affairs Quarterly* 27 (September): 128–44.

Morone, James. 2003. *Hellfire Nation: The Politics of Sin in American History*. New Haven, Conn.: Yale University Press.

National Abortion Rights Action League (NARAL). 2001. "A State-by-State Review of Abortion and Reproductive Rights." www.naral.org.

National Gambling Impact Study Commission. 1999. "Final Report." http://www.casin-gambling-reports.com/GamblingStudy/.

National Gay and Lesbian Task Force. 1996. *Capital Gains and Losses 1996*. Washington, D.C.: National Gay and Lesbian Task Force.

Nolan, James L. Jr. 2001. *Reinventing Justice: The American Drug Court Movement*. Princeton, N.J.: Princeton University Press.

Normand, Jacques, David Vlahov, and Lincoln E. Moses, eds. 1995. *Preventing HIV Transmission: The Role of Sterile Needles and Bleach*. Washington, D.C.: National Academy Press.

Norrander, Barbara, and Clyde Wilcox. 1999. "Public Opinion and Policymaking in the States: The Case of Post-*Roe* Abortion Policy." *Policy Studies Journal* 27: 707–22.

———. 2001. "Public Opinion and Policymaking in the States: The Case of Post-*Roe* Abortion Policy." In *The Public Clash of Private Values*. Edited by Christopher Z. Mooney. New York: Chatham House.

O'Connor, Karen. 1996. *No Neutral Ground? Abortion Politics in an Age of Absolutes*. Boulder, Colo.: Westview Press.

Pagano, Michael A., and Ann O. Bowman. 1997. *Cityscapes and Capital*. Baltimore: Johns Hopkins University Press.

Page, Benjamin I., and Robert Y. Shapiro. 1983. "Effects of Public Opinion on Public Policy." *American Political Science Review* 77 (March): 175–90.

Park, Kee Ok. 1997. "Friends and Competitors: Policy Interactions between Local Governments in Metropolitan Areas." *Political Research Quarterly* 50 (December): 723–50.

Peterson, Paul. 1981. *City Limits*. Chicago: University of Chicago Press.

Pierce, Patrick A., and Donald E. Miller. 2001. "Variations in the Diffusion of State Lottery Adoptions: How Revenue Dedication Changes Morality Politics." In *The Public Clash of Private Values*. Edited by Christopher Z. Mooney. New York: Chatham House.

Polikoff, Nancy D. 2000. "Raising Children: Lesbian and Gay Parents Face the Public and the Courts." In *Creating Change: Sexuality, Public Policy, and Civil Rights*. Edited by John D'Emilio, William B. Turner, and Urvashi Vaid. New York: St. Martin's Press.

Polner, Robert. 1999. "The Art of the Deal/Museum, City Negotiating." *Newsday,* September 28, p. A7.

Rosdil, Donald. 1991. "The Context of Radical Populism in U.S. Cities: A Comparative Analysis." *Journal of Urban Affairs* 13: 77–96.

———. 1998. "Rethinking Local Policy Analysis: The Challenge of Culture to Political Economy." Paper presented at the annual meeting of the Midwest Political Science Association, Chicago, April 23–25.

Rosenthal, Donald B. 1999. "Regime Change and Gay and Lesbian Politics in Four New York Cities." In *Culture Wars and Local Politics*. Edited by Elaine B. Sharp. Lawrence: University Press of Kansas.

Ross, Marc Howard. 2000. "Culture and Identity in Comparative Political Analysis." In *Culture and Politics*. Edited by Lane Crothers and Charles Lockhart. New York: St. Martin's Press.

Schneider Mark, and Kee Ok Park. 1989. "Metropolitan Counties as Service Delivery Agents: The Still Forgotten Governments." *Public Administration Review* 49 (July–August): 345–52.

Sharp, Elaine B. 1994. *The Dilemma of Drug Policy in the United States*. New York: HarperCollins.

——. 2002. "Culture, Institutions, and Urban Officials' Responses to Morality Issues." *Political Research Quarterly* 55 (December): 861–84.

——. 2003. "Local Government and the Politics of Decency." *Social Science Quarterly* 82, no. 2 (June): 262–77.

——. 2004. "Local Culture and Social Capital: Exploring Validity and Predicting Connections." Poster presented at the annual meeting of the American Political Science Association, Chicago, September 2–5.

——, ed. 1999. *Culture Wars and Local Politics*. Lawrence: University Press of Kansas.

Smith, Kevin B. 2001. "Clean Thoughts and Dirty Minds: The Politics of Porn." In *The Public Clash of Private Values*. Edited by Christopher Z. Mooney. New York: Chatham House.

Smith, T. Alexander, and Raymond Tatalovich. 2003. *Cultures at War*. Orchard Park, N.Y.: Broadview Press.

Stafford, Tim. 1998. "None Dare Call It Sin: How Mississippi's Bible Belt Succumbed so Quickly and so Completely to the Gambling Industry." *Christianity Today* 42, no. 6 (May 18): 34–39.

Statistical Abstract of the United States. 1980. 101st ed. Washington, D.C.: U.S. Government Printing Office.

Statistical Abstract of the United States. 2000. 120th ed. Washington, D.C.: U.S. Government Printing Office.

Stern, Henry. 2002. "Portland Considers Nude Dance Restrictions." *Oregonian,* November 20, p. C1.

Stone, Clarence N. 1989. *Regime Politics: Governing Atlanta, 1946–1988*. Lawrence: University Press of Kansas.

Tauber, Judge Jeff, and C. West Huddleston. 1888. *Development and Implementation of Drug Court Systems*. Washington, D.C.: National Drug Court Institute.

Terry, W. Clinton III. 1999. "Judicial Change and Dedicated Treatment Courts: Case Studies in Innovation." In *The Early Drug Courts*. Edited by W. Clinton Terry III. Thousand Oaks, Calif.: Sage.

Thompson, William N. 1997. *Legalized Gambling: A Reference Handbook*. 2d ed. Santa Barbara, Calif.: ABC-CLIO.

"Update: Syringe Exchange Programs—United States, 1998." 2001. *Journal of the American Medical Association* 285, no. 21 (June 6): 2709.

Wald, Kenneth D., James W. Button, and Barbara A. Rienzo. 1996. "The Politics of Gay Rights in American Communities: Explaining Antidiscrimination Ordinances and Policies." *American Journal of Political Science* 40 (November): 1152–78.

Weitzer, Ronald. 2000. "The Politics of Prostitution in America." In *Sex for Sale*. Edited by Ronald Weitzer. New York: Routledge.

Willen, Liz. 1999. "Giuliani: It's No Show/BMA Told to Pull Exhibit." *Newsday,* September 23, p. A5.

Witt, Stephanie L., and Suzanne McCorkle. 1997. *Anti–Gay Rights: Assessing Voter Initiatives*. Westport, Conn.: Praeger.

Wohlenberg, E. H. 1992. "Recent U.S. Gambling Legalization: A Case of State Lotteries." *Social Science Journal* 29: 167–83.

Wolfe, Alan. 2003. "Invented Names, Hidden Distortions in Social Science." *Chronicle of Higher Education,* May 30, p. 13.

Woliver, Laura R. 1999. "Abortion Conflicts and City Governments: Negotiating Coexistence in South Carolina." In *Culture Wars and Local Politics*. Edited by Elaine B. Sharp. Lawrence: University Press of Kansas.

Index